THE DRINKERS' GUIDE TO WALKING

Edited by Nicola Hodge

PROTEUS
London & New York

PROTEUS BOOKS is an imprint of
The Proteus Publishing Group

United States
PROTEUS PUBLISHING COMPANY, INC.
747 Third Avenue, 14th Floor
New York, N.Y. 10017
distributed to the trade by:
CHARLES SCRIBNER'S SONS
597, Fifth Avenue
New York, N.Y. 10017

United Kingdom
PROTEUS (PUBLISHING) LIMITED
Bremar House,
Sale Place,
London, W2 1PT.

ISBN 0 906071 20 8

First published in UK July 1980
Re-printed February 1981
© 1980 by Proteus Publishing Group
All rights reserved.

Printed and bound in Great Britain by
Butler & Tanner Ltd, Frome and London,

Acknowledgements

The editor and publishers would like to thank the following individuals and organisations who have greatly assisted in the development of this book:

General Research

Tim Locke, Peter Gerard-Pearse, Chris Barton and Dave Rimmer

Maps and Illustrations

Bill Goodson

Line Drawings

Pauline Hodge

Cartoons

Peta Maughan

Advice and Assistance

Ron Andrews and Alfred Palmer of the Ramblers' Association

Research on Individual Walks and Inns

Sharon Barnfield, Michael Brecher, Michael Carr, Gustav Dobrzynski, Kevin Dunford, Geraldine Ellis, Peter Griffin, Eldred Jones, Tim Locke, George Loucaides, Nick O'Brian-Tear, Alison Peake, Roland Richardson, Camilla Sheffield, Daniel Shrimpton, Stephen Skelly, Greg Stickley, Nick Varley and Paul Whitcomb.

The English Tourist Board from whose collection some photographs have been reproduced, and the British Tourist Authority for allowing us to use them.

Cook, Hammond and Kell Ltd for supplying the Ordnance Survey Maps.

The Reference Department of Marylebone Library for its interest and co-operation.

Design Camilla Sheffield

Layout and Paste-up Bill Goodson

Introduction

THE DRINKERS' GUIDE TO WALKING has been written for all walkers, whether they be experienced ramblers or city-dwellers moved to stretch their legs on a hot summer's day. Starting with the basic premise that our native countryside provides something for everyone, we have tried to cover a wide range of interests, from real ale to ecclesiastical architecture. Wherever possible, we have tried to gear the walks to the average family, with 2.2 kids and not necessarily a car and, in selecting the pubs, we have taken into account their attitude towards children. Indeed we would like to point out that we do not regard ourselves as competitors with Camra, and that our pubs have been chosen as much for their location and their food, as for their beer.

Carefully prepared by our research team, the walks reveal both specialist knowledge and particular prejudices. Unfortunately this edition is not as comprehensive as we would have liked; partly because of the enormous task of developing a national walk book from scratch, and because this is only the first in a range of Proteus leisure guides. Scotland in particular may feel hard done by, but, in case Proteus is held responsible for any Anglo-Scottish skirmish, I would hastily point out that we hope to restore the peace by the next edition.

Considerable trouble has been taken to ensure our route descriptions and maps are as accurate as possible. Unfortunately, such details have a particular tendency to change, as the countryside is ever-changing, thanks both to Nature and to Man. We would like to encourage readers and users of the DRINKERS' GUIDE to send us their suggestions for improving the book, as well as information on any errors or alterations found (via the publisher) so that improvements and corrections can be incorporated into THE DRINKERS' GUIDE TO WALKING mark 2. I should like to draw your attention to the back of the book, for details of how you could make a valuable contribution to future editions.

The book has been divided into regional sections, with each walk clearly and precisely located on an overall map of Great Britain. The Guide offers a wide variety in terms of distance, the amount of effort required, and the kind of places of interest to be found en route, and we have given some indication of this at the beginning of each talk-round.

Nicola Hodge
Summer 1980

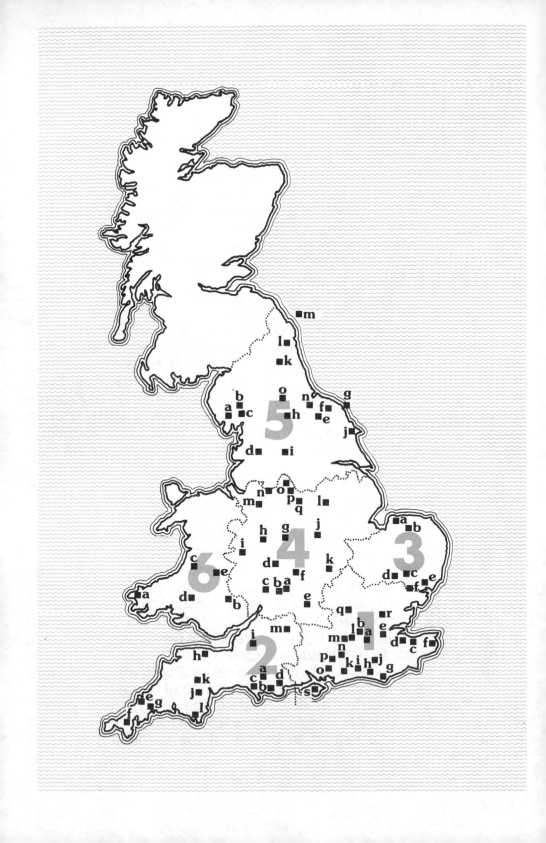

The Index to the Walks

WALES — SECTION 6

Key for the Maps

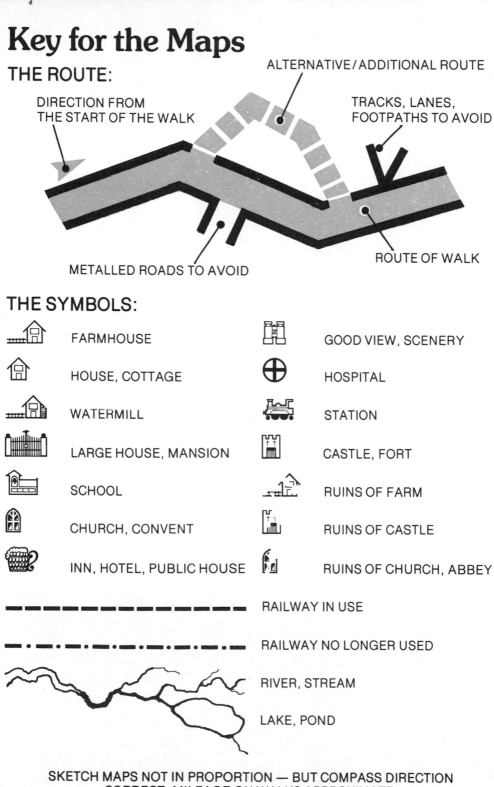

THE ROUTE:

DIRECTION FROM
THE START OF THE WALK

ALTERNATIVE / ADDITIONAL ROUTE

TRACKS, LANES,
FOOTPATHS TO AVOID

METALLED ROADS TO AVOID

ROUTE OF WALK

THE SYMBOLS:

FARMHOUSE

HOUSE, COTTAGE

WATERMILL

LARGE HOUSE, MANSION

SCHOOL

CHURCH, CONVENT

INN, HOTEL, PUBLIC HOUSE

GOOD VIEW, SCENERY

HOSPITAL

STATION

CASTLE, FORT

RUINS OF FARM

RUINS OF CASTLE

RUINS OF CHURCH, ABBEY

—— —— —— —— —— RAILWAY IN USE

—— · —— · —— · —— · RAILWAY NO LONGER USED

RIVER, STREAM

LAKE, POND

SKETCH MAPS NOT IN PROPORTION — BUT COMPASS DIRECTION
CORRECT. MILEAGE ON WALKS APPROXIMATE.

The South-East

The area which comes under the wide umbrella of the south-east forms some of England's most green and pleasant land. Evidence of the vast tract of forestland which used to sweep across from the Kentish coast right through to Hampshire can be seen today in the New Forest and on the North and South Downs. However the soil beneath these mighty oak trees has always been rich in iron and nowadays supports lush and fertile pastures.

All the counties we have included in this section have their characteristic and sometimes contrasting charms. The dainty prettiness of Surrey, the beech-covered chalk hills of the Chilterns, the quiet agricultural lowlands of Bucks and Berks, along with the dense woodlands of Epping Forest.

Architecturally the south-east begs to be noticed; the various fortifications along its coastline, its picturesque villages as well as the more obviously imposing attractions of a Knole or a Penshurst.

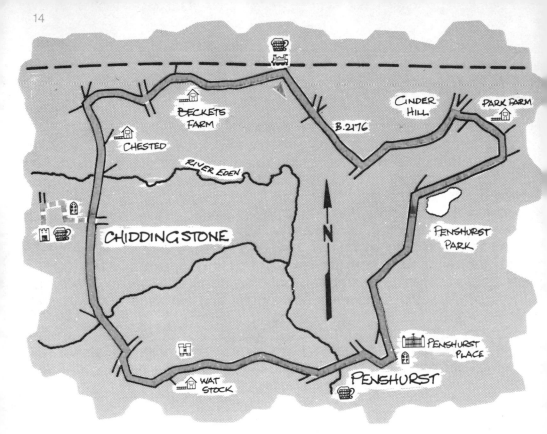

1a Penshurst

The District

About six miles north-west of Tunbridge Wells, the village of **Chiddingstone** takes its name from the 'chiding stone', made from sandstone, before which nagging wives were said to have been hauled up and judged by the assembled villagers. The picturesque row of half-timbered 16th and 17th century houses is now the property of the National Trust. The village goes back to 9th or 10th century, though it became closely connected with the Streatfield family with its squire and patron until it was finally sold to the National Trust just before the Second World War. It remains unspoilt; its post office is recorded in a deed of 1453 and enjoyed the role of the Manor House of Chiddingstone for several centuries. It was bought by Anne Boleyn's father in 1517.

Chiddingstone Castle is a mock Gothic creation, built about 1800. It houses some interesting pictures and furnishings, and boasts important collections of Jacobite and Stuart items and Japanese lacquerwork.

Catching a bus in Chiddingstone is an interesting experience: it arrives twice a week, on a Saturday and Monday though even locals have not been able to figure out anything approaching a timetable.

Penshurst Place is a great medieval manor house surrounded by a walled and terraced garden. It offers a fine collection of 17th and 18th century ephemera and several imposing halls and state rooms, and is open to the public throughout the summer. Home of the Sidney family (De L'Isle) since 1554, the manor is said to be haunted by the Black Prince, Henry VIII gorging himself and Queen Elizabeth I dancing. But perhaps a more credible ghost is that of Sir Philip Sidney who died at the manor in 1586. **Penshurst** also offers a fine parish church, on which work was begun in the early 13th century. Many of the graveyard's tombstones carry curious, anecdotal inscriptions.

How to Get There
By car from London A20, turn right onto A224 and onto A21 (Sevenoaks and Tonbridge bypasses), then onto A26 at Southborough sign. After 1 mile turn right onto B2176 to Penshurst. From Surrey via A25, through Crockham Hill and Bough Beech. By rail to Tonbridge or Tunbridge Wells, then bus to Penshurst.

The Penshurst/Chiddingstone Walk
A gentle though fairly long stroll (about 7½ miles) through the magnificent parklands of Penshurst Place to the picturesque village of Chiddingstone, returning along the Chiddingstone Causeway.

The walk begins at Penshurst station, opposite the signal box. Turn left onto a small tarmac road, proceeding down it in a south-easterly direction (this is beginning to read like a copper's notebook!). This road meets the B2176 at a T-junction, with an oast house facing you. Turn right onto the B2176 and, walking up the incline, lined on either side by fir and spruce trees, you will arrive at another T-junction. Turn left towards Cinder Hill. This minor road, skirted on either side by more fir and spruce trees, will take you to a fork in the road. Bear right, and take the footpath (opposite the small red postbox) on your right.

The footpath is easily recognizable as a wide dusty track lined with Christmas trees. It leads up to Park Farm, with its square, white-painted Victorian farmhouse. Pass the farm and descend the slope until you reach a six-bar metal gate with a stile attached to its left side. Cross the stile and continue straight towards a junction with a footpath and a bridleway. Go right heading west onto Martin's Drive, a tree-lined track that leads through Penshurst Park.

Reaching a fork in the path, take the stile on the right-hand side, then turn left. This route takes you down past a lake, bearing ▶

The Inns

Castle Inn, Chiddingstone

About the Inn: Standing at one end of a row of timbered Tudor houses that is Chiddingstone, this tavern is a particularly fine example of 16th century domestic architecture. It was bought in 1712 by Thomas Weller, a tailor, who started the inn with his brother in about 1730. 250 years later it is still the centre of village life. Seating is placed out in the garden during summer months.

Beers and Food: Wide selection of hand-pumped real ales including Fremlin's, Young's and Shepherd Neame. Bar snacks and hot and cold pub grub, plus a magnificent country-style menu in a traditional restaurant: many specialities, including smoked chicken, home-made pâté, pancakes stuffed with prawns, local pheasant, venison and hare. Amazing wine list.

Spotted Dog, Penshurst

About the Inn: On Smart's Hill, a little off the walk route. Built 500 years ago, but just recently licensed, this is a very attractive inn with plenty of olde worlde atmosphere ▶

westward around the lake. Enter a large wheatfield on your right. As you cross a stile halfway up the field the facade of Penshurst Place looms directly in front of you with the lake to your left. Cross the pasture bearing right to the next stile that will lead you up onto the B2176, about 200 yards outside the village of Penshurst. On entering the village you turn at a T-junction, heading towards the post office, St John's Church and Leicester Square (how did *that* get into this walk?). Alternatively, you can walk left up Smart's Hill and towards **The Spotted Dog Inn.**

Though slightly off the route, The Spotted Dog is worth the detour. Built 500 years ago but only recently licensed, it already boasts its very own ghost (landlord Desmund Leppard suggests you ask Mrs L about *that*) and a growing local reputation for fine handpumped real ales served in a warm and friendly atmosphere.

Leaving the church, turn right and right again, retracing your steps a little back up to the main road, past the public conveniences on your left. Take the footpath on your left, a small metalled lane. This leads across the River Eden on a small, three-arched bridge. Fishing permits for the river are available at £1 per rod from Salman's Farm close to the bridge.

After the bridge take the right fork uphill to Wat Stock. A marvellous view, of the surrounding woods and farms sloping away down the valley, complements this attactive collection of 16th century farm buildings. Passing the main farmhouse on your left, you will reach a fork. Take the track straight ahead as it bears gradually to the right. It leads up to a footpath and bridleway marked by a six-bar metal gate and stile. Cross the stile into a field, walk diagonally through the field to a second stile and cross over a small country road continuing on the footpath and bridleway. The path takes you over a tiny stream, almost silted up, and up to a footpath to the right which is clearly marked by an iron gate and signposted for Chiddingstone.

Follow the route to Chiddingstone, turning left for the castle. If you want to avoid the castle, continue the walk by taking the footpath next to the small cemetery, bearing north-east down the metalled footpath past a football pitch. If you visit the castle, a visit to **The Castle Inn**, tucked away in one corner of the castle's lea, is a must. Justly famed for a wide selection of handpumped real ales, its pretty courtyard garden and an amazing menu of real country cooking (accompanied by the most comprehensive wine list of any inn in the south of England), this inn should not be missed.

Meanwhile, back at the football pitch, you are about to cross the River Eden again. The track becomes gravelled on the other side of the river; it leads to two wooden gateposts. Just past these on the right is a stile. Cross this and bear right along the right perimeter of the field.

The route continues straight across three fields, over stiles between each, until it enters Chested, a hamlet of a few cottages. At Chested turn left onto a metalled road and over a stile, past which the path bears left. This runs over two more stiles. Take the one to your right, up towards Beckett's Farm, and walk through the farmyard (the farmer is friendly), picking up the footpath between two hay barns. Cross a cowfield (the cows are just as friendly) to a stile on the right side of the field. This leads into a small field, then into a large wheatfield, where you turn sharp left, skirting the field until you reach a track taking you through the field and beside a large timber yard. A path carries you along the timber yard and back towards Penshurst station. Just by the station is **The Station Inn**, a Victorian stone tavern which offers a warm, intimate welcome, particularly to children — for whom it has a special garden.

and superb view from the rear. Two bars, open fires, oak panelling and furniture, with many interesting antiques casually strewn about the place.

Beers and Food: Fremlin's Bitter, Tusker Bitter drawn by handpump. Bar snacks.

Station Inn, Penshurst

About the Inn: Victorian heavy stone building, almost domestic in style. Small bars with round tables and chairs. Simple, cosy setting. Special childrens' garden. The atmosphere is of a small farmhouse, and Evelyn Smith keeps geese and chickens at the back to complete the effect.

Beers and Food: Worthington's Bitter and Special Mild, Carlsberg lager drawn by handpump. Basic bar snacks only.

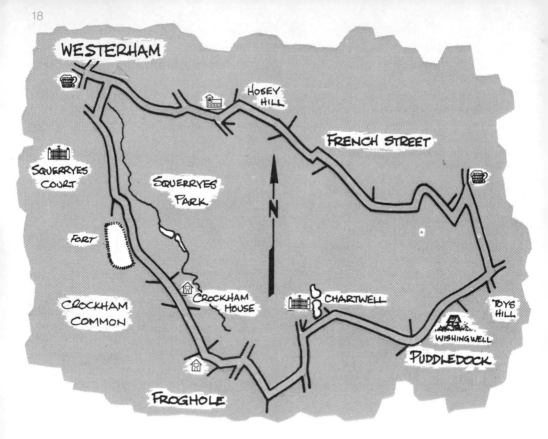

1b   Westerham

The District

Westerham is the most westerly village in Kent; its houses are huddled around the village green, in which stands a statue of General Wolfe. Indeed, both Wolfe and Sir Winston Churchill have connections with Westerham. James Wolfe's birthplace — with its collection of Wolfe memorabilia — is now called Quebec House, and is open to the public. Squerryes Court, on the west side of the village, is a red-brick country mansion which was used by Wolfe's family. **Chartwell**, the home of Sir Winston, is about 2½ miles south of the village. It has been preserved much as it was during his lifetime, and retains the atmosphere and the superb views over the Kent Weald that moved the statesman to his renowned hobby of painting.   Many of Churchill's

paintings can still be seen in the house.

The village is also connected with William Pitt, the Younger; this great predecessor of Winston Churchill once lived in a heavily timbered building close to the Market Square, which is the oldest part of Westerham. St Mary's Church, on the Green, was considerably restored in 1882, but retains interesting relics of its medieval history, including a most unusual spiral stairway leading to the top of the bell tower.

How to Get There

By car, A22 from London. A25 via Oxted to Westerham. By rail, hourly services from London (Victoria) to Oxted (on East Grinstead to Edenbridge line), bus from Oxted station to Westerham.

The Westerham Walk

In the summer, lunch on the village green at Westerham can be taken, courtesy of **The Grasshopper Inn**, a famous and beautiful tavern with a tradition for hospitality that goes back to the 12th century. Having wined and dined to excess, what better than an easy, 6 mile stroll along the richly wooded landscape surrounding this charming village, to work off the fat?

Cross the Green and the far road to join the signposted footpath to Hosey Hill.

The Inn

Walk along the alleyway and over the river at the end. Cross the stile at the end of the path into a field and walk through the field to a second stile on the brow of the hill.

Catch your breath and enjoy the view! Follow the path over to the left of the field towards a wooden fence; take the gap through the fence and onto a well-worn path down beside a cottage garden and along past a high brick wall.

Turn right at the junction towards a green in front of the primary school. Follow the track that bears to the left, signposted for French Street. Fork left down the track into the woods, then right up along a path deeper into the woods. Climb the hill to where the path divides and turn right. Go along the edge of the wood to emerge at the top by a road, then walk down to French Street Village. Do *not* head for

►

The Grasshopper Inn, Westerham

About the Inn: Lying against the village green, this is one of the most famous taverns in the area. A fabulous coaching inn, the Grasshopper was once a boarding point for the daily coach service between Westerham and Fleet Street. This most attractive and friendly free house is managed by John Thirkell, who delights in offering a wide range of real ales pulled from the wood by real Wedgwood pulls — insured for £500 each! The inn's three bars feature beamed ceilings and open fires, with Churchill and safari relics adorning the walls. Jukebox; children welcomed.

Beers and Food: 22 different beers and ales — including Sam Smiths, Everard's Old Original, Bass, Trophy and Youngers No 3 — most handpumped by John Thirkell's

►

Hornshill; instead continue down past the cluster of cottages into the valley. Pass a beautiful house on the right and continue right following the lane that climbs another hill.

At the fork turn left up towards the cottage on the hillside. Take the path directly ahead up and into the woods. Follow this path all the way to the top, where it runs into a glade, with a seat to the right, and a private memorial to two brothers killed in the First World War on the left. This is the National Trust Weardale Estate. ·Continue through the woods and onto a road, turning left towards **The Fox and Hounds Inn** where you turn left and walk down the road to the bottom of the hill and a crossroads. Turn right towards Puddledock, passing a wishing well on the left of the track. Continue downhill into the valley.

In the floor of the valley, take the signposted footpath towards Chartwell House. This leads through an iron gate and then left across a farmyard, passing several oast houses on your right. Then take the lane which leads to the drive for Chartwell.

The House is well worth a visit, and is open to the public from the beginning of March to the end of November. If not visiting the house, or after your visit, turn left at the main road at the end of the drive, then onto a lane leading off to the right towards Crockham Hill (this path is marked on a stone just before you reach it, beside a house and wooden gate).

The lane continues for about 2 miles, past private houses and gardens, eventually bearing right onto a main road at the top of a steep hill. Cross the main road, taking the footpath leading up to the woods to your left. Climb the hill, taking the top right hand track where the path forks towards forest and scrubland. In front of the old house at the top, cross the drive and take the right path leading down into the woods. Turn right onto a track at the end and take the next footpath on the left downhill. This path leads through rhododendron bushes, continuing downhill to Crockham House. Take the stile opposite that leads to Squerryes Court Park, crossing the field and a second stile

onto a track leading to a third stile, which passes a fort on the extreme left.

Take the third stile onto an uphill path. which leads to a junction marked for Kent Hatch. At the junction take the path to the right leading over another stile, across a field towards a cricket pitch and pavilion. Walk past this pitch, having taken two more stiles en route (a great one for stile junkies, this walk!) and over — you've guessed it! — another stile. Bear right down the hill into the valley. Turn left at the bottom by a house and walk along the lane past a pond and back towards the main road through Westerham village. Walk up to the main road and turn right to pass the shops and houses at the 'lower' end of the village. Alternatively, just before the main road, take the path leading away to the right over a field and onto the other side of the river — crossed at this point by a stone bridge. Follow this path until you reach a track leading off to the left back up to the alleyway opposite the village green and The Grasshopper Inn.

prized Wedgwood pulls. Home-made hot and cold bar snacks, full table d'hôtel and à la carte menus in the upstairs restaurant.

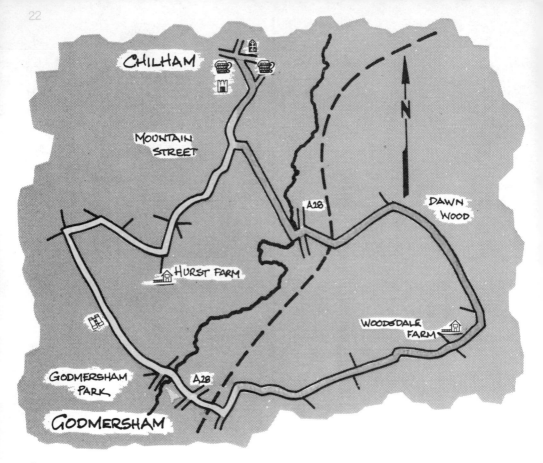

1c Godmersham

The District

Godmersham Park, set in oak forest land beside the River Stour in Kent, is comprised of little more than a well-kept lawn and a red-brick mansion. In the 1790's it belonged to Jane Austen's brother Edward, and Jane's love of Godmersham is reflected in the fact that she used it as the background for her novel *Mansfield Park*.

Two miles to the north is **Chilham,** one of Kent's most picturesque villages, huddled around a small square and bordered by lime trees. A somewhat self-conscious beauty spot, with its tea-rooms and antique shops vying for attention, nevertheless Chilham is an impressive sight, with its massive castle keep, the adjacent Jacobean mansion and the turreted church tower.

A constant stream of pilgrims trudged through Chilham in the Middle Ages — nobles, merchants, peasants, monks and nuns — all bent on getting a good look at Thomas à Beckett's tomb in Canterbury Cathedral. In fact, religion seems to have played a significant role in Chilham's history; for the bones of a still-more-ancient martyr were hidden away in the church at Chilham, after Henry VIII had dissolved the monasteries. However when restoration work was being carried out in 1860 and the coffin was opened, it was found to be completely empty.

Chilham Castle grounds are open to the public daily, and contain Jacobean terraces, a water garden, peacocks, swans and displays of jousting and birds of prey. There is a rumour, incidentally, which says that if the herons are not back from their spell abroad during the winter months by Valentine's Day, evil will befall the castle and its occupants.

How to Get There
Godmersham is on the A28 between Ashford and Canterbury.

By rail, from Charing Cross direct to Chilham, or go to Ashford and catch a 601 bus to Godmersham (hourly service).

The Godmersham Walk
This is a pleasant ramble of about 5½ miles across the rolling country around the River Stour, and incorporating part of the North Downs Way along the edge of Forestry Commission land.

The walk begins at Godmersham Post Office, next to the bus stop. Cross over the main road, the A28, in a north-westerly direction. You should now see a metalled lane turning off the A28 (it has grassy banks and is edged by a white fence). Follow this lane until it comes to a bridge over a stream. Directly in front of you is a red-brick lodge. Go through the gate to the right of this, into the grounds of Godmersham Park. Straight ahead is a metalled path leading to the front of the main house, but do not follow this unless you have pretensions of grandeur and well-polished shoes! Instead make a diagonal turn to the right, over well-kept lawns, to a low iron fence. Here you will see a small gate and to its left a sign indicating a footpath to the left, uphill. Go through the gate, (dogs should be kept on a leash, so as not to annoy the sheep) and follow the fence uphill in a north-westerly direction.

A little further up there is a sign marked 'Footpath to Chilham', but you should ignore this and continue to follow the line of the fence, going through any gates or fences which you encounter. Lovers of Close Encounters of the Floral Kind should look out for wild Daffodils, Clementines, Primroses, Anemones and Cowslip along the way.

As you pass a house to your right, look back over your shoulder for a good view of Godmersham Park. Soon you will pass a clump of trees to your right just before a metal gate. Go through the gate and take the right-hand fork. After about 100 yards, you will see a sign indicating the North Downs way. This track is grassy underfoot,

▶

The Inns

The White Horse Inn, Chilham

About the Inn: As already mentioned, this pub has an interesting history. It also has a ghost, named Samson, who is believed to be a former priest of Chilham and who was unfrocked during the Reformation. This sinister spirit reputedly appears bright and early in the morning, presumably in the hope of getting a quick drink before opening time.

Beers and Food: Full range of Whitbread beers. A cold buffet of seafood and meats is served over the bar. Steaks are available in the separate 'log cabin' dining area.

The Alma Inn, Chilham

About the Inn: Situated opposite Chilham station, the Alma was first built as a railway hotel in 1854; the year of victory of the battle at the River Alma in the Crimea. It is a typical early Victorian building, and the interior, with its sash windows, remains unaltered. Pool and electronic games are among its more modern attractions.

Beers and Food: A free house with a choice of four real ales, three pump and one gravity dispensing. There is a comprehensive menu, from substantial Ploughman's lunches to hot snacks, such as cheeseburgers; and three-course meals, including delicious roast duckling.

and should be followed to the edge of the woods.

Pass through a gate at the edge of the wood and turn left along the way-marked Forestry Commission bridlepath. Bear round to the right and at a North Downs way milestone, start making your way downhill. At the bottom of the hill you will see another milestone: here there is a good view of a farm and some oast houses, across the fields.

Oast houses are a phenomena peculiar to both Kent and Sussex, dating back to the 16th century when brewing with hops first began in England.

However, you should turn left at this second milestone and follow the path as far as a signpost to the right, indicating 'Private Road to Hurst Farm'. Here the track widens onto a metalled road, with telegraph poles and a fence to the left. Soon you will see a cluster of attractive houses to your right, and eventually the wall of Chilham Castle grounds on your left. At intervals you will be able to see through the wall to a private fishing lake, and you may even catch a glimpse of a couple of armourclad knights, risking death by the sword in front of hordes of camera-clicking sight-seers. Keep following the wall as it bends to the left, with woodland to the right. After a while the road turns right, but you should carry straight on. This is Mountain Street and leads into the square at Chilham.

The White Horse is at the lower end of Chilham square, in front of the church. Great excitement was caused at this 15th century inn when, in 1956, a massive inglenook fireplace was uncovered, with carvings now established as being over 1000 years old. The white-washed, half - timbered building started its filmic career as an extra in *Moll Flanders,* and its inn sign bears a portrait of a white horse, which is a copy of George Stubbs painting, hanging in the Tate.

After sampling the liquid pleasures of olde-worlde Chilham, you should go back down Mountain Street and retrace the route until the end of the castle wall; as far as the houses on the left. There is an unmetalled track turning off to the left, by a milestone, and at the end is a sign marked 'FP 23' which points across an arable field.

Follow the line the sign indicates, until you come to a hedge, which you should go through, via a stile. Follow this hedge round to the right with the River Stour now to your left. Eventually you will see a bridge going over the river just to your left, which takes you out to the A28. Turn left along the road, and then right at a track marked 'East Stour, Farm Road'.

Follow this track under a railway bridge, passing a hay barn to your left. Turn left just past the barn, and go up the hill to the edge of the wood, following it round to the right in a wide arc. At the point where a line of trees join the edge of the wood, go into the wood and follow the bridlepath uphill, bearing left. The path comes out at a field, where you should follow a tractor track to the right. This takes you down through a gate and through Woodsdale Farm, passing a white building to the left. Continue uphill, and where the path forks carry straight along the unmetalled track. It goes uphill, bounded to the left by a fence, and goes over the crest of a hill, to the right. Ignore a path forking to the right and soon you will notice banks appearing on either side of the track. Go through a gate, and bear left, keeping the house on your left. A private metalled road, Eggerton Lane, begins by this house, and you should follow it past various buildings, until the railway is immediately to your right. Where the railway goes over a bridge there is a forked signpost, and you should follow the 'Chilham' arm, under the bridge. This takes you through Godmersham and comes out next to the Post Office on the A28.

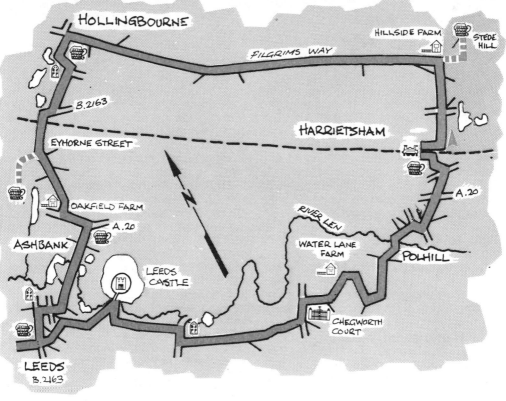

1d   Harrietsham

The District

Nestling in the heart of the Kent Downs, **Hollingbourne** is a quaint village full of Tudor charm and architecture, though the village dates back originally to pre-Norman conquest days. It boasts a large, 16th century manor just off the winding main street, made of Kentish rag and sandstone. For centuries the manor house has been the home of the Culpeper family, squires of the village whose family history is well-documented in the local All Saints Church. There has been a church on this site, near the bottom of the village, for over a thousand years, though the original structure was badly damaged in a great earthquake in 1382. Most of the restoration work dates from the mid-19th century.

Hollingbourne is haunted by a wild rider, seen but not heard in daylight, heard but not seen at night. Some say that he is the ghost of the Lord of Hollingbourne House, who died while attempting to make his horse jump the iron gates of the manor.

Eyhorne Street is a hamlet which is really a tiny suburb of Hollingbourne. Though not featured on our walk, it boasts two fine inns in **The Sugar Loaves** and **The Windmill**. About three miles south-west of Hollingbourne is the small village of **Leeds**; its houses are fine examples of early Victorian building, shaped from heavy, attractively weathered stone. **The George Inn** is one of the focal points of village life, situated in a hollow at the main crossroads. Certainly, the village's greatest attraction to visitors is **Leeds Castle**, the oldest and one of the most romantic of England's stately

▶

homes. First built in stone in the reign of William the Conqueror's son Henry I, this formidable baronial fortress came into Crown possession in the Middle Ages. At the beginning of this century the castle had spent 400 years in private ownership, but has recently been lovingly restored and rededicated to the nation by Lady Olive Baillie. In its time, the castle's splendid state rooms and gardens have been the setting for many a royal romance.

How to Get There

By car, from south London A20 (M20) to Harrietsham station; from Folkestone and Dover A20 westwards. By train to Harrietsham station; the walk begins at the station.

The Harrietsham Walk

A long (almost 9 miles) hike across the Kent Downs, offering extensive views of an area designated officially as of Outstanding Natural Beauty. It coincides in part with the Pilgrims' Way, which was the medieval route pilgrims took from Winchester to Canterbury.

Begins at Harrietsham station. Take the footpath on the north side that leads past the station into a large wheat field. In the far left corner of the field two large grain silos stand out against the sky; there is also a lake to your right. Climb to the top of the field, up to a hillside farm, in front of which is a crossing (for **The Ringlestone Inn** turn right here to Stede Hill). Turn left at the

crossing, keeping the Dutch House to your right and emerge onto the Pilgrims' Way heading north-east. The Pilgrims' Way is a wide bridlepath and footway, marked by an acorn symbol. You follow it all the way to Hollingbourne.

Entering Hollingbourne off the Pilgrims' Way you reach a T-junction with the B2163; **The Pilgrims' Rest Inn** is on the left. A 15th century tavern that began life as three cottages, it is a most fortuitous find: a warm, friendly atmosphere, excellent beer and nourishment make it a resting place not to be missed. Once past the inn turn left, following the main street through Hollingbourne to All Saints Church. Take the right footpath alongside the church, bearing south-east through a field. At the country road turn right under the railway bridge and walk down to Eyhorne Street. Where the road turns right into Eyhorne Street, take the footpath on the left, clearly signposted 'Footpath to A20'.

Follow the footpath passing through two fields towards the A20. There turn left and descend the hill, in the dip of which is **The Park Gate Inn.** Just before the inn, a footpath on the right takes you through a small wood, down to a lake and bird sanctuary, with Leeds Castle on your left. Having past the lake you cross a four bar wooden gate and climb a hill to a marker post painted yellow. This marker points to three footpaths; take the middle track. Follow this track through a cricket ground up to St Nicholas Church in Leeds. Walk

through the graveyard onto the B2163.

Turning left at the main road, bear south-west down to The George Inn. At the back of the inn a footpath on the left leads up to a country road. Cross this road and follow the track down to Leeds Castle. From the castle turn left, crossing the field immediately beside the castle and a small stream. Climb the stile that leads to a small wood which, in turn, takes you up to a country road. Here turn right along the road until you reach a telephone box. From here you can check with your broker on the latest stock market prices, before turning left and following the path towards St Margaret's Church.

Follow the footpath through the church graveyard (this is certainly a ghoulish walk!) and into a field, bearing right of a small wood. Cross the stile where the wood meets a hedge surrounding the field, and walk into an orchard. Take the clearly signposted track back into the wood, and follow the signs through the woods and over a stile; up the hill to a second stile. Turn left here, bearing east into another wood and down a slope onto a country lane and Chegworth Court.

Turn left, then take the metalled bridleway on your right past Chegworth Court. Follow the bridleway down to Waterlane Farm. At the farm building turn left up a metalled lane which climbs quite steeply. Follow this path north-east and where it meets a track bear right onto the path to Polhill. Crossing a small stone bridge brings you to a winding track bearing eastward which meets a small country road. Turn right here, and where the road bends to the right take the middle footpath which twists off to the left. This footpath

The Inns

Ringlestone Inn, Stede Hill, Harrietsham

About the Inn: Situated on a picturesque road at the top of the Kent Downs, this inn is about three centuries old, with an interior furnished with antiques. An inglenook fireplace, exposed beams and brickwork and a Sackville sideboard from which drinks are dispensed. Once owned by two eccentric women who discouraged unwelcome custom at the point of a shotgun, the inn boasts a ghostly lodger who creeps around the cellar steps.

Beers and Food: Fremlin's Bitter and Tusker Bitter, Bass Bitter drawn from the cask; draught Guinness, many keg beers and lagers. Range of hot and cold pub grub, including basket meals and a dining room offering an à la carte menu on Friday and Saturday evenings.

Pilgrims' Rest, Hollingbourne

About the Inn: A 15th century tavern which had its name changed (to the King's Head) during the reign of Henry VIII. An open fire and intimate bar complement the warmth of the staff's welcome. Children welcomed on patio.

goes through pastureland and is flanked by hedges. It leads eventually to the A20, with Harrietsham straight ahead. Follow the road through the village and turn right back to the station.

Beers and Food: Fremlin's Tusker and Shepherd Neame Master Brew, a sweet, well-hopped tipple, handpumped. A selection of other draught beers and lagers, including Whitbread Trophy, McEwan's Export and Heineken. Stella Artois and Strongbow cider. Range of fresh sandwiches and snacks and full menu (starters; steaks, chops, gammons or kebabs) for lunch or dinner except Sundays.

Park Gate Inn, near Eyhorne Street

About the Inn: Rather isolated free house off the A20, in the midst of sheep grazing pastureland. Jacobean exterior and interior; low ceilings, exposed beams in the two open bars. Lawn with wooden furniture in summer, children welcomed in garden. Coach parties positively discouraged.

Beers and Food: Seven draught bitters including Stones, Ansells Festival, Shepherd Neame and Fremlins. A la carte meals in the restaurant; plus full range of sandwiches and bar meals.

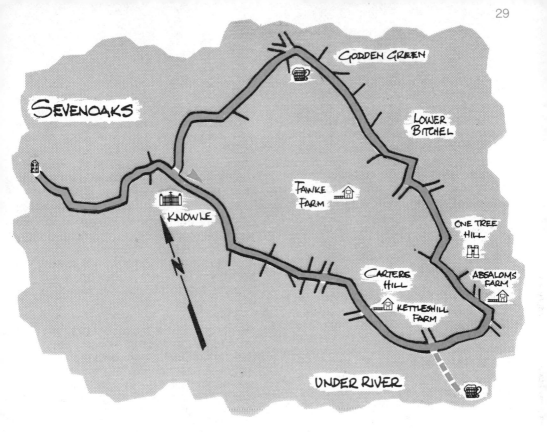

1e Sevenoaks

The District

Sevenoaks is a largish Kent town. Popular as a residential area for London commuters, it retains much of its rural atmosphere, having a lovely market and an easy leisurely pace in the comings and goings of the townspeople. Whether this pace was the reason for the popularity of that slowest and most graceful of sports, cricket, or vice-versa; it has been a great local interest now for 250 years. A nearby village where there was a thriving cricket-bat making industry was, and still is, called **Bat and Ball**.

One of the oldest and most famous boys schools in the country is Sevenoaks School, though the town is substantially older and it wouldn't take a genius to guess that the original settlement was in, or close to, a clump of seven oaks.

How to Get There

By train to Sevenoaks British Rail station, then bus 402, 431, 454A, 471 or 483 to Sevenoaks Bus station. By Green Line coach 705 or 706 from Victoria Coach Station London, or from Tunbridge Wells or Tonbridge to Sevenoaks Bus station.

To the start of the walk, turn left out of the Bus station and out onto the High St. Turn right along High Street and left along Buckhurst Lane. Follow the footpath signposted to Knole through the Park. By car, take the A21 from London and then the A2021 into Sevenoaks and turn off the High St into Knole Lane. Follow to Knole Car park £1 through the park.

►

The Sevenoaks / Knole Walk

Some of this walk can be wet and muddy in winter, so care and wellies should be taken. Start in Knole car park next to Knole House. Knole is an astonishing country house that looks more like a medieval township than anything else. Set in its beautiful parkland, it was first of all the property of Thomas Bourchier, an Archbishop of Canterbury, who built it between 1456-1486.

Subsequently owned by Henry VII and Lord Leicester, it was given by Queen Elizabeth I to Thomas Sackville in 1566 whose descendants have lived there ever since.

Vast is not the word for it, known as the Calendar House' it has 7 courtyards, 52 stairways and 365 rooms. Three hundred and sixty-five rooms — just think about it a minute and wonder what it must have been like to have been an aristocrat. Games of hide-and-seek could take up to a fortnight to finish. Think of the hoovering, dusting and polishing and the heating bills (phew!).

When you go inside, which you *must,* the interior is no less astonishing. A list will suffice, because there are guides and guide-books. Especially notable are the plasterwork ceilings, the marble chimney pieces, the painted decorations on the Great Staircase and in the Cartoon Gallery, the almost infinite number of paintings, many by famous artists, the magnificent tapestries, the unique and beautiful silverwork and the enormous amount of, well, furniture (Elizabethan and since). When the bed in the King's Bedroom was made, the construction and materials cost £40,000 at 1970 prices. Just think what that would be in 1980 prices, plus its antique value of course. Enough to make you insomniac at any rate. One thing I rather liked was the set of curved billiard cues (for cheats perhaps?). Fourteen rooms are open to the public and worth every penny of the £1.50 adult admission.

And now, after your researcher's exuberant enthusiasm, you can begin the walk, brimful with culture and probably exhausted already. From the car park walk down to the left along the walls, leaving the house on your right, and up along the tree-lined metalled roadway. Watch for the really very tame deer, but beware — they can bite. Follow the wall to the corner of the garden, where the road bears right past an odd little octagonal house. Just after this, fork off to the right on a gravelly track that disappears on your right, turn left onto another metalled track. Ignore turnings to your right and follow through very tall trees. Cross straight over a crossing onto a track of earth and stone.

Leave Knole Park through the gate ahead and, crossing the road, take the footpath opposite, through a plantation of cropped trees. At the far edge of the wood, cross the stile into a field, which looks like an assault-course for horses. Strike out diagonally for the opposite corner to your right, though if the field is being used by these horses keen on the glories of Badminton, you're advised to go around the edge. From this field at the top of Carter's Hill, there are good views across the Sevenoaks Weald so stop briefly to catch your breath and think 'Isn't England wonderful', but not for too long — it might rain.

In the corner of the field is a stile, cross it and turn right down a path on the right-hand bank of the gully. There are lots of bluebells here in spring. Follow the path downhill. At a big water tank the path joins the bridleway — you continue downhill passing old badger sets under tree-roots, and the path widens into a farm track just before Kettleshill Farm buildings. Ten out of ten for observation if you can spot the peacocks here.

Turn left onto the bridleway that skirts the

The Inns

garden of the house — this can be muddy in winter (and summer) so careful. Join a gravel driveway at Black Tharles and follow to the road. Turn right to go to **The White Rock** in Underriver, where you can have a pint and a sandwich to give you the necessary energy for the uphill stint to come. To continue the walk, go back to where you came out onto the road and turn right along the lane marked 'Shipbourne 2½ miles'. Walk along this quiet lane, past the cricket field on you right and an orchard on your left, to a junction where you turn left up the No Through Road. Turn left again at the oast houses and long barn of Absalom's Farm and follow the stony track uphill. Past the houses on your right, in the paddock below the Tudor House, you may see llamas — yes llamas! But keep your distance, as they can spit a long way and very accurately.

Where the track levels out, turn sharp right up a private drive and public footpath. Walk past White Rocks and follow the track to the left of the garage. Turn left up the steep bank between two stout trees and then turn left to continue climbing up a steep path and, when you are almost above White Rocks, turn right, away from the edge. In a few yards, you'll meet a track (there's a wooden bench to your right) but turn left along the track to a concrete bench with One Tree Hill engraved on it. Sit down here and rest, while enjoying the best views on the walk and patting yourself on the back for having got this far.

Then walk directly away from the bench and the view across the clearing, leaving the clump of gorse on your left. Follow the path gently downhill to the National Trust 'One Tree Hill' sign. Continue in the same direction with the field on your right. Go gently up again with the barbed wire fence on your right to Starvecrow House, where you turn left along its stony drive, still through woodland. At the lane, turn left and follow it down and then up.

Turn right just before Fawke Farm House along a concrete stone track, which becomes properly metalled. At the farm buildings, turn sharp left. Opposite the bungalow, Nether Fawke, turn right

The White Rock, Underriver

About the Inn: It is a modest 200 year old and very typical Kentish farmhouse pub — both rustic and snug. It's on the Sevenoaks Weald, under Carter's Hill, in a pretty village and its interior is as traditionally attractive as its exterior, with exposed oak beams, exposed stone walls, panelled bar and parquet floor. Mr Dennis Leahy welcomes walkers.

Beers and Food: A variety of Ind Coope beers with Friary Meux and Burton's hand-drawn. Good home-made sandwiches and sausages.

The Bucks Head, Godden Green

About the Inn: An immediately welcoming pub with a very friendly atmosphere. It is opposite the Green (where you can sit, weather permitting) and near the pond. Its interior boasts exposed beams and an inglenook fireplace and Mr Chandler has a very fine copper collection — jugs, pans etc. Anna Ford came here once!

Beers and Food: It's a Courage pub, with hand-drawn Directors. All other pub drinks and chilled wine by the glass. Lunchtime snacks are many and varied both hot and cold — sandwiches, steaks, scampi, pizzas, sausages, baked potatoes, shepherd's pie, pasties, quiche and oddly, Danish curry and savoury rolls. Coffee is also served.

through the gap in the holly-hedge and walk across the field, over the stile and into a second field, walk slightly left across this to a stile, climb over onto a path through woodland. At the crossing of paths, go straight over. At the second crossing, go straight over again, keeping the wooden fence on your left. When the path meets a bridleway, turn left and follow (it becomes metalled) past houses and emerge onto a road in Godden Green.

You will see **The Bucks Head** opposite; so panting with thirst, you will ignore its pretty redbrick exterior (with rings to tie horses to) in your hurry to reach the bar. However, armed with your pint of Directors and one of the many very substantial snacks on offer, you may feel inclined to sit out on the green or near the pond and then take a look around.

From the door of the pub, turn right along the road and then take the left fork to Sevenoaks. However, after a few yards, turn left and take the track through the gate. Follow the main stony track over a crossing and through the rhododendron bushes. Pass a large field on your right and go through the gate back into Knole Park. Follow the metalled track down and then gently up through an avenue of trees to Knole House and either your car or the path back to Sevenoaks.

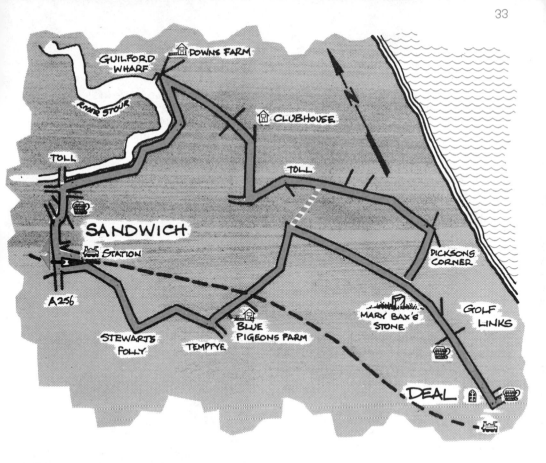

1f Sandwich

The District

Now a couple of miles from the sea, **Sandwich** was one of the original Cinque Ports and England's main harbour for the export of wool during the 13th century. The Guildhall and the surrounding market square form the nub of Sandwich; many of the town's 16th and 17th century buildings having over-hanging upper stories, a characteristic of Elizabethan architecture.

Sandwich has a one-way system round its closely-knit streets designed to infuriate the impatient motorist, and the town is perhaps best explored on foot. Look out for the Barbican, the toll-gate leading to the bridge over the Stour; and the parish church of St Clements, with its fine Norman tower.

There is safe swimming at Sandwich

Bay, plus a long stretch of sandy beach, where you are more likely to see a redshank or a ringed plover, than a coach party of day-trippers tucking into hot dogs.

Nearby **Deal** is a more popular holiday resort, although it too has its old quarter with many ancient buildings arranged cheek to jowl in the narrow lanes. A modern pier and steep shingle beach, which gradually levels out towards the ruins of Sandown Castle, supplement the town's attractions. **Deal Castle** itself, erected by Henry VIII to defend England in the event of a French invasion, contains a museum filled with local finds.

How to Get There

By rail, from Charing Cross direct to Sandwich. Alternatively, trains run from ►

Ramsgate to Sandwich. By road, take A257 from Canterbury, or the A256 from Ramsgate.

The Sandwich Walk

This is a straightforward coastal walk along the east Kent coast from Sandwich to Deal, across land that gently shelves into the sea. To the north the sand dunes and salt marshes of Sandwich Bay are famed for their wild fowl.

Come out of Sandwich station, and walk down the short approach road; turning left at the end and then immediately right. This is the A256 going into Sandwich. The quickest way to get to the toll-bridge is to turn right, at a street called The Chain, which leads onto the High Street. This takes you to the square, just by the river; where to the left of the Barbican (the toll gate arch) you will see an excellent old inn, namely **The Admiral Owen.**

Named after a veteran of the Napoleonic Wars, The Admiral Owen was originally constructed in the 14th century as a monastery. Whether the monks' sideline in fermenting wine got out of hand remains idle speculation; but the fact is you are unlikely to notice such habits (!) here today.

From The Admiral Owen walk to the right of The Bell Inn, and pick up the footpath leading from the car park over a grassy field. The River Stour is navigable here and pleasure cruisers are sometimes available for hire. Keeping the river to your left, walk past some willow trees, to a children's playground. The Stour curves round to the left, and you should cross a footbridge, with a short stretch of the river snaking away to the right. Keep to the earthy path; the river curves away for a while, and then rejoins the path. Eventually the path leaves the river altogether and crosses Guilford Wharf, and here you should go through a wooden gate on a grassy bank.

With Downs Farm now ahead of you, turn right into a metalled road. This road curves round and takes you past Royal St George's Golf Club. This part of the walk is good for bird-watching, but take care not to be knocked out by a low-flying golf ball whilst gawping at a Plover, a Sandpiper or a Sandwich Tern.

Just past the clubhouse the lane joins the access road for the golf club and you should turn right here. This takes you down to a road, onto which you turn left. It passes alongside a small tributary of the Stour and leads to the Toll House, which has a sign indicating 'Private Road to Sandwich Bay Estate'. Follow this road past part of the estate and, at a modern white villa, take the unmetalled track to the right, which continues along the line of the road. Where the track divides, take the path which forks slightly to the right, not the one which is at almost 45 degrees. This path takes you to the end of the Royal Cinque Port Golf links.

Eventually you will see a solitary brick building behind a small grassy incline. Bear left here and follow the line of its bank, keeping the fence to your right. After a while you will come to Mary Bax's Stone, a small gravestone with well-weathered writing.

The story goes that as Mary was walking along this track, which used to be the ancient Sandwich to Deal highway, she was accosted by a drunken sailor who brutally murdered her. The stone marks the actual spot of the crime. Keep following this track, with the golf course still to your left and very soon the club's nineteenth

The Inns

hole will appear like a mirage on the horizon. **The Chequers** is the half-way mark between Sandwich and Deal (don't panic, you're getting a train back!) and in fact used to be called The Halfway House, but was reputedly re-christened as a result of some more of those wayward monks using it as a cashpoint for their cheques.

Anyway from here you should continue along the well-defined track to Deal; passing several houses and the Cinque Ports Clubhouse to the right. Take the first right-hand turning, and walk down to a T-junction. Here you will see a cul-de-sac and Sandown Road to the right. The remains of Sandown Castle are just visible on the seafront, and the pub of the same name is just down the road.

The sea is responsible for the gradual erosion of this castle; built by Henry VIII at the same time as Deal, as part of his campaign to Keep Britain Safe, after having quarrelled with the Pope. All that remains of the site nowadays is a rock garden, which offers good views over Pegwell Bay to Ramsgate and across the sandhills to Sandwich.

Follow Sandown Road back towards Deal and, at the next major road intersection, turn left and then right. This road leads onto the seafront, with Deal Castle a little way down to the right. After inspecting the castle, retrace your steps to the pier and take the road leading back into town. Look out for a small road to the right indicating Deal railway station where you can catch a train back to Sandwich. Trains are frequent; and Sandwich only one stop away.

The Admiral Owen, Sandwich

About the Inn: Situated in the centre of Sandwich, with room for cars by the river, this timber-framed building has much to recommend it. There are two bars, both with heavy wood tables and chairs and decorated with interesting photographs, documents and old clocks.

Beers and Food: A Truman house with draught and keg bitter available. Good range of sandwiches at this 'ere pub in Sandwich, plus excellent value basket meals.

The Chequers, halfway between Sandwich and Deal

About the Inn: Over 400 years old, the Chequers is an old smuggling inn, which is rumoured to have an as yet undiscovered tunnel to the beach, and a piano-playing ghost. The black and white building has been modernised and nowadays includes several Spanish-style arches. The pub's hosts are Mr & Mrs Humphreys from West Ham, who have made this pub quite a centre of entertainment, despite its remote location.

Beers and Food: A free house with a comprehensive range of beers, including the popular Scottish and Tartan, and real ale on occasion. Separate restaurant. Snacks, including scampi, available over the bar. The pub operates a take-away service.

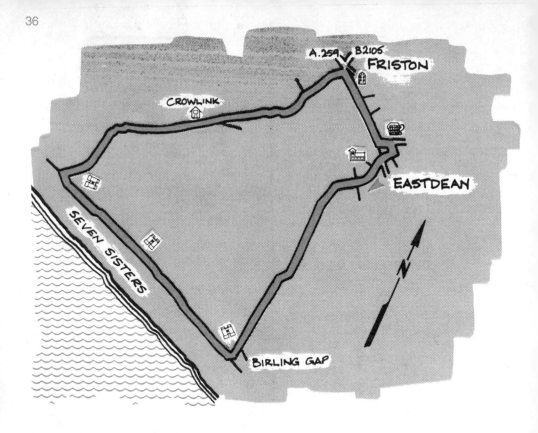

1g East Dean

The District

The village of **East Dean** occupies a secluded position on the South Downs and consists of several attractive flint-built cottages, grouped around a green. The church and the pub vie for being East Dean's most remarkable feature: the church has a fine, late Saxon tower and three foot thick wall, whereas **The Tiger Inn** (more of which later) is reputedly the oldest pub in Sussex.

The road south from East Dean leads to **Birling Gap**, which is the only point of access to the sea between Cuckmere Haven and Beachy Head. This dip between the lofty cliffs used to be a favourite with smugglers, and at one time the authorities actually blocked the passageway with a gate and a portcullis. Many ships have

been wrecked on the perilous rocks beneath, and the story goes that the vicar of East Dean narrowly escaped death in 1813, when a huge section of the cliffs gave way and vanished into the grey-green sea.

Eastbourne, 3 miles to the east, still has the aristocratic air of a once highly fashionable watering place, with its grand Victorian and Edwardian houses along the parade. Eastbourne is sheltered by **Beachy Head**, the highest and most easterly point of the South Downs, and from where, on a clear day, it is possible to see the Isle of Wight.

How to Get There

East Dean is on the A259, between Seaford and Eastbourne. Trains run frequently between London (Victoria) and

Eastbourne; and from here you can catch a green bus (112) to East Dean.

The East Dean Walk

The instructions for this walk are short and straightforward, as you simply go beyond Birling Gap and over the brows of the famous Seven Sisters chalk cliffs, before turning inland. However, although these paths are clearly defined, and along protected land; take care, as blustery weather conditions can make the going more treacherous.

From the pub, **The Tiger Inn**, cross the green to the opposite side and bear left on the path leading uphill, past the old School house (*not the sharp left turn*). Continue past the old Bakehouse, up the track and through a farm gate. This track leads uphill to a rise and across the fields in the direction of Birling Gap. Veer right in view of the village in the hollow, following the public footpath, indicated by arrows on the gate posts, to the cliff's edge. You are now approaching the first sister, endearingly named 'Went Hill', and the way continues over three sisters to a cairn and a seat on the top of the third hill. Note the horizontal lines of flint in these chalky cliffs, as well as the scrubby growth of hawthorn and other wild shrubs, characteristic of the chalky downs.

From the summit of the third sister, turn right downhill and head directly inland, passing Crowlink. At Friston, a tiny village perched on a hill, turn right onto a footpath behind the church, which will take you back into East Dean.

The Inn

The Tiger Inn, East Dean

About the Inn: An ideal starting point for walks over the South Downs; the inn is situated on the edge of the village green. Reputedly the oldest pub in Sussex, The Tiger Inn is a two-storeyed flint building, painted white and adorned with various plants and flowers. It derives its name from the Lord of the Manor's coat of arms, although years later it was discovered that the cat was actually a leopard and not a tiger! The Kitchen Bar reflects the inn's age, with its sturdy oak beams and stone floor. The fire in this bar, which originally came from nearby Friston Place, dates back to 1622 and at one time a tax of one penny had to be paid every time it was lit.

Beers and Food: A Courage house offering a good pint of Directors. The Landlord, Mr Conroy, ensures a friendly welcome for walkers by providing morning coffee or hot toddies (as the weather or inclination dictates!). The menu is changed twice-yearly, and the steak and kidney pie is popular in the winter, and the smoked mackerel and liver pâté in summer.

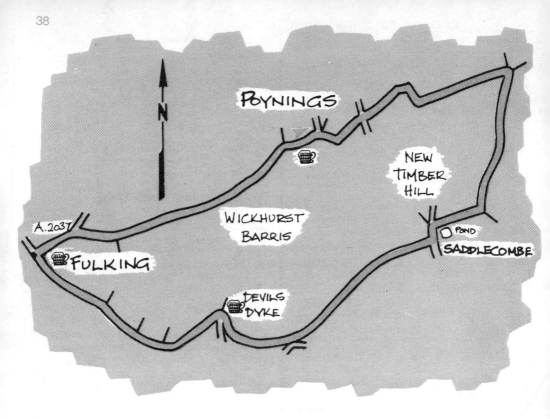

1h Poynings

The District

Poynings, a picturesque village on the Sussex Downs is named after the Poynings family who were notable servants of the crown until Tudor times. Its Holy Trinity Church dates from the late 14th century.

Nearby **Pyecombe** once a centre of the iron industry, still boasts an active smithy which produces a great variety of iron objects including 'Pyecombe hooks': shepherds' crooks made of iron for which the village was renowned in the nineteenth century. The smithy was once haunted by witches, the exorcism of which is celebrated every year on November 23rd.

Devil's Dyke is a famous 45 degree scarp and an important centre these days for hang-gliding.

How to Get There

By car A23 from London to Poynings turn-off. Train to Brighton and then bus to Poynings (fairly good service).

The Poynings Walk

This is quite a long (about 6 miles) and hilly walk with fine views over the Weald.

We begin at **The Royal Oak** in Poynings, a comfortable 19th century inn in a picturesque spot below Devil's Dyke and, after a few pints of Pompey's Royal, we are ready for off. Turn left out of the pub down to the T-junction with its interesting circular shelter. Turn right to a second T-junction. Cross the road and take the footpath which climbs steeply through the scattered trees and gorse bushes.

At the brow of the hill this path is crossed by another. Turn right here and follow it around the left side of the valley into Saddlescombe, a small farming hamlet.

Go through the buildings, past a well on the left, round the pond and on to the road. Opposite on the left there is a public footpath which leads around the hill on the right-hand side of Devil's Dyke valley, and then up through more gorse to the brow of the hill. Here the path joins the South Downs Way and there is a marvellous view stretching from Saddlescombe in the foothills across the whole of the Sussex plain as far as Brighton. Devil's Dyke, legend has it, earnt its name because Old Nick himself, frightened by the ever-increasing number of churches in the area, tried to dig a trench out to sea in the vain hope of flooding the area. He was scared off, however, by the flame of a candle lit by an old woman in Pyecombe which he (rather stupidly) took to be the rising sun. His attempt to drown his problems was thus thwarted. He would have been better advised to do what we are doing, to follow the path round the head of the dyke to **The Devil's Dyke Hotel,** and to drown his problems there instead, with a few pints of Bass. This inn has a garden from which the weary traveller can watch the hang-gliders rushing like lemmings over the top of the scarp.

The path leads further along the edge of the scarp and over a wire fence by a stile. After a second stile the path forks and the right-hand one takes us down to Fulking. Head for the left-hand side of the village where you will find **The Shepherd and Dog.** There is a fresh water spring beside the pub and John Ruskin recommended the waters for health and long life, urging the villagers to build a fountain here. If you don't fancy trying the waters, then try the ales in the pub instead. From Fulking there is a path beside the road which leads all the way back to Poynings and **The Royal Oak.**

The Inns

The Royal Oak, Poynings

About the Inn: Built in the late nineteenth century, this is a comfortable tavern resting in a picturesque spot below Devil's Dyke, which can be viewed from the large beer garden. Darts can be played.

Beers and Food: Local Pompey Royal as well as Watney's Ales and the usual wines and spirits. Extensive selection of bar snacks.

Devil's Dyke Hotel, Devil's Dyke

About the Inn: Situated on the top of Devil's Dyke and frequented by hang-gliders, of which pictures decorate the walls. Beer garden with a panoramic view. Pool and darts.

Beers and Food: Stones, Bass Charington and Mild, Black Label lager. Try the Bass. Lots of bar snacks including a good Ploughman's lunch which is excellent value at 75½p.

Shepherd and Dog, Fulking

About the Inn: At the foot of the Downs and over 300 years old. Inside, the ceiling is low and bow-beamed. Open fire. There is a large beer garden on both sides of the stream where those faint-hearts who are tired of beer can take John Ruskin's advice and sample the water. Darts are played, though it is a bit dodgy with the low ceiling.

Beers and Food: Watneys, Ben Truman and Carlsberg as well as lots of bottled beer, wines and spirits. Many bar snacks (though unfortunately not on Sunday).

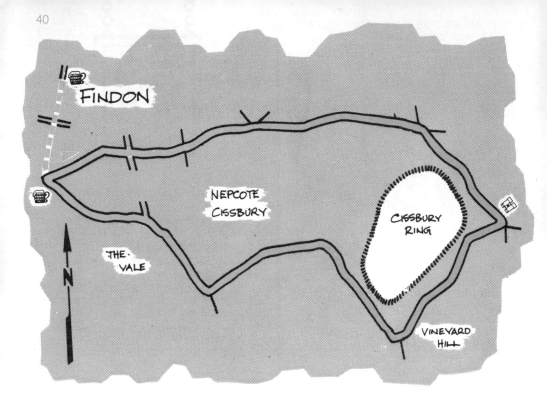

1i   Findon

The District

Findon is a beautiful small village in a narrow valley just north of Worthing. It contains some fine old buildings made of flint and its Norman Church of St John the Baptist is a fascinating jumble of different architectural styles, with a chimney rising from the roof of the nave. The winners of many famous races have been trained at the Downs Training Stables including Grand National winners in 1912, 1913 and, more recently, 1962.

To the east of the village (on the walk) stands **Cissbury Ring**, an Iron Age fort dating from around 200 BC. In the west part of the fort there are flint mines dating from some 2000 years earlier. The defences consist of a massive rampart and ditch with a small counterscarp bank on the outer lip of the ditch. Its highest point is 602 feet, and the ring has been variously used since the Iron Age by the Romans (who refortified part of it), the Saxons and even the British Army in the Second World War!

How to Get There

By car, the A24 from London. By train to Worthing then a bus to Findon which stops outside The Black Horse.

The Findon Walk

This walk is short, only 2 - 3 miles, and gentle so you've got no excuse to leave granny in the car.

The Black Horse Inn in Findon High Street is the starting place for this walk and some Pompey Royal or their strong country bitter should put you in the frame of mind to try anything, let alone a quiet country stroll! Turn left out of the inn, up the road to the left and first right up to the village green. Take the footpath across Nepcote green, which has been the site of a sheep fair since 1790, and back to the road which continues up towards Cissbury. Where the surfacing ends, turn right up to the Ring, then left up a sloping chalk path to the top of the hill. From here there is an excellent view as far as Worthing. Continue through a gate and down the path which soon divides into three.

Take the right-hand path which leads you round the head of a wooded valley to the top of Vineyard Hill. Turn right where the path meets another on the other side of the valley, which takes you back to the Ring. It is worth having a look at this iron-age fort, and from the top of it there is a superb view of Findon and the surrounding countryside. Many prehistoric artifacts have been dug up around here, and there was reputedly a Saxon mint, the site of which has yet to be discovered. During the war, an anonymous donor sent a chalk head to Worthing Museum saying it had been dug up at Cissbury. This proved to be true, but the fact that its origins were somewhat less than ancient was clear from the Hitler moustache which it sported!

The path continues round the Ring and down to the car park. Cross the park (actually a large field) to the far right-hand corner and cross the stile to the footpath. This goes back to Findon, turning into a track and then joining a road. Take the road to the right and turn left and walk right up the High Street to the Square. Here, **The Village House Hotel**, previously a school, a hospital and a morgue, now has six different varieties of real ale guaranteed to sate even the most jaded of hikers' palates!

The Inns

Black Horse Inn, Findon

About the Inn: Quite a recently built pub, but no less friendly for all that. The locals (including Josh Gifford, who recently won £¼ million pounds on the pools!) are involved in many fund-raising events for local pensioners. There is a beer garden outside and within there are many old photographs of the village as far back as 1890.

Beers and Food: Pompey Royal and Strong Country Bitter for real ale enthusiasts, mild and lager. Many snacks, salads and sandwiches. In winter hot bar meals for around £1 (eg curry, lamb casserole).

Village House Hotel, Findon

About the Inn: Dating back to the 16th century, this attractive Tudor tavern has been, in its day, a school, hospital and a morgue, Presumably this last is where the two ghosts — one male, one female . — originated. There is a lawn outside, a patio with a goldfish pond and accommodation for nine within.

Beers and Food: A choice of no less than six real ales, all hand-drawn, as well as many bottled beers, wines and spirits. Many bar snacks and full à la carte meals available in their 30 seat restaurant.

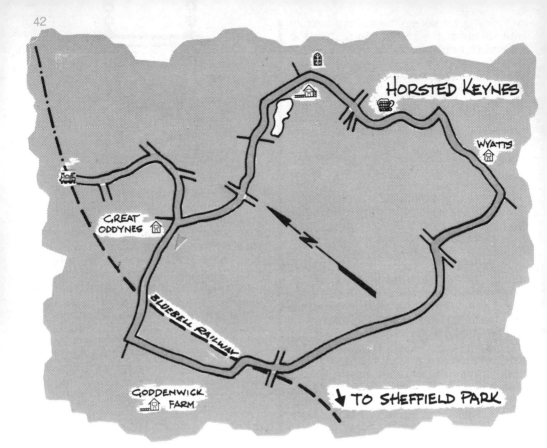

1j Horsted Keynes

The District

This is, above all, *the* walk for railway enthusiasts and families wanting to combine fresh air with a fun activity for kids from nine to 99, as the saying goes. The village of **Horsted Keynes** takes its name from a Norman baron, and its church has many Norman features. But perhaps its greatest claim to fame is being the larger of two stations on the famous Bluebell Line, which sets off from **Sheffield Park** at the southern end of the line.

Set in the heart of the Sussex Weald and running for 5 miles through some of its most beautiful countryside, the Bluebell Railway is a living museum for the steam train and has become one of the major attractions in south-east England. Operated and maintained by the Bluebell Railway Preservation Society, a voluntary organisation, the railway boasts one of the largest collections of vintage railway stock in the country, with authentically preserved stations to match.

Sheffield Park itself is not a village, but a lovely period station, and a magnificent 18th century garden laid out by Capability Brown, featuring all manner of exotic trees and shrubs, lawns, an avenue of hardy palms arranged around five lakes decorated by ornamental bridges, waterfalls and a mass of waterlilies.

How to Get There

Horsted Keynes is 3 miles north of Sheffield Park, off A265. By car, drive to Sheffield Park on A22 from East Grinstead and London, then onto A275; from Lewes take the A275, and from Brighton turn right onto A272 and then onto A275. From Sheffield Park take the Bluebell Line to Horsted Keynes. By train to East Grinstead or Haywards Heath, then Southdown Bus 170 to Church Street, Horsted Keynes.

The Horsted Keynes 'Bluebell Line' Walk

A gentle 4 mile walk with a ride on the Bluebell and a visit to the splendid gardens at Sheffield Park form the highlights of a day out.

The walk begins at Horsted Keynes station after a ride up the Bluebell Line from Sheffield Park if you come by rail. The train journey takes about 15 minutes. Follow the station road south to a T-junction, turn left to a second junction and then turn right. Look for a track to the right leading to Great Oddynes Farm. Leave the farm behind you via a footpath which follows a line of trees down to a pedestrian railway crossing. Cross with care to a gate, and over the gate into a field.

Walk straight through this field, leaving by a gate and stile in the far right corner, then follow a line of trees around to the left and across a wooden bridge over a brook.

Cross the ploughed field to a double gate to the left of some trees, and then pass through the gate into another field. Walk along the left perimeter of this field towards Goddenwick Farm. Leaving the farm on your left, join the track that leads down over a brook and up to a railway bridge. Do *not* take the bridge, but instead follow the track round to the right, which offers some excellent views of the steam train passing under the bridge.

The path joins a wider road; turn left under a bridge and look for a gate into the woods on your right. Take this gate through

The Inn

Crown Inn, Horsted Keynes

About the Inn: Set close to the station at the northern end of the Bluebell Line, this inn lies beside the village green. Built in the early 19th century of stone, its entrance is dominated by a huge yew tree. The inn boasts two spacious, comfortable bars and a large collection of kegrings.

Beers and Food: Watney's Stones real ale, Stag Bitter on draught. Carling Black Label on draught. Small, inexpensive restaurant and usual bar snacks.

►

to a large field. Follow the right perimeter of the field towards the woods, the path swinging to the left with the field. You will see a wide gap in the woods on your right; take this gap through the trees into the fields on the other side.

Continue along the line of trees to a large house. Just before the house turn left into a new field towards a gate. Cross over the gate onto the road; follow the road to the left, immediately looking out for a footpath on the right. Take this footpath over two stiles into a field, cross the field and over another stile into a gap in the woods ahead. Climb to a white cottage. Turn left past the cottage and up a winding path, up to, and past, tennis courts. Take the first right into the car park of **The Crown Inn**, an early 19th century stone tavern.

Kick off your shoes in one of The Crown's spacious bars, enjoy a draught of Watney's or Stone's real ale to mask the odour, then drag yourself out onto the path opposite the inn towards the village school and church. At the church follow a path to the left then turn sharp right down the hill to an elegant private house beside a water-mill. Follow this path alongside a lake towards a timbered barn. Turn right just before the barn, past the head of the lake and then turn to the left. Follow the track down to a black creosoted barn and onto a road, then turn right over a bridge, then left onto a footpath leading back up to Great Oddynes Farm.

The route has taken you full circle; turn right back to the road, then left and left again back to Horsted Keynes station.

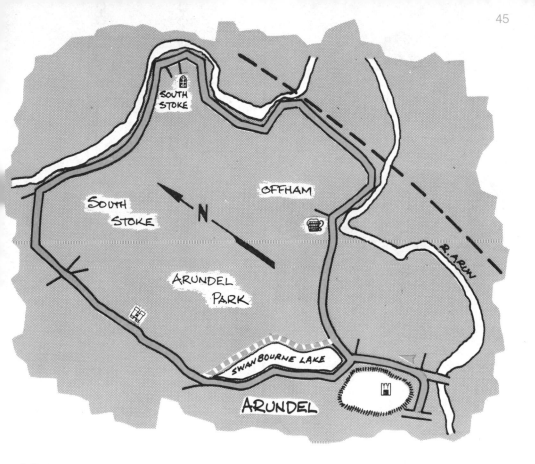

1k Arundel

The District

The **Arun** region on the south coast of England is an ideal area for family visits, whether for a day or a fortnight's holiday. Along the coast are dotted some of the country's most popular holiday resorts, like **Bognor Regis** and **Littlehampton**, while inland the fertile South Downs are pierced by the lazy River Arun.

Arundel itself is a magnificent medieval town in a tranquil setting, justly famous for the old saying 'there are many beautiful places in the world, but there is only one Arundel'. It offers a huge variety of places of interest, a charming gentle walk through some of the county's most impressive countryside and a number of fine traditional alehouses (as well as more modern watering-holes). Unquestionably, the town is dominated by **Arundel Castle**, a mighty Norman stronghold steeped in history and legend. Besieged three times, it was finally laid to ruins by the Roundheads during the Civil War and magnificently restored at the beginning of the 19th century. Its baronial apartments, with their fine collection of portraits, are open to the public from April to October.

Aside from the castle Arundel boasts a **toy museum**, off the High Street in the main square; a **crafts and heritage museum**, also off the main square; and an industrial history museum called **Chalk Pits Museum** in Amberley, about 1¼ miles outside the town. It also boasts the most complete complex of surviving 14th century buildings in England, at **Arundel Priory**. It is the

►

home of the Wildfowl Trust's newest centre, which lies between Swanbourne Lake and the River Arun and will ultimately consist of almost 1,500 wildfowl from many parts of the world.

How to Get There

By car, on A29 from London or A27 from Littlehampton and Brighton. The castle is within walking distance of the BR station in Arundel, served from London and most Southern Region stations in the general area.

The Arundel Walk

A pleasant walk, about 4 miles long along the South Downs starting from the historic town of Arundel. Those wanting to stay overnight could do worse than try **The Norfolk Arms**, a charming traditional hostelry and Georgian coaching inn, built by the Duke of Norfolk in 1783. Visited both by the author G K Chesterton and the monarch Queen Victoria, the inn's landlord David Horridge takes pride in its fine restaurant and real ales.

The walk begins to the right of the castle, by the large car park. Follow the road north along an avenue of trees towards a humpbacked bridge, and watch for a turning on the left. Those with dogs should take this turning and follow a well-defined path. Others may continue towards the humpbacked bridge, keeping some old stone barns on your left. Cross the bridge over the River Arun (this point offers a fine view of Swanbourne Lake) past a 'No dogs please' sign. Both these paths enter a wood and merge. Continue until you reach a fork in the path, then take the right-hand fork up

The Inns

Black Rabbit, Offham

About the Inn: On the approach road to Arundel from Offham, lying beside the bank of the River Arun, this charming 16th century inn was a watering-hole for soldiers in the Middle Ages. About a century ago a group of navvies drunk the inn dry, barracaded themselves inside and murdered the landlord and his wife. They were hung two days later for their efforts, and it is rumoured that their ghosts still haunt the Guinness barrels! Probably the most famous pub in the South of England (at least according to the landlord) it can certainly be described as family-run: 10 members of Brian Kirby's brood help out, and the atmosphere benefits from their enthusiasm.

Beers and Food: The whole range of McEwans and William Youngers beers, dry Blackthorn cider and Guinness on draught. Home-made hot and cold snacks every day of the year and French cuisine in the beautiful restaurant.

Norfolk Arms, Arundel

About the Inn: Built in 1783, a picturesque Georgian coaching inn with 35 bedrooms (all mod cons including colour TV). Pool and table tennis, children welcomed. No music.

Beers and Food: King & Barnes Sussex Bitter (a well hopped ale) and Pompey Royal handpumped from the barrel. Good selection of pub grub and a hotel restaurant offering excellent table d'hôte and à la carte menus.

47

the side of the valley, through an open cluster of deciduous trees.

Follow the path out of the trees to the brow of the hill; the ground here is covered by gorse bushes. From this vantage point the views of the castle and its grounds to the south and the wide, sweeping Arun valley are majestic. Large chalk cliffs fill the distance to the left, with South Stoke and Burpham to the north-east.

Follow the path down the hill towards the River Arun and along its right bank along the footpath to South Stoke, a small village which is little more than a group of farmhouses and barns. Continue along the river bank as it twists its way back to Arundel and the sea; passing Offham to the right. The route takes you into the gardens of **The Black Rabbit**, an early 16th century inn steeped in history and truly classic ales. Beyond the inn the path leaves the river bank and leads onto the road running south back to the town centre.

The walk is well-defined, signposted and trodden, but none the less enjoyable for that.

White Swan, Arundel

About the Inn: On the Chichester Road this neat 16th century inn, a canopied black and white building fringed by woodland, was once a haven for pilgrims and the landed gentry alike. Its most famous occupant, a ghost named Jupp, has overstayed his welcome by several centuries. Landlord Gordon Groves is no mean shot with a harpoon (slow payers should avoid this place!) and trophies commemorating his feats adorn the walls.

Beers and Food: King & Barnes and Bass real ale handpumped, plus a unique version of a Bloody Mary (no, they don't use real blood!). Extensive bar snacks and good restaurant with table d'hôte and à la carte menus.

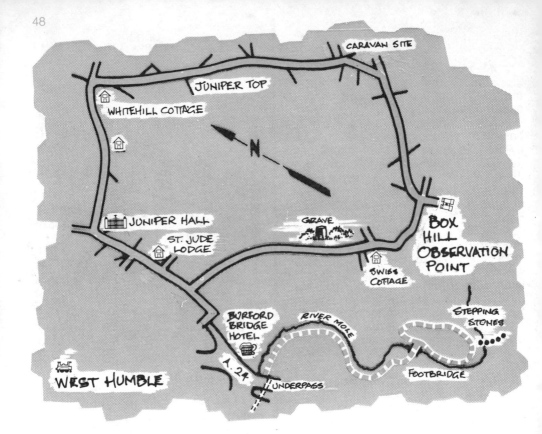

11 Box Hill

The District

Probably the most popular viewpoint and picnic area in the Home Counties, **Box Hill** has been open to the public for more than half a century and is now owned and maintained by the National Trust. A dramatic rise on the North Downs above the River Mole, it offers a breathtaking, panoramic view down over Dorking and across the South Downs. The chalk cliff-top takes its name from the native box trees on the western side, and is the site of a famous picnic in Jane Austen's novel *Emma*. The novelist and poet George Meredith lived in **Flint Cottage** at the foot of the hill from 1867 to 1909.

Juniper Bottom is one of several parallel valleys which run up to the edge of the escarpment; the sides are thickly studded with junipers, oak, ash, beech, yew, whitebeam, firs and box tree. The wood of the box tree, of which there are many varieties, is very close grained and particularly suitable for musical and mathematical instruments. Beneath the hill, between it and Juniper Bottom, is the site of **Labelliere Grave**. A major of that name, one of the area's foremost eccentrics, was buried there in 1800. At his own request he was buried head downwards because, he claimed, the world was topsyturvy and he wanted to be the right way up at the end.

The viewpoint, 563 feet above sea level, can be reached by a number of routes; a steep ascent from Burford Bridge or a zigzag path from the same spot, and easy climbs along the northern approaches from the Headley Road and Mickleham.

How to Get There

By car, from London to Kingston and Esher, then onto A24 Leatherhead to Dorking road. By train to Box Hill and West Humble, then walk through the pedestrian underpass under A24 to the car park opposite the Burford Bridge Hotel.

The Box Hill Walk

A shortish walk (about 3½ miles) exploring the countryside beneath the hill. The area is liable to be very crowded on a fine summer's day, though the route seeks to avoid the worst of the crowds. Almost better to visit the area on a dull day, in which case be prepared for some muddiness.

The Burford Bridge Hotel was the site of Lord Nelson's emotional farewell to Lady Hamilton before the Battle of Trafalgar, and also where Keats wrote the last part of his poem *Endymion*. As the result of extensive modernisation it has lost some of its charm, but continues to serve fine ales and fare. From its car park, turn left up the metalled road past St Jude Lodge cottage, which is the road cars take up to the Observation Point. Carry on along the road towards Juniper Hall.

All the entrances right and left are now to private houses. At the Hall turn right and pass the back entrance to the Hall and another cottage on your right. Reaching White Hill Cottage, turn right along the footpath. Here the path forks, the right fork being a bridlepath, the left a footpath barred to prevent horses straying onto it. Take the footpath and climb a steep, grassy slope to the plateau at the top. Cross the plateau and take the right-hand opening through the trees to descend along a heavily wooded path. This path bears slightly to the

The Inn

Burford Bridge Hotel, Box Hill

About the Inn: Developed from a humble tavern in the middle of the 17th century, the hotel was popular as a country retreat for the fashionable, particularly in literary and artistic circles during the 18th and 19th centuries. Robert Louis Stevenson wrote part of *Kidnapped* here. An imposing Georgian building, with an open air swimming pool and beautiful gardens to the rear, bordering on Box Hill. Attractive antique furniture and Nelson memorabilia on the walls. Overnight accommodation for 60.

Beers and Food: Young's Special and Watney's London Bitter handpumped; Guinness, Tuborg, Carlsberg and Ben Truman on draught. The complete range of food, from humble snacks and simple pub grub to elaborate restaurant fare. Reasonable prices.

▶

right (there is a barbed wire fence on your right) and, after some distance, you will see two tree trunks lying across the path, with a caravan site just visible to your left. This is a warning to turn away from civilisation, so bear right which brings you out to... a car park!

Cross the car park and, on reaching the main road, turn right. This leads to the Observation Point and a series of magnificent views that almost make up for the odious popularity of the place. Just along the roads is a large cafe offering expensive, virtually inedible junk food (a must for lovers of expensive, virtually inedible junk food!). Those who can hold out should take the pathway to the left just before the cafe. This path is well-marked by numerous small white posts, preventing parking in front of Swiss Cottage. This path leads down through the woods, past cranky Major Labelliere's grave, onto the open chalk path downhill, bearing left back to the car park. This track tends to be very slippery after rainfall.

pedestrian underpass). Just before the entrance to the underpass, climb a stile on your left and follow the river, selecting your own spot in this large grassy meadow. Those wishing to see the Stepping Stones, which according to legend is where the Romans and the Canterbury Pilgrims forded the river, should continue to follow the river to the green iron footbridge. Cross the bridge and turn right to the stones. This area is a great spot for a paddle in summer as the water is slow running and quite shallow.

If you fancy a picnic away from the crowds there is an ideal spot by the River Mole. Turn left at The Burford Bridge Hotel and walk towards Dorking (and the

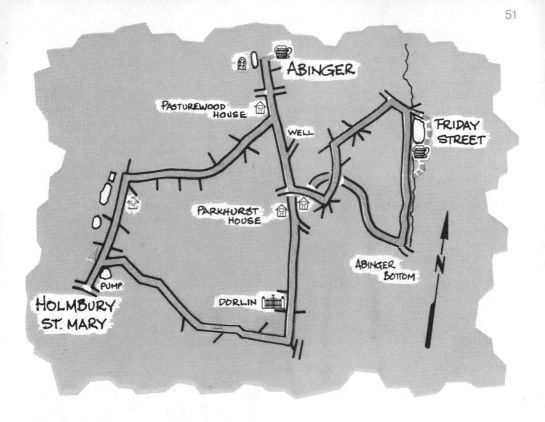

1m Holmbury St Mary

The District
Situated in a superb setting in the heart of the Surrey Hills, **Holmbury St Mary** lies close to Leith Hill. To the south-west, on **Holmbury Hill,** the ramparts of an Iron Age camp have been unearthed. These Iron Age people probably hunted wild boar in the Wealden forest below, and made primitive pots and utensils, the remnants of which have been excavated. The village offers a fine view of the Weald. The church of St Mary was designed and bequeathed by George E Street in 1879 as a memorial to his second wife. Art treasures in the church include an 800 year old altar cross, and two Italian pieces: a Madonna and Child triptych and sculpture.

The route passes through the hamlet of **Friday Street,** set in a pinewood valley and part of the vast Wotton estate. The lake was formed by damming the River Tillingbourne.

How to Get There
By car, on the A25 from London and Guildford, right just past Abinger Hammer onto B2126 to Holmbury St Mary. By train, to Dorking then either 417 Ramblers' Bus or 412 Green Line bus to Holmbury; or to Guildford and 412 Green Line to Holmbury.

The Holmbury St Mary Walk
About 4½ miles (the alternative route adds a mile) through the rolling landscape of the Surrey Hills. A quiet district with the countryside very much the main attraction.

On the left, just past the church of St Mary in Holmbury, there is a pond with an

►

old-fashioned water pump by it. Turn left here, and take the path straight ahead through the trees. When you see the derelict house on your right, look for a square pool just a little further on, to the left. Turn right here and take a steep climb along the edge of the woods with a new spruce forest on your left. As the woods bear left, keep straight ahead on a downhill track. At the junction of tracks, continue straight over (or around) a stile, on to a path which eventually bears left towards Pasturewood House and some cottages. Turn left onto a metalled road, and continue for about a half mile to **The Abinger Hatch.** A beautiful traditional hostelry opposite Abinger Common's Norman church and Village Green, it offers a wide range of handpumped real ales and choice of bar snacks or restaurant menu. If your boots are muddy, take the side entrance into the inn as this has a flagstone floor — the front entrance leads to the restaurant and is carpeted.

After a satisfying lunch retrace your steps along the main road and continue past St James's Well, now unfortunately not in working order. At the Y junction on the left, take the left path alongside the garden of a house. Continue until you reach another junction, take the left fork along a road with a horse barrier across it. You may see horses being exercised opposite. Cross the road and take the path straight behind the exercise ring. Where the main paths cross (the ground rises before you) go right.

At a junction of 5 paths, bear left (do *not* take the path sharp left — telephone wires run overhead along the correct route). Continue down to the main road and turn right towards Friday Street Lake.

At this point you may, if you prefer, take an alternative route. Cross the bridge and turn right into the woods, continuing along the clear path which follows the line of the back gardens to The Stephen Langton Inn and neighbouring cottages. After approximately half a mile, fork right to cross a stream by the plank bridge, which will bring you back onto the main path — at which either turn right for the inn, or left to continue the walk. This area, especially the upper reaches, is extremely popular in the summer as a picnic area (every other person seems to emerge from the undergrowth toting a wicker basket!).

At the lake, the main walk continues with a right turn. On the left is The Stephen Langton Inn. Although boasting a pleasant bar and good food, we are not featuring this inn as, despite its name, it is more of a family restaurant than a noteworthy watering-hole. The paths meets a metalled road, on which turn right and follow the route uphill back to the house.

At the main road turn left and, with Parkhurst on your right, walk straight ahead off the main road along a path leading to a steep-sided bridlepath. At Dorlin go straight ahead (the path to the right is private estate property) and just before the main road, turn right on a footpath which you can follow downhill all the way back to Holmbury St Mary.

The Inn

Abinger Hatch, Abinger Common

About the Inn: In the heart of open, rolling countryside and sited opposite a Norman church, the Village Green and the original stocks (still used for those who forget to pay), the inn exudes an inviting and friendly atmosphere, landlord, Michael Cuthbert, enthusiastically offering a wide and changing selection of fine real ales. Charlie Chaplin once stayed here. Exposed oak beams, a beautiful open fireplace and flag-stone floor complete the traditional feel of an inn which is the best country pub in a 15 mile radius (the landlord has sworn to this fact on a bible). A large lawn, on which children are welcomed, and a cosy dining room. Darts; live music on Monday and Saturday evenings.

Beers and Food: A free house, the Hatch offers a wide selection of real ales — King & Barnes ordinary and Old (during winter) ale, Pompey Royal, Badger Best (a moreish Dorset concoction), John Smith's Yorkshire Bitter and Courage Directors, all handpumped — and enjoys experimenting. Good pub grub, buffets and full dinner in the restaurant, carvery lunches during summer months.

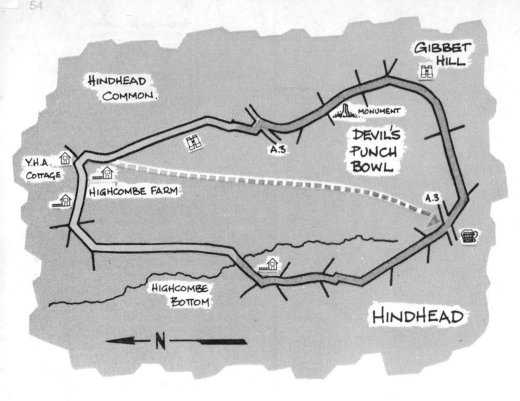

1n Hindhead

The District

The Devil's Punch Bowl, known to the Anglo-Saxons as Wolf's Den, rests beneath the old London to Portsmouth road, once one of England's major coaching routes and a notorious attraction for outlaws and highwaymen.

The walk begins in **Hindhead**, the highest village in Surrey and a former home of Sir Arthur Conan Doyle, creator of Sherlock Holmes (The Undershaw Hotel has an exhibition of Doyle memorabilia). Crammed with antique and bric-a-brac shops, Hindhead is in the heart of 'fat farm' country; at nearby Grayshott Hall and Forest Mere the rich and desperate queue to pay hundreds of pounds a week for the privilege of drinking hot water, eating grapefruit and sweating off the inches against a magnificent Hampshire landscape.

6 miles north-west of the village are **Frensham Ponds**, a popular area for picnicking and for yachting, sailing model boats or just tanning on a lazy summer afternoon.

How to Get There

By car, A3 from London (with a spectacular view down onto the Punch Bowl about a mile outside Hindhead). Free public parking by the start of the walk. The nearest BR station is Haslemere (about 4 miles away), with National bus routes 219 and 268 between the station and Hindhead.

The Hindhead/Devil's Punch Bowl Walk

The walk is a combination of two National Trust walks (Devil's Punch Bowl and Gibbet Hill); it begins at the NT's Hillcrest car park, where individual leaflets on these walks can be obtained (price 5p). The walk is muddy and quite steep in parts, so granny should be discouraged from wearing her satin stilettos.

Nervous souls can steel themselves with a pre-walk lunch and aperitif in the attractive, Tudor-style **Devil's Punch Bowl Hotel** in Hindhead, which offers good, fresh food from a varied menu, ranging from inexpensive pub grub in its bars, to haute cuisine in its immaculate restaurant.

The Devil's Punch Bowl walk takes in the Punch Bowl itself, a breathtaking basin plunging over 300 feet from the highest point in Surrey, and Gibbet Hill, the scene of a gruesome highway murder and the summary execution of its three perpetrators in 1786. The murder spot is marked by a contemporary stone monument; the execution site by a cross. The hill affords spectacular views of the Punch Bowl and much of Surrey, Hampshire and West Sussex. On a clear day a vast panorama, from the Chilterns north of the western end of the London Basin to the South Downs, is visible; on a murky day you have enough trouble seeing your feet!

The Inns

The Devil's Punch Bowl Hotel, Hindhead

About the Inn: Off the London Road (A3) in Hindhead, a beautiful century-old Tudor-style coaching inn with three bars, features an open fire and an excellent French restaurant with seating for 130.

Gardens at rear in use during the Spring and Summer. Newly refurbished accommodation for 24. A genial landlord in David Coombs and his friendly staff help make this a delightful locale for lunch or dinner.

Beers and Food: Pompey Royal and Trophy Bitter hand-drawn, Heineken and Kaltenber lagers, Guinness, Trophy Key and Worthington E on draught. Good, fresh pub grub at reasonable prices (Sarnies 35p - 60p, Ploughman's lunch 70p, salads around £1.25) and haute cuisine restaurant between £7.50 and £10 per head. Dinner and dance on Wednesday, Friday and Saturday.

The walk begins at the National Hillcrest car park, opposite The Devil's Punch Bowl Hotel. Care should be taken as the route does *not* follow the marked nature trails for much of the way. The car park is the last opportunity for a civilised leak for 5 miles!

Walk through the car park and follow signposts for the Devil's Punch Bowl Nature Trail. At the first crossroads there are two left trails and one to the right. Take the second on the left, which descends the Bowl quite steeply between heather and holly bushes. Holly is common throughout the valley, bearing male and female flowers on separate trees. The clusters of small white flowers can be seen in May, the female only bearing the Christmas berries. After about ¼ mile the path forks into two, a gentle track along the rim of the Bowl on the left, a descending path to the right. Take the right fork down into the valley.

The next mile or so is for the fairly adventurous. Having left the beaten track, the path takes you through woodland, sometimes steep and over foliage and tree stumps — which are home to such insects as millipedes, centipedes, beetles, woodlice (lovely on toast!) — or under low-hanging trees. The woodland is very varied, featuring at least a dozen different kinds of trees including Whitebeam with grey/green leaves, Scots Pine, Oak, Birch and Mountain Ash, which has bright red berries in autumn, on which blackbirds and thrushes dine out. At times the path is barely distinguishable, but it is never completely deserted.

Follow the path as it descends the western side of the basin. Straight over one crossing, then over a second, after which the path veers to the right. About 400 yards past the second crossing there is a grazing field for cows to the right of the path, and a ¼ mile further a quaint farmhouse. A 150 yard stretch of the path alongside the farmhouse is often boggy, but a handy diversion just above the main path bypasses this.

At the farmhouse take the right fork descending alongside the front entrance of the farm. A brook on your right closes towards the track as you descend down to the basin. Where they meet, at the floor of the basin called Highcombe Bottom, take the log footbridge across the brook and follow the ascending path. The floor of the basin is pitted with marshy areas kept constantly wet by springs. Many kinds of ferns and mosses grow in these damp places, and the area has been colonised by quick-growing birches. Blue Tits, Coal Tits, Siskins and Gold-crests feed among the trees.

The path veers to the right, following a blue National Trust marker (there is also a marker showing a sharp left fork, which should *not* be taken), and becomes steep and stony as it climbs towards the eastern rim of the Punch Bowl. Gibbet Hill dominates the horizon on your left as you climb to a crossing. Turn right (this time *against* the direction shown by the NT marker). The Path is a little muddy for about ½ mile, with marshes in places to the right of the track. It passes a small farmhouse on your left, then climbs again.

Reaching a junction with Highcombe Farm to your right and a cottage used as a Youth Hostel to your left, take the right fork past the farm, keeping the large farmhouse on your right. This track broadens slightly into an asphalt path. About a 100 yards past the farmhouse a leafy trail bearing a 'No Horses' notice forks downhill to the right. This can be taken by those who prefer to avoid a steep climb; it cuts off about a mile from the walk and leads directly back to the car park.

The athletic and those goaded by their children will follow the asphalt path up out of the basin. A ¼ mile past Highcombe Farm is an opening in the bushes to the right which offers a beautiful view of the Punch Bowl and a secluded spot in which to flake out.

The path climbs steadily for another ½ mile, then a sharp left leads you onto a steep track through thick, bushy terrain up to the A3. Lovers of brambles and stinging nettles can enjoy a handful as they climb. Cross the main road diagonally to continue in the same southerly direction on a clay path that hugs the road. With Gibbet Hill behind you to the left, keep straight along the clay path (there are several viewpoints en route), passing over several crossings until the path brings you back to the opposite side of the A3, the car park entrance.

On your right, about ½ mile after joining the clay path, is the stone monument commemorating the savage murder of an unknown sailor nearly 200 years ago, and the nearby hangings that gave Gibbet Hill its name.

Mr Welbourne, landlord of **The Woodcock** in Churt Road, will welcome exhausted walkers with hand-drawn Gales real ale and a carvery-style cold buffet.

The Woodcock, near Hindhead

About the Inn: On Churt Road, Beacon Hill, near Hindhead, a turn-of-the-century inn in the midst of National Trust grounds, the outside is a bit off-putting, but a pleasant surprise awaits within. Charming atmosphere, roomy with an open fire, it offers pool and bar games, taped music. Barclaycard and Diner's Club accepted.

Beers and Food: Gales real ale, special bitter (the second strongest in Britain), hand-drawn. Wide range of food, lunch and evenings, hot meals and extensive carve-your-own buffet. Home-baked bread. Children welcome (if eating).

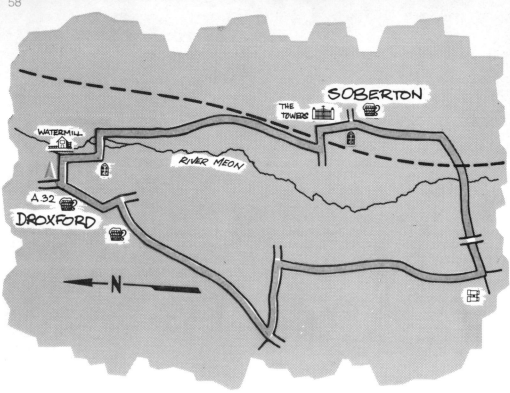

1o Droxford

The District

Near a pleasant chalk stream, **Droxford** is set deep in the Meon Valley in Hampshire, north of Portsmouth and east of Winchester. The Norman village church, which boasts two original Norman doorways, is mentioned in the Domesday Book.

In the later years of his life Isaak Walton, the famous fisherman, spent much of his time at Droxford Rectory, where his son-in-law was the rector. Winston Churchill and General Eisenhower were based in Droxford for much of the period immediately before the D-Day landings on Normandy, and lived in a railway carriage stationed on the disused line which is passed on the walk. They frequently dined at **The White Horse,** one of our featured inns.

How to Get There

By car along the A32 north from Fareham. By rail, to Fareham station, then a bus which stops just outside the station to Droxford.

The Droxford Walk

A gentle stroll (though it may be muddy in patches beside the stream) through the chalk valley of the Meon. Roughly 3 miles, which hardly allows the legs to get a good stretch between featured inns.

Cars can be parked in the square at the bottom of the hill on the A32 in Droxford. The bus from Fareham station stops in the square, by the National Westminster Bank.

Walk uphill out of the square towards the road leading right. Take this route past the picturesque timbered building. At the end of the road, take the footpath to the right. On the corner an old watermill, with sluice gates beyond it, turns incessantly, as it has for hundreds of years. Pass over a stile into the grounds of the village church, whose several interesting features include two Norman doorways.

Keep to the left through the church grounds and make for a stream passing over two smaller streams. Immediately after the second footbridge turn right over a stile, which leads into a ploughed field. Keep straight, crossing three fields and their respective stiles, until you reach a road. The more athletic can make an historic detour after the second field to the left, towards the disused railway sidings which played host to Churchill and American General Eisenhower during the final planning for D-Day.

If you have taken the route towards the railway cutting, walk along the cutting and turn right towards a bridge. At this stage a steep scramble up the embankment and back onto the road will make many of the more athletic wish they weren't, and the less wish they were. (You just can't win, you see).

From the road turn left up into **Soberton** and The Towers, a large stone country house with castle-like battlements. Turn right, following the road round towards the old church. **The White Lion**, in Soberton, looms large and welcoming in the church square by the village green. It dates back to the early 17th century. The village square makes a pleasant viewpoint, with the church to the west, The White Lion to the south, and The Towers to the north. In front of the church take a stile on the left into a ploughed field; cross the field to its far corner (or, if muddy, follow its left-hand perimeter) towards a swing gate.

The Inns

White Horse Inn, Droxford

About the Inn: A free house situated in the High Street. John and Rose Bristowe host a magnificent 16th century inn which is proud of its female ghost, recently featured in the National Geographical magazine! Tudor-style with adjoining stables, the inn offers three bars with open fires, a cosy atmosphere, and the kind of furniture you can really sink into. A dining room for 30, a good jukebox, a wide variety of pub games (including a novelty from Sri Lanka of all places!) and a courtyard for use in fine weather complete a perfect hostelry.

Beers and Food: No less than 10 different real ales, too numerous to itemise, and a full complement of spirits, malt whiskies etc. Extensive selection of lunchtime bar snacks, home-made goodies and substantial fare from an à la carte menu. Booking needed for weekend dining.

White Lion, Soberton

About the Inn: On the village green by the church square in Soberton, a three cen-

Immediately past the gate turn right onto a track that passes under the railway bridge towards the stream (this is a popular spot with local fishermen, swans and ducks). Cross the stream and keep to the right of the field.

Following the field round to a stile, keep straight, crossing another field and climbing a stile to reach the A32. Cross this main road carefully and walk towards another stile and up a slight hill. From a track running along the brow of this hill the wide sweep of the Meon Valley's panorama stretches for miles, beyond Droxford and Soberton. Follow the track to the right down to the road, then left along the road towards a T-junction.

Turn right along the road into Droxford, passing **The White Horse**, at which the famous war leaders enjoyed many a gastronomic distraction from the hectic business of winning the war. After sampling each of the inn's 10 real ales, saunter on towards Droxford Square. A hundred yards beyond the Square is **The Baker's Arms**, an Ind Coope house of distinction.

tury-old establishment with a small paved garden to the rear.

Beers and Food: Ind Coope and Friary Meux real ales. Fresh pub grub.

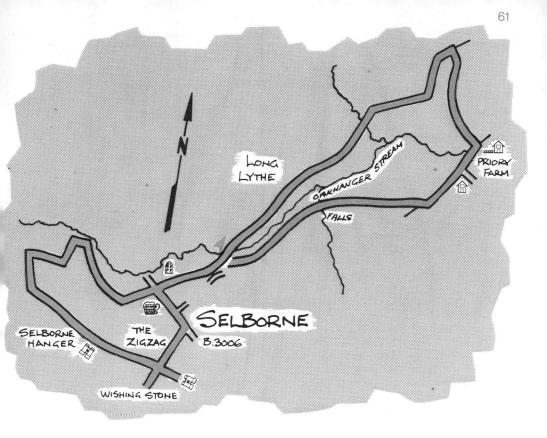

1p   Selborne

The District

Considered by many the classic English village, **Selborne** lies in the heart of Hampshire's fertile farm land. It owes much of its reputation to the 18th century naturalist, the Reverend Gilbert White, whose *Natural History and Antiquities of Selborne* is still regarded as an incomparable record of English country life.

White spent most of this his life in Selborne, and his former home, in the main square, is now a museum. Its gardens feature a renowned sundial.

The village boasts an antique shop and a craft centre. St. Mary's Church, to the north-west of the village, dates from 1180 and was originally erected on the site of an even earlier church. Restored in the 19th century, its churchyard contains the grave of Gilbert White and a massive yew tree which is about 1300 years old. Priory Farm stands on the site of Selborne Priory, founded in 1232 as a house of the Augustinian Canons and endowed to Magdalen College, Oxford in 1484.

The village stands in over 200 acres of National Trust land.

How to Get There

By car, A31 (Alton by-pass) from Farnham, turn onto B3006 for Selborne. BR station at Alton, then bus (Petersfield service 252) to Selborne.

The Selborne Walk

Selborne lies at the foot of a steep scarp-face of chalk which sweeps across the

►

southern edge of the village. The walk is made up of two self-contained circular routes that begin and end at the main car park. They total about 4½ miles of fairly easy terrain, and can be walked together or individually.

In the pretty village square just by the car park is **The Queens Hotel**, a charming stone and brick inn which boasts the largest range of wines, spirits and liqueurs in the county. A Queenburger Welsh Rarebit in the adjoining Buttery, washed down with a pint of draught Courage Directors' Bitter has what it takes to fuel the most slothful hiker for the task ahead.

The walk begins past the church to a stile. Descending, keep away from the road and bear left over a small bridge, over one of the two headwaters of the Oakhanger stream. Cross over a second stile leading to the ash wood, a National Trust area, then follow a well-defined path through the hanger and over two stiles. Leaving the wood, climb another stile into a field called Long Lythe, which you follow along the northern perimeter until it turns sharply left. Cross here to a brook, which can be crossed over some planking. Climb the stile and head uphill into the woods, following fencing surrounding the woods.

Turning right and climbing a stile, then passing through a gate, you eventually reach a well-defined track that leads, over a stile, into a field. Follow this track along the side of the field and over yet another stile (lovers of stiles, this is the walk for you!). Turn sharp right onto a dust track that leads down to Priory Farm, which stands on the site of a 13th century priory which was suppressed by Pope Innocent VIII in 1486.

At Priory Farm turn right along the road and track past a white bungalow. The track is prone to muddiness after rainfall. Follow the track uphill over a gate and a stile and onto a metalled road which leads through woods, on the opposite bank of the stream, to the Long Lythe. The spot offers excellent views of the valley and the twisting stream for camera fiends, and welcoming benches for the footsore. The track, known as Dorton Lane, crosses a small brook with rapids and falls, continues down to a

The Inns

Queens Hotel, Selborne

About the Inn: Situated in the delightful unspoilt village centre. Originally called The Compasses Inn, it probably had connections with the Augustinian Priory. Gilbert White's famous history of Selborne refers to the fact that The Compasses Inn was the scene of a wild weddy party in 1783. Built of stone and brick, with an adjoining Buttery, the inn offers overnight accommodation, a blend of ancient and modern bar games and a small functions room suitable for parties. The Lounge Bar is heated by a huge open fire.

Beers and Food: Courage Directors and Best Bitter available on hand pump, three types of lager, two ciders and JC also on draught. Boasts the largest selection of wines, spirits and liqueurs in Hampshire. Excellent bar food (including delicious fresh smoked Cornish mackerel) at reasonable prices and restaurant with full à la carte menu (last orders 8.45 pm).

Selborne Arms, Selborne

About the Inn: Large garden with rabbits, guinea pigs, parakeets, budgies; children very welcome. Has its own rugby team.

wooden house and rejoins the path towards the church.

At this stage the self-satisfied will retire to the comforts of **The Selborne Arms,** a highly recommendable tavern offering excellent home cooking (stew cooked slowly over the large open fire - a mouth-watering speciality). Originally a cottage, The Selborne Arms has been offering rest, repasts and recreation to travellers for 150 years.

The gritty, indefatigable, obsessive walker (get off your behind, that means YOU!) will be raring to complete the course.

Pass through the car park and follow the sign pointing to the Zigzag, the easy path up the hanger constructed by Gilbert White in the 18th century. From the top there is a splendid view of the village through the beech trees. A few yards east opens up a panoramic view of the heathland of Woolmer Forest and the Blackdown Hills near Haslemere.

Retrace your path to the Wishing Stone and walk straight ahead along the crest of the hanger. Passing a memorial signboard on your left, descend and turn right at the NT sign, along a path that leads into a lane. Continue to Gracious Street (ignoring a stile on the right-hand side of the bend), then turn right. At the end of this long side street, flanked by interesting stone buildings, turn right into the main street and walk back towards the car park.

Interior is timbered with flagstone floor.

Beers and Food: Courage Directors Bitter hand-drawn. Fabulous home-cooked inn food, with stew, slowly cooked over large open fire, a speciality.

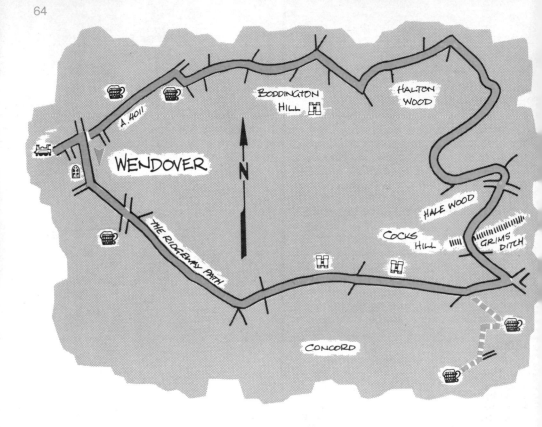

1q Wendover

The District

Wendover lies on the edge of the Chilterns at the junction of the Icknield Way and main London-Aylesbury road. With its many half-timbered cottages and red-brick buildings this old town has attracted much attention throughout the ages. Robert Louis Stevenson was so taken with the town that he recorded his impressions for posterity in *An Autumn Effect*.

Bosworth House, in the village street, is a popular visiting spot despite the fact that most of its sixteenth and seventeenth century wall paintings have been moved to the Victoria and Albert Museum in London.

The fourteenth century church, though much restored, still proudly displays its original tower.

How to Get There

From London, take the A413 and turn onto the A40 for Wendover. Alternatively take the A413 south from Aylesbury. By rail to Wendover station on the London-Aylesbury line.

The Wendover Walk

This is a fairly long walk of about eight miles but, by way of compensation, it takes you round some of the most breathtaking scenery in the Chiltern area.

The walk begins at the station, and you go left down the High Street past **The Red Lion Hotel** (the alternative starting-point). Just before the mini-roundabout near the hardware store, look for the Heron path on the right. This pleasant path along the side of a steam takes you past St Mary's church. Turn left here into Church Lane and down to the T-junction where you turn right to find **The Wellhead Inn**. Approximately 100 yards before the inn you will see a 'No Through Road' on the left. On your left as you walk down the lane you will see, in the distance, Boddington Hill. At the top of the lane, just past the dairy farm, you will see the Ridgeway Path (signposted by white arrows with white acorns above them). Follow this path as it forks left just above the farm. Two hundred yards further on take the right-hand fork and, making sure you follow the Ridgeway Path signs, you will eventually come to a triangulation point. Keeping this to your left continue straight on until you come to a signpost warning against the theft of timber. Should you feel in need of refreshment at this point, keep going straight on until you reach some cottages; turn right and right again at the road to find **The Gate Inn**. At this point take a right turn and go through the gate into a field. Make straight for the white house and turn left down a path just before the road. Follow this path across two fields and over a stile, and then turn left down a path just before the road. Follow this path across two more fields and over another stile and then turn left at the T-junction to take you past Grim's Ditch, an example of ancient man's endeavours.

Once across Grim's Ditch the footpath brings you to a black gate and a road on top of a steep hill. Turn right onto the road then after 30 yards go left to rejoin the Ridgeway Path. Following the left-hand fork you skirt the edge of a wood. At the fork in the road bear right and go over a stile. Continue on until you come to a sign saying NO HORSES, then fork left round the side of the hill. The vast fir trees on both sides make for a spectacular horizon.

The Inns

The Red Lion Hotel, Wendover

About the Inn: Situated in the High Street this beautiful half-timbered building dates back to the seventeenth century. The original fireplace still remains.

Beers and Food: With Youngs and Morlands Bitter available, the discerning drinker should be well-satisfied. For those requiring solid refreshment the Red Lion Special Menu will no doubt whet your appetite, once you have got used to smoked haddock being called a 'Fraddy'.

The Gate Inn, Lee Gate, Near Great Missenden

About the Inn: Located near the Ridgeway on the edge of the Chilterns. The original building dates back to 1620, reflected by the heavy beams and open fire. For the ghost hunter, a harmless lady ghost allegedly haunts one of the rooms. Furthermore, legend has it that somewhere in the grounds there is a hidden cache of gold.

Beers and Food: If you find treasure-hunting thirsty work, then a choice of Wadworths Old Timer, Hook Norton Best Bitter or Old Hooky should satisfy the inner man.

From the snack bar, steaks, lasagne and moussaka can be obtained. During the summer they have a barbeque.

At the T-junction, turn right, heading uphill. At the top there is a large circular car park. Turn sharp left here and walk along the top of Boddington Hill. Should you look carefully you will see the remains of an old fort. Head back towards the car park and, keeping to the Wendover side, you will find a track leading steeply downhill. Continue straight down here to Beech Wood Lane. At the end of the lane veer left then right at the T-junction. At the A4011 turning go left to Wendover.

The Wellhead Inn, Wendover

About the Inn: Originally a pub for the workers on the railway, it is now a popular country inn. The cosy atmosphere and friendly service ensure regular custom and, 3 times a year, the local hunt uses it as a meeting place.

Beers and Food: Being a free house it has a wide selection of notable ales and normal pub grub.

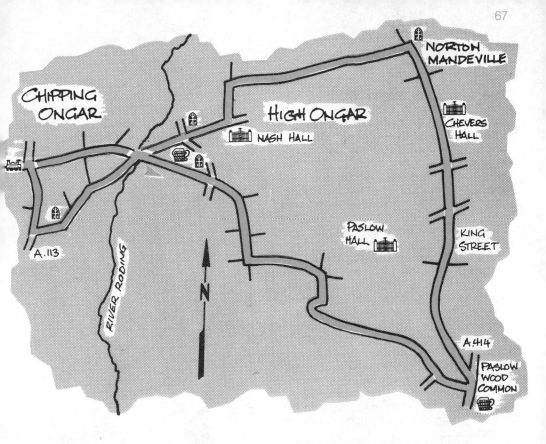

1r Chipping Ongar

The District

To the east of Epping, **Chipping Ongar** lies in rolling Essex countryside, and is crossed by the River Roding.

'Chipping' is an old English word for market, as this small Essex town used to boast a fine market adjacent to the Norman castle. If the old market has gone, there is also little left of the castle, besides an earthy mound and a water-filled moat. However the High Street still has an ancient appearance with its gabled houses and overhanging stories. Of interest too is the Congregational Church where, it is presumed, David Livingstone was trained before he went Africa-wards. The daughter of a former vicar of this church has the dubious distinction of having composed 'Twinkle, twinkle, little star', the bane of a generation of nannies. **High Ongar,** 1 mile to the east, is comprised of a picturesque row of timbered cottages.

Chipping Ongar is within **Epping Forest** district; an area which used to be covered by a vast expanse of hunting land belonging to the King. The forest with its shady glades and rough heathland, is nowadays home of black fallow deer, badgers, foxes, nightingales and hawfinch.

How to Get There

Chipping Ongar is reached by tube; it is on London Transport's Central Line. By car the A11 converges onto the M11, turn off at junction 7 and take the A122 into Chipping Ongar.

▶

The Chipping Ongar Walk

This is a relatively easy ramble over the valley of the Roding. The paths can sometimes be muddy, so wellies are probably a good idea. From the underground station, turn left and walk up the station drive to the main road (A128). Turn right and after ½ mile you pass Budworth Hall to your right. There are several car parks here, if you are starting by car. Cross over the road by the pedestrian crossing, and continue in the same direction.

Just past the Co-op grocery turn left towards the church. Skirt round the church to the right, before turning left down a drive. Keep to the central path where the driveway divides and then veer to the left to join a farm track. Carry straight on, ignoring a turning to the right, and cross over the park to turn left into the next track (by a metal kissing gate). Proceed to the end of the hedge, making sure you keep to the left of the hedgerow and cross over a stile. The path now leads downhill to the River Roding, and then climbs up again, in the same direction.

The path passes through some buildings in a close, and continues to a road. Turn right here and walk along for a few hundred yards to pick up a footpath on the other side of the road. This path veers to the right, uphill, towards a gap in a tree-line on the horizon.

After the trees continue downhill, passing through a gate, and turn left, with a stream to your right. Follow the path, through the water meadows for about ½ mile, before turning right near some derelict buildings. Go through the hedge and turn left; following the path to the end

of a thin wooded strip. Cross over a stile and follow the path through hedges onto the road. Straight ahead, a couple of hundred yards along, is a T-junction, where by turning right you arrive at **The Black Horse Inn** on Paslow Wood Common.

You're now near enough half-way round to start thinking about a little drop of self-reward; so choose your pint from the range of local ales (Adnams Bitter, Greene King Abbot and Fullers London Pride) available, and take it into the garden for a breather!

On leaving the pub, retrace your steps to the road junction and take the bridleway opposite the farm. Initially the track is through hedges and small trees but, where it opens out you should cross over a stile and bear left across a field. (Regrettably there is a barbed wire fence across the field, but do your best to get over it in one piece). At the edge of the field, you should head out onto the road to pick up a footpath on the other side, beside a gas pipeline enclosure. The path leads onto another main road, which you should cross, and then keep heading north along the track, to the right of farm buildings. Continue downhill across a stream and aim for the distant church spire. A stile leads you into the churchyard of Norton Mandeville Church.

Keep to the left of the church and exit through the front gate, turning left along the gravel track. Follow this fenced track, which veers to the left after about $2/3$ mile, and then comes out onto the main road opposite North Weald village hall. Turn right and walk through the village of High Ongar to **The Red Lion**. Stop for a drink because I'm sure you won't want to be chipping away at this walk any 'onger!

Come out of The Red Lion and pick up the footpath on the right-hand side of the pub, passing behind it, downhill, with woodlands to your right. Recross the bridge you crossed at the start of the walk and continue uphill over a stile, with a hedge on your left. Go through the metal swing gate and keep following the track, past a tennis club, to a lane leading onto Chipping Ongar High Street. Just to your right is the station, and a ¼mile left are the Budworth Hall car parks.

The Inn

The Red Lion, High Ongar

About the Inn: The street in which this old inn is situated is rumoured to have formed part of the route Henry VIII took when sneaking off for clandestine lunchtimes with Jane Seymour, at neighbouring Jericho Priory. The inn itself was erected some hundred years after Henry's death, and photos taken in Edwardian times show it used to have a pantiled coach house. The oak-beamed interior has an interesting old carving of a Saxon king, whereas in a yard at the back of the inn there is a barn-owl avairy, believed to be unique in Essex.

Beers and Food: An Ind Coope house. The pub offers various hot meals, such as home-made steak and kidney pie and roasts, as well as the usual snack menu.

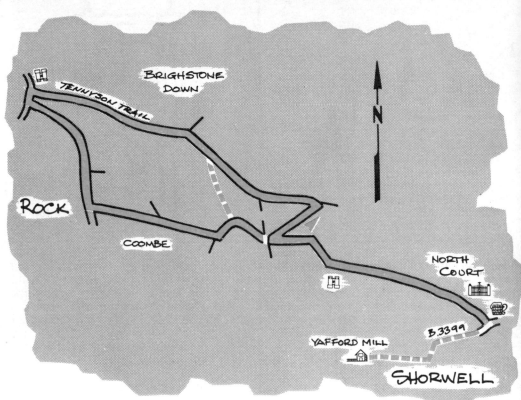

1s Shorwell

The District

The Isle of Wight's dominant topographical feature is the central chalk ridge of downland. At **Brightstone Down,** which is one of the landmarks of our recommended walk, the ridge attains its highest point — 700 feet above sea level — and affords some of the most extensive views on the island

The thatched and stone cottages clustered around The Crown Inn are typical of **Shorwell,** our starting point. St Peter's Church, on a hill in the centre of the village, dates back to 1440; its many unusual features — a medieval stone pulpit, 17th century pews, brasses and gun chamber — make it well worth a visit. The village boasts three magnificent Elizabethan houses: North Court, above the church and surrounded by trees; West Court, an early

Tudor residence now used as a farm; and Wolverton Manor, a Jacobean mansion on the stream at **Yafford.**

How to Get There

Hovercraft from Portsmouth (Clarence Pier) to Ryde; hydrofoil from Southampton (Royal Pier) to Cowes; ferry from Lymington to Yarmouth. Buses to Shorwell from each of these destinations.

By car: from Yarmouth, the A3054 east, right onto B340, right in Calbourne, keep left and veer onto B3399 to Shorwell; from Cowes, A3020 south, into Newport then B3323 to Shorwell; from Ryde, A3054 to Newport then B3323 for Shorwell.

The Shorwell Walk

The walk takes you across the chalk downlands between the villages of Shorwell and Brightstone; it begins at **The Crown Inn** in Shorwell, in the expansive beer garden in which in summer you can catch a glimpse of the wild life gathered around its trout stream, and in winter pneumonia. The trail is normally dry, though stout shoes are recommended.

The Crown Inn, a ghost-free (at least that's what the landlord swears!) three century old tavern, will set you on course with a fine home-prepared lunch and sherry drawn from the wood.

Beyond the inn's car park a bus stop claims to hail buses hourly on their way to Newport. Follow the path past the bus stop towards a row of houses; on the right, between the houses, a footpath leads up through a gate and onto a hill. Just at the top, a trail follows the brow of the hill, giving an impressive view of the sea. Take the left fork along the brow of the hill, until you reach the end of a first field, which is split by a hedge.

At the end of the field take a gate towards a second, south-facing field and keep to the top of the field until you reach a stile which leads into a third field. Cross the field to its far corner. This point marks the end of the valley. Crossing over the valley to the base of North Hill. a natural chalk cliff, pass through the gate, then turn sharp right ►

Crown Inn, Shorwell

About the Inn: Nestling in the heart of Shorwell, one of the most popular inns in the south-west corner of the Isle of Wight. A genuine rural house that shows its Tudor ancestry in low, beamed ceilings and heavy oak panelling; it offers open fires and is complete with antique furniture and leaded windows. A large beer garden at the rear boasts its own trout stream, which is a gathering place for wild fowl and doves. Darts in winter and background music. Children welcome in the garden.

Beers and Food: A variety of real ale drawn from the barrel and draught sherry. Good country-style food including bubble & squeak, home-cooked gammon and hot snacks in winter, a wide range of salads through the summer. Fresh sandwiches always available.

around the edge of the hollow and up the hill, keeping the perimeter of the field on your left. The trail leads to a barn, and offers a view across the water to the north towards Portsmouth.

At the barn, turn left along the track towards a stone marker at the top of the hill. Sweeping views, of Portsmouth and Portland Bill to the north-west of St Catherine's Light, of Shorwell and Brightstone and a magnificent stretch of coastline westwards to Freshwater are available, courtesy of a clear sky. Continue on your path downhill towards the cluster of pine trees; namely Brightstone Forest. The nearby site of an ancient Roman villa is on your left as you descend into the valley.

After about a quarter mile you reach a road; turn left into the village of Rock; a track veering to the left takes you up past a group of thatched barns. Turn left past the barns through a field; leave the field by a gate and follow the path to the right that climbs the hill. From the top of this hill you can enjoy a fine view of the valley leading down to North Court. Pass through a gate and re-cross the field on the saddle of the hill to a second gate; take that gate and continue along the brow of the hill until it is split by long hedgerow. The walk has taken you full circle. Take the south-facing side of the field, to the right, and cross the field keeping to the top. Crossing over a gate at the end of the field, you have arrived back at the public footpath that takes you down between the houses and back onto the road.

The Crown Inn has been welcoming weary travellers since 1650; your good deed done for the day, settle back and enjoy some real ale and fine company in one of the most popular landmarks in the area. Incidentally, one other popular landmark is Yafford Mill, a short walk along the B3399 from The Crown Inn. It is one of the few remaining mills, for at one time every village on the isle had to grind flour and cattle food; and is still turned by water from the stream in the grounds of North Court. The mill is open from Easter to October.

The South-West

The south-west peninsula, carved out over the centuries by stormy seas, possesses inland features quite as striking as its coastline. The solemn plains and downlands of Wiltshire with their stark reminders of a prehistoric age give way to the softer contours of the Dorset hills. From the mysterious Isle of Purbeck into the heart of Hardy country, Dorset remains unspoilt.

Somerset is a county of contrasts; the genteel farmlands, the eroded limestone of the Mendips and, to the far west, the bleakness of Exmoor.

From the Mediterranean climate of its southern coast to the treacherous mists of Dartmoor, Devon has a wide appeal. Finally, the Cornish coastline bounded by rugged cliffs is home to both sheltered coves and powerful Atlantic breakers.

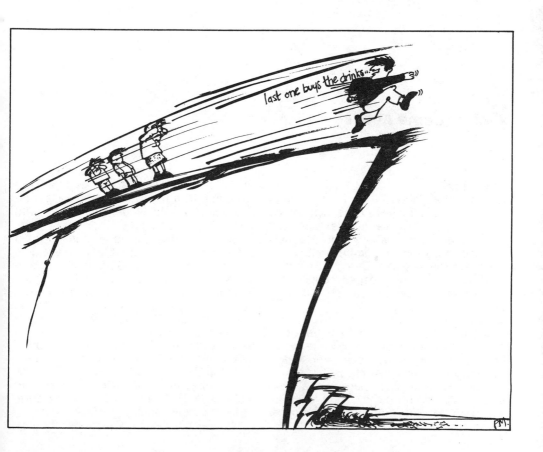

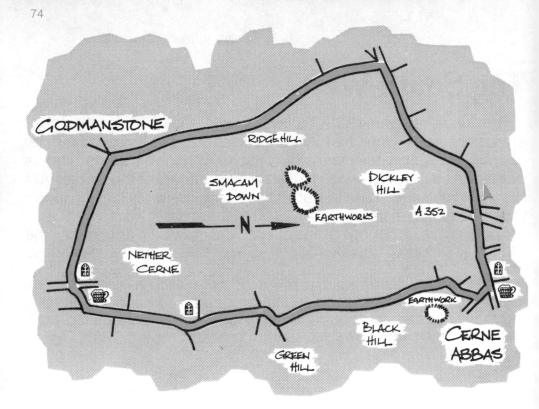

2a Cerne Abbas

The District

Cerne Abbas is set in the heart of rural Dorset, the area that was used as a setting by Thomas Hardy in his writings, especially in *The Woodlanders* where **High Stoy Hill** (3 miles north) and **Melcombe** (Melbury - 5 miles east) are featured. Cerne Abbas itself is an attractive town steeped in history. It has a fine 14th century church with 14th century wall paintings and a good Jacobean pulpit. In the churchyard, there is a wishing-well, reputed to have been created in a miracle by St Augustine, when he needed water for baptism. (It must have been quite fun being a saint...) While still on matters ecclesiastical, there was a Benedictine Abbey from 987 - 1539, some of which still remains, notably the gatehouse. Much of the fallen stone has been pilfered

and reused by the villagers for their own housebuilding; indeed there are fine examples of half-timbered houses with projecting upper stories.

But of course Cerne Abbas' biggest boast is the **Cerne Giant**. A club-wielding caveman figure, he is 180 foot tall,and was probably cut in the chalk hillside during the Roman occupation in the 2nd century. However, his origin and purpose remain unknown. Many theories have been mooted, the most obvious of which is that he's a super-virile fertility symbol (not a lot of imagination needed there) but others range from the Devil (again fairly obvious - we all know what he's like with his sex and violence) to Hercules (a little more obscure, but in the same mould).

Naturally myths and legends abound.

Visiting the giant is said to increase fertility, and a girl wanting many children should actually sleep on the giant's phallus. With the advent of Christianity, these pagan rites were frowned upon and the ever-dominating presence of the Phallic Giant must have been an embarrassing reminder of a pagan past. Indeed anyone visiting the St Augustine-installed wishing well was supposed to turn their back on the Phallic figure before they made their wish. Maintained by the National Trust, the Giant is best seen from the A352 to Sherborne.

How to Get There
By rail to Maiden Newton station which is on the main London (Waterloo) — Weymouth line. A bus service runs from Maiden Newton to Sydling St Nicholas, but only on Wednesdays and Saturdays. Cerne Abbas is on the A352 between Sherborne and Dorchester.

The Cerne Abbas/Godmanstone Walk
The walk starts in Cerne Abbas. Walk west along 'Sydling Rd' towards Sydling St Nicholas. Walk along this pleasant lane for about a mile, passing on your left, one of the finest examples of a medieval field system in Great Britain. You can see several tiers of almost perfectly preserved terraces, which give a good impression of the appearance of agricultural Britain before enclosure brought tree-lines, hedges and fences to section off the land. Follow the lane up to the sky-line and continue until you reach a slightly staggered cross roads, where the land begins to dip quite steeply and a track-cum-path crosses it. Turn left here, through the gate and follow the track along the ridge. After about a mile, the track dips away to the right — keep straight on here by going through a gate on the left through the hedge and continue in the same direction (with the hedge now on your right). Head towards towards a gate on the other side of the field. Go through it and turn left, keeping close to the hedge, until you come to two gates, one on your right and one on your left. Take the narrow right-hand one keeping to the edge of the field, until you get to a small wood. Climb the gate in the corner on the left, and then turn right to continue in the same direction. Go along the edge of the field until, in front of a water tank, a track crosses. Turn left down it, sharply downhill into the village of

The Inns

The Smith's Arms, Godmanstone

About the Inn: Set in the beautiful Cerne Valley this pub is, as mentioned, the smallest licensed premises in England, its most famous customer also being its first - Charles II in 1665. Since then though, many people from all over the world have visited this attractive little 15th-16th century thatched tavern on the banks of the River Cerne. Inside it is naturally very small, but is perhaps one of the cosiest interiors you will ever see, with its open fire and fine collections of brass and copper and other interesting objects. However, if it is crowded (!) there is a beer-garden with roses and bedding plants where you can enjoy drink.

Beers and Food: A good variety of Devenish beer, with real ale (straight from the barrel) some keg beers, lager, Guinness and draught cider. Bar snacks include sandwiches, local pâté and Ploughman's.

The Red Lion, Cerne Abbas

About the Inn: On Long St in Cerne Abbas, one of Dorset's most beautiful villages; The Red Lion Inn is of old foundations but was modernized in 1895 and given a Victorian frontage with leaded, stained glass windows. Inside there is an open fire in the pine-panelled bar and a good collection of 1870-80 photos of the village. Darts, shove-halfpenny, and cribbage can be played, and the skittle alley can be hired for parties. There are three double rooms (each with a shower) and children are welcomed for meals.

Beers and Food: A cask-conditioned bitter (hand pump) and a range of national keg-beers. But, more importantly, there is a choice of over 80 malt and blended

Godmanstone.

The pub, **The Smith's Arms** is on the road to your left. It is without question the smallest pub in England and stands little more than 4 foot high at its thatched eaves. It is 10 foot across inside and 4 foot from door to bar. All in all this is obviously not the best place for the Cerne Giant to take his girlfriend for a quiet drink. One of the few one-bar pubs in the country, Charles II stopped here to reshoe his horse (it was a smithy before) got thirsty while waiting and promptly granted it a licence. Oh! to be a King...

To continue the walk, turn left from the pub along the road until you reach an old house called 'The Mill'. Just before this is an alley leading to a footpath across fields to Cerne Abbas. Follow this over two footbridges and a stile. After the stile turn immediately left — this takes you through a gate and round the back of Nether Cerne. Don't turn left into the hamlet; instead the walk continues between two hedges along a slightly overgrown and very ancient path signposted to Cerne Abbas. After the next stile, walk across the field: the path continues three-quarters of the way up the field just underneath the plantation. Go through the gate under the telegraph wires. Walk through the farm between the silos and then fork left. Continue and go through the gate, heading for another gate (in the hedge) about three quarters of the way up the field (ie the upper of the two gates). After this gate, follow the left-hand side of the hedge and leave the field by the gate in the corner at the top to meet a track. Turn left along this and after ½ mile, climb the stile under the telegraph pole. Turn right, skirting the hedge.

Aim for another stile on the far side of the field at the top and follow the track round the right-hand side of the farm, where you meet a lane. Turn left along it back into Cerne, turning left into the centre of the village and **The Red Lion**. Here you can rest your eyes from these instructions, your feet from the walk and ease your parched throat with a well-deserved pint in The Red Lion Inn, chased by one of a range of 80 whiskies.

whiskies, at least a couple of which you should try to sample. Grills, soups and other cooked dishes are available from the bar, along with salads, toasted sandwiches and Ploughman's with local cheese.

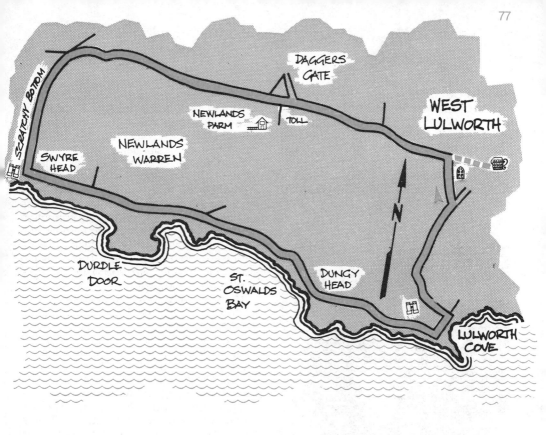

2b   Lulworth

The District

This part of the Dorset coastline is generally accepted as being an area of Outstanding Natural Beauty. It's wild and rugged and has been battered by a cruel sea for eons. Though the sea is winning, it is the visitor who is the real winner, because the result of this fight is a spectacular if not brash coastline. From the craggy arch of **Durdle Door** to the almost landlocked **Lulworth Cove,** this stretch of rocky coast is a geologist's paradise. Rich in fossils of many kinds, these cliffs are witness to a great geological upheaval way back in the mists of time. Some of the fossils found in the last century gave experts their first clues of the sizes and shapes of some prehistoric monsters and the twisted, 'folded' rock strata showed the primeval force, unleash-ed in the forming of the world as we now know it. 'All very well and good' you might say, 'so what?'. The fact is that the contorted rock formations make this a dramatic walk and if you find a fossil, I'll bet you will be well pleased. You should however, be extremely careful about not dislodging rocks onto people below, about not deforming this beautiful stretch of coast, and about not deforming yourselves, by falling off cliff edges, which in places are crumbly. While over-adventurous fossil-hunting is dangerous, the walk is safe.

►

How to Get There

By rail to Wool station, which is on the main London (Waterloo) — Bournemouth — Weymouth line. There is a connecting, although infrequent, bus service to Lulworth.

By car, leave the A352 between Wareham and Dorchester on the B3070 (or B3071) for West Lulworth.

The Durdle Door/Lulworth Cove Walk

The walk starts in **West Lulworth,** which is a fairly touristy village, especially in summer, though it is pleasant enough and is a good place for cream teas, crab salads and local ices. If you approach from the north, you will see a lane, signposted Winfrith Newburgh. You go past the church, walking up this quiet and pleasant lane for about a mile until it swerves to the right at Dagger's Gate. Turn left here, down a turning, signposted to Durdle Door, Walk through Newland's Farm and immediately after the track turns right, take the left-hand track along the stone wall and follow for about 250 yards, when you will see a gate on your left (the gate-post is marked with a yellow arrow). Go through the gate and take the path to the coast, following the yellow arrows. You are now walking along Scratchy Bottom and you are warned not to

sit on any ants' nests for a rest; you know what you'll get if you do. At the coast, the views are staggering — but, remember to keep well in from the edge of the cliff. Turn left along the coastal path.

Soon you will see the spectacular landform of Durdle Door — a natural arch eroded by the sea — a sinister and awe-inspiring sight even on calm days. The weakest part of its folded strata formation has been worn away and sometime in the future the archway will be whittled too wide for the arch to be supported. Then only the stack will remain, so you'd better take photos while you can.

There are steps down to the beach here, a good place for swimming and sunbathing on sunny days.

The main track veers inland — however, keep to the coastal path. Sometimes in summer, this path from Durdle Door to Lulworth Cove is alive with many butterflies including Lulworth's own local butterfly — the Lulworth Skipper. A toffee-gold colour, it contrasts nicely with the Marbled Whites, the Chalkhill Blues and the Graylings, all of whose colours are hopefully obvious. When you walk over the brow of the next cliff, you will see Lulworth Cove, The cove, almost an inland sea, is all but surrounded by 400 foot high cliffs and the starkness of these windswept clifftops contrasts strongly with the protected peace of the cove.

This calm peace means that bathing and rowing are popular here. The path slopes back down into West Lulworth.

A detour before the pub to the Fossil Forest, round the beach to the other side of the cove, will make you feel that you've deserved your pint all the more, and is certainly well worth the effort. The Forest consists of fossilized tree-stumps with hollowed out trunks, which are large enough to hold several people at a time. Again, care should be taken NOT to deface or destroy.

And so, back into Lulworth where, it's said Keats wrote his last sonnet, so if you feel all overcome by the beauty and splendour of the walk, have the courage to put pen to paper and see what flows. A sonnet has 14 lines, so it's not too strenuous. (If you think the results are good enough, send off

your efforts to us at Proteus).

Walk back up to the village and **The Castle Inn.** This pub, in the sleepy and almost entirely thatched part of the village, is named after the castle at East Lulworth, 2¼ miles to the north-east. The castle was burned out in 1929, but much remains intact. It is tall and foursquare and is tinged with romance and mystery. Before the fire, luminous red spots appeared on a wall in a bedroom (the scene of a grisly death?) and, though many attempts were made to obliterate and remove the spots (even going as far as knocking down and rebuilding the masonry) they continued to appear. Spooky, eh? The renovated stables house the family's art collection, and a nearby chapel (1786) was the first Roman Catholic church to be legally built in England after the Reformation. However back to the pub...

The Castle Inn, West Lulworth

About the Inn: Opposite the village green, it is a 16th-17th century thatched pub, covered with winter jasmine — a very attractive exterior. The public bar is plain but traditional — a low-ceilinged room with a flagstone floor, while the lounge is cosy, with an open fire, oak beams and copper-banded barrels on the bar.

The ghost of a lady, who hanged herself in the garden, has been seen by several locals.

It's a friendly pub with darts, dominoes and a good atmosphere. Some accommodation is available.

Beers and Food: Devenish Bitter, Whitbread Tankard, Viking Lager, draught Guinness and perhaps most importantly, draught cider from the barrel. At the bars, there are hot snacks in winter and a cold buffet in summer.

There is an excellent restaurant, noted throughout Dorset which has a good à la carte menu — well worth trying out.

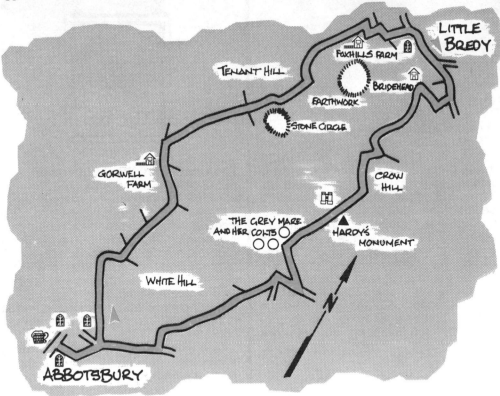

2c Abbotsbury

The District

Abbotsbury is a fairly sleepy and picturesque village situated between Blagdon Hill (Blackdown) and Chesil Beach — the twenty-mile ridge of shingle that stretches from here to Portland to the east. Its 16th and 17th century thatched cottages made it a natural choice for locations in the film of Hardy's *Far from the Madding Crowd.*

It boasts a wider variety of interest than one might think such a small village could or should, catering to tastes botanical, archaeological, historical, architectural, religious and especially ornithological (phew!). I'll explain: what has brought visitors and tourists to Abbotsbury more than anything else is its **Swannery.**

Fleet Lagoon lies to the landward side of Chesil Beach and its here you find the Swannery in particular, and a Bird Sanctuary in general. The Swannery is the home of 560 or more swans and it was set up by monks from the Abbey in 1363 (for food purposes, it's thought). There are hides for watching the birds and, naturally, dogs are not allowed. (Open daily mid-May — mid-September 10.00 — 4.30).

The Benedictine **Abbey of St Peter** was founded in a fit of conscience in 1026 by Orc, one of King Canute's henchmen. With imported monks from Cerne Abbas, it grew in importance and profits, necessitating the building of the second largest **Tithe Barn** in England. Built in the 15th century, it is stone-buttressed and thatched, with reeds from the Fleet, though nowadays only half is in good condition.

All that remains of **Abbotsbury Castle,** burnt down in 1914, are its sub-tropical gardens. Beautifully laid out, they contain lily ponds and peacocks and about 7000 plants for all you Percy Throwers. Well worth visiting — especially when the camellias and magnolias are in flower. (Open mid-March — September, Monday — Saturday, 10.00 — 5.30. Sunday 2.00 — 7.00).

How to Get There

By car, leave the A35 (Bridport - Dorchester road) at Winterbourne Abbas, and follow via Portesham to Abbotsbury. By bus, either from Weymouth to Abbotsbury or from Dorchester to Winterbourne Abbas, then its a 1¼ mile walk to Little Bredy, where you can start the walk if you want.

The Abbotsbury / Little Bredy Walk

This walk can be started either in Abbotsbury or in Little Bredy, so, for ease, the walk is divided in two.

Abbotsbury to Little Bredy

From Market Street, take Back Street, which is opposite **The Ilchester Arms** and the Post Office Stores, and walk about 100 yards past a chapel on your left and, just before a tiny thatched cottage facing the street, take a path on the left. After 20 yards, fork left, ignoring a patch veering steeply uphill. Continue on along this path — it takes you up onto the ridge, passing through two gates and ignoring side turns. Continue to a hedge with a barn on your left and go through a gate and fork right, passing some ancient earthwork or other on your left. Here you may rest for a while (to let the older members of the party catch up), but not for long - you've only just started. At the top are two gates: go through the right-hand one, skirting a fence on your right, along a faint track. At the end of the field, turn right along the hedge for about 50 yards, then take the first left down a track onto a lane. Turn left here down to Gorwell Farm. When you are opposite the last house here, turn right through a gate and walk uphill. Go through a second gate and keep to the left-hand side of the hedge — i.e. straight up the side of the field. At the top, continue on through a gate, along a hedge and into the next field over a stile.

The Inn

The Ilchester Arms Hotel, Abbotsbury

About the Inn: Both ancient and modern are combined in The Ilchester Arms Hotel, with its old English coaching inn exterior and its up-to-date facilities and comforts within. Its old stone features were included by the BBC in their *Diary of a Village* series for Westward T V

In the past, the inn has welcomed two of Queen Victoria's children who slept in what is now the Royal Bedroom (huge, by all accounts!).

Beers and Food: Mr John Thornicroft, your host, is keen to maintain this tradition of hospitality and, along with hand drawn Devenish Bitter and Wessex Best Bitter, he offers splendid, hot, locally baked cottage loaf rolls with Dorset Blue (!) cheese as well as home-made pasties. The latter are so popular that the cook can't always keep pace with demand (so be there first!). In summer, a drink in the leafy garden with its good sea-views is recommended.

Here is the Kingston Russell Stone Circle — something fairly important may or may not have happened here a long, long time ago — who knows? Anyway, look to a large group of trees, surrounding a tumulus, at the right-hand edge of this field and, at the near corner, you will see a stile. Cross this and walk diagonally to the right to the other side of this ancient wood and cross another stile out of it. Walk downhill about 20 yards and then continue downhill on a track to Foxhills Farm. Turn left here onto a semi-metalled lane and follow for about three-quarters of a mile, eventually coming down into Little Bredy. At the road turn right, and pass the church on your right, arriving at the junction. You are now half-way round and, as everyone knows, going back is always quicker than coming.

Little Bredy to Abbotsbury

At the fork in the road go right (signposted to the cricket ground), leaving the telephone box on your left. Walk about 200 yards and then turn right over a stile into the cricket ground. The path continues straight up through a gate, follow it right up the hill and then round it. When you see the wood, keep on your left and, at its corner, swing left, so that it's still on your left. Walk past Crow Hill Farm. Ignore both the farmyard smells and a descending fenced track on your left, and continue straight on. To your left now, as you walk along is the Valley of Stones. However, this is out of sight, so the information is for knowledge-seekers only. What you can see though, is the Hardy Monument — a rather ugly tower. It offers superb views for miles in all directions and was built in 1844 as a viewpoint and memorial to Thomas Hardy. He was, however, not the Thomas Hardy one instinctively associates with Dorset/Wessex, but he was Nelson's flag-captain, immortalized at Trafalgar. Unreliable historical sources trace the origin of the phrase 'Kiss me quick' to him. His home was in Portesham, also on the left, a very pretty village with a green. 150 yards along the track are two gates — go through the right-hand one and keep the hedge on your left for 400 yards. The Grey Mare and her Colts are here — not livestock as you might imagine, but monoliths and stone circles. While on an archaeological note, you may be able to see, (though its a good mile and a half away to the left, below the Hardy Monument) the Hell Stone — 'the Stone of the Dead'. It's a neolithic burial chamber and of some importance due to its good condition. Follow onto a lane and turn left (to the right is Gorwell Farm's drive) onto another lane. Turn right and walk for 200 yards until the lane swings left — here go through a gate on the right-hand side of the lane keeping along the line of the hedge to the bottom of the field, then at the fence, turn right for 250 yards to find a gate. Go through it and pick up the continuation of the track. Head down towards a field with a narrow gate in the corner. Go through it and follow down onto a lane. Turn left into Abbotsbury. By now, whether this is the end or the half-way point of your walk, you may well want some refreshment. and you are entitled so make your way to the inn.

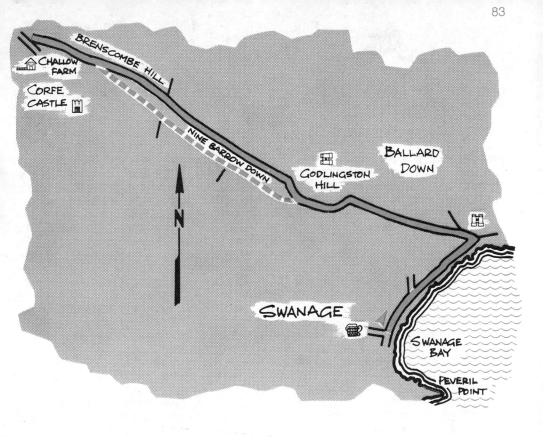

2d Corfe

The District

This walk is in the Isle of Purbeck, an area naturally cut off from the rest of Dorset by the Purbeck Hills. The stone from this corner of the county is greyer than that from the farmed quarries of Portland, giving the area a wilder and more rugged look. The houses and cottages in Swanage, and especially in Corfe, are largely made from this stone, many of them being topped with lichen and moss-covered roof-tiles.

An area of quiet seclusion, it is a natural haven for all kinds of wild life. There is little or no industry beyond quarrying and with Swanage being a smallish and fairly select resort (with no Butlins etc) the Isle of Purbeck remains unspoiled by both pollution and tourism.

It should be STRONGLY emphasized that in the whole Purbeck area, especially along the coastline, it is *very dangerous* to tamper with any metal objects you might find, as there are still unexploded bombs and mines hereabouts.

This walk is NOT circular, going from Swanage to Corfe (or the reverse), but there is an efficient hourly bus-service to get you back to the start. Soon, steam railway enthusiasts will be reopening the Swanage-Wareham line, making the return all the easier, though this is not the case as yet.

How to Get There

By car, take the A351 from Wareham, through Corfe to Swanage. From Bournemouth and Poole, go over the Sandbanks ferry and drive via Studland to

➤

Swanage. The nearest BR station is Wareham and then there are hourly buses to Swanage. At Corfe return by bus to either Wareham or Swanage.

The Swanage Walk
The walk starts in Swanage, a quiet, pleasant and unpretentious resort, though cruel critics have been heard to say that it is the kind of seaside town where people come to die. Ignore them. Mentioned in the Domesday Book (though not probably as a resort); it was the scene of England's first ever important naval victory when Alfred the Great's fleet trounced the Danes in 877 AD, driving the tattered remnants of the invaders' fleet onto the dangerous rocks of Peveril Point for good measure. Since then the powers that be have seen fit to be a little more merciful and have equipped this promontory with a coastguard and lifeboat station.

Further round the coast at Durlston Head you can see a 40-ton stone Globe — a little heavy, possibly, for contemporary Atlases. Tilly Whim Caves here are also worth a visit. When in Swanage years ago, your humble researcher encountered to his great surprise, a dromedary being taken for a constitutional by his mistress. Whether it's still an inhabitant of Swanage, remains to be seen, but be warned.

Start the walk on the seafront and walk north towards the massive cliffs of Ballard Down. Walk along the seafront until you reach a telephone-box near the 'Ocean Bay' building. Here the road swings inland but the walker keeps right and along the concrete walkway. When this ends, continue for 300 yards or so along the beach until you see a wooden handrail on your left (naturally) leading to the clifftop. Climb the wooden steps. At the fork go right onto the coastal path. Follow this path until it is about to swing to the right to go over Ballard Down Cliffs towards Handfast Point and Old Harry Rocks. (These rocks, populated by many and varied sea birds are pure-white chalk stacks and arches carved from time immemorial by the sea. Care should be taken near the edge of the cliff — accidents will and do happen). But don't

follow the path here, unless you fancy a detour for the wonderful views; instead fork left for 20 yards to a stile, which you climb over. Once over this stile, don't follow the path steeply uphill over Ballard Down, but turn immediately left onto the path which skirts the right-hand side of the fence. When the path crosses to the other side of the fence go through the kissing-gate and continue until a fork, where you go left over a stile and onto a lane. Turn left along this lane and after 50 yards go over yet another stile (this walk, as you may have noticed is very good for your leg muscles) on the right-hand side of the lane, which takes you onto a track. Follow this track and after ½ mile, fork right up the hill and onto the ridge. (If it is very windy, you may prefer to fork left staying on the lower path, though this way is not half as exciting). From the ridge there are wonderfully dramatic views in all directions. Behind to the left is a panoramic view of Swanage Bay and to the right you can see across the heathlands of the Studland National Nature Reserve towards Bournemouth. This Reserve surrounds a freshwater lagoon, the Little Sea, and is the habitat of many different kinds of wildlife, notably the smooth snake, the sand lizard, many species of birds, many butterflies (the Painted Lady and the Clouded Yellow in particular) and 600 or more species of flowering plants. (Yes, you're right, this information comes from a guide-book, we didn't count these plants, but presumably somebody must have done).

Continue along the top of the ridge until, after maybe 3 miles, you come to a TV aerial, where there is a fork. Here take the left-hand track down into a lane. Turn left again and this brings you into Corfe. This old grey-stone village takes its name from the Anglo Saxon word for 'to cut', standing as it does in a natural break or 'cut' in the Purbeck Hills. With this strategic advantage, a castle was inevitable; indeed Corfe was fortified since Alfred the Great.

A place curiously linked with villainy, it was here that in 978 AD, Prince Edward the Martyr was murdered by his stepmother Elfrida, who then enthroned her son — none other than the infamous Ethelred the Unready. Evil King John used the by-now Norman-built castle as a prison for his and the Red Baron's political enemies and also as a treasury for his ill-gotten loot. In the Civil War, the Castle was an invulnerable stronghold, staunchly defended by Royalist Lady Bankes and her men and it only fell into Parliamentarian hands through the treachery of a traitor from within the castle walls. The Roundheads destroyed as much of the castle as gunpowder could, leaving the very substantial ruins we see today (open daily Mar — Oct, afternoons only Nov — Feb).

And now after the history lesson, there will be a break for refreshments. Make your way to The Castle Inn in East Street, where Mr Trevor Thomas and his wife Pat will welcome you with hand-drawn Tankard and Trophy bitters and a goodly selection of cold snacks and basket meals.

The Castle Inn, Corfe

About the Inn: In East Street, Corfe, this inn was reputedly built as such in the 14th century, making it the original village inn. Built of Purbeck stone with a white, rendered front (this is shortly to be restored to its original stone exterior), it has a stone roof and the original stone porchway. Very much a Corfe building. The interior (one large bar and one smaller) retains the traditional atmosphere with two inglenook fireplaces, the original oak-beamed celling, stone walls and a flagstone floor. It is supposedly haunted — the till opens of its own accord, people claim to have had their hair pulled and footsteps have been heard in empty upstairs rooms. However, be brave (give the exact change, wear a hat and ear-plugs) and enjoy a cosy drink and snack.

Beers and Food: Whitbread beers — Tankard and Trophy straight from the barrel and draught cider, lager and mild. Cold snacks, sandwiches, Ploughman's lunch etc and a selection of basket meals. Morning coffee is served.

2e   Padstow

The District

In medieval times, **Padstow** was a thriving port and one of the most important towns in Cornwall. Its shipbuilding industry gradually declined as steam and turbine vessels replaced the old Padstow schooners. The trade of the town was largely in timber and later, fishing. Now it is a quiet residential town, but still retains many narrow, winding streets and old stone buildings. Many boats still sail from here, but the sand bar across the estuary prevents large vessels using the harbour.

St Petroc was a saint of Irish origin who came to Padstow in 518. The church ascribed to him was founded in the 13th century, although only the tower remains from that period. The rest was enlarged and rebuilt in the 15th century. Note the sculptured effigy of St Petroc on the chancel wall, and the carved sedilia in the south aisle. The town also boasts an ancient well in Fentonluna Lane, renovated in 1592 — the date is marked on a stone at the top with older lettering around the sides. **Abbey House** on the North Quay, is an ancient building from which a subterranean passage was built to connect it with the monastery which, until 981, occupied the upper part of the town. **Raleigh's Court House** on the South Quay, was where Raleigh held his court and collected taxes in his office as Warden of Cornwall. It dates from the 16th century.

Every year on May Day in Padstow, an ancient and somewhat grotesque ritual takes place called 'Baiting the Hobby-Horse'. The hobby-horse, a fearsome full-length mask crafted from canvas and wood, is kept by the landlord of The Golden Lion. At one minute past midnight on the first of May, the ''oss' is brought out and so the dance begins. Another dancer baits the horse with a club of celtic origin called the 'Teaser'. The dance continues through the town until dawn, when the horse virtually dies, symbolising the end of winter and the birth of the summer. Slightly bizarre, but fascinating, this is one of the most genuine surviving folk customs in England.

The Camel Estuary, winding between grassy cliffs on one side and sandy dunes on the other, is a beautiful stretch of the walk especially at high water.

Just outside Padstow there is a **Tropical Bird Sanctuary** which houses about 200 species of bird, with more being bred there all the time.

How to Get There
From Exeter, A30 to Bodmin then A38 to Wadebridge and A39 to Padstow turn-off. Train from Exeter to Bodmin then bus to Padstow.

The Padstow Walk
This is a long walk — about 7½ miles, with a few digressions for those who wish to take them — but a very pleasant one indeed.

We begin, after sufficient refreshment within, outside **The Ship Wright Inn** on the north quay. Take the ascending metalled road to the recreation ground and continue to the top, passing through the metal gates that commemorate the Queen's Silver Jubilee in 1977. Follow the obvious coastal path to the rocky inlet of **St George's Well,** a perennially-flowing spring in the rocks. The path climbs steeply to **Gun Point** and continues to **Harbour Cove** where there is

The Inn

The Ship Wright Inn, Padstow

About the Inn: An old brick building located right on the harbourside. The Ship Wright's is very much a fisherman's pub. The simple and functional interior, with its oak beams, stone floor and large open fireplace, is enhanced by the friendly atmosphere and the agreeable array of refreshments on offer. Sit out on the paved courtyard at the back, complete with tables, chairs and rose bushes.

Beers and Food: Best bitter (on keg) and the ordinary draught from St Austell Brewery; plus draught Guinness, draught Strongbow and draught Harp. Take your pick from the grub available at the bar — cornish pasties, plaice and chips, and fresh mackerel salad, for example — or sample the delicious fare available in the separate restaurant.

►

a particularly fine beach. From here there is a fine view of **Doom Bar** the sand bar which goes across the entrance to the estuary. Legend has it that this was the work of a mermaid who, having been the ancient protectress of the town, was mortally wounded by a young man with a bow and arrow. Dying, she flung a handful of sand at the town and cursed the place. Thus the bar was formed.

Climb to the footpath along the coast with a fence on the right to begin with, until you reach a stile. Follow the sign over the stile and up the lane past a house to another gate. With the life-boat houses to

Go through the gate down a metalled track, then through another gate, turning right on to a road past Lellissick farm. Coming to another stile (which if crossed, would lead you up to Gunver Head) turn sharp left down the road and then left again past Crugmeer. About 30 yards along there is a signpost indicating a footpath to Padstow. Go through the gate and along the path through fields until it meets a road. Here go downhill under the bridge, passing Prideaux Place on the right, (a 16th century manor on the site of the old monastery) then left down Fenonluna past the well. Here one can turn right to visit the Bird Sanctuary, or continue down into the town via Fore Street and Market Strand, which lead back down to North Quay and **The Ship Wright Inn.**

the left, follow the path up to the old life-boat station at Hawker's Cove, where the small plateau affords an excellent view. Continue up the path through brambles and over the stile at the top, past the observation post and Daymark Conny (an old tower) at Stepper Point. The cliffs here are 227 feet high. Continue round the coastal path to Pepper Hole and Butter Hole before turning left through a wooden gate and leaving the cliff tops.

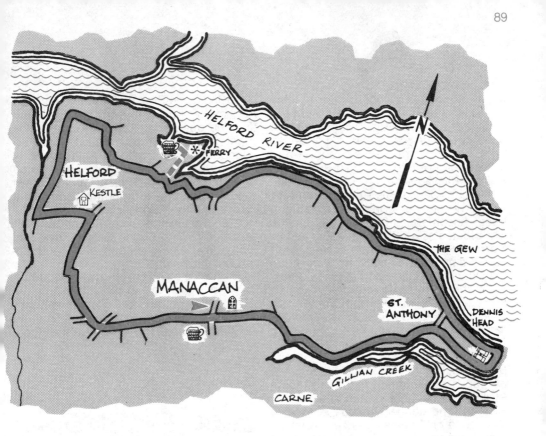

2f Manaccan

The District
Manaccan stands on a hill in that still as yet unspoilt area of Cornwall, The Meneage. The town achieved fame at one time, giving its name to Manaccite — titanium ore — which was discovered here in 1791. (The ore has since been re-named Gregonite). **The parish church of St Manaccus** (a saint of dubious origin — Manaccus in Cornish means the Monk, so perhaps the church was built near the cell of an old celtic hermit) has one surprising feature: an ancient fig tree that grows out of the south wall near the tower. It has been there for some 200 years.

During the Napoleonic wars, Captain Bligh (of *Mutiny on the Bounty* fame) came to this area to survey Helford River for the Admiralty. Taken for a French spy, he was arrested by the local constable who dragged him to Richard Polwhele, Vicar of Manaccan and the magistrate. Polwhele was at tea, and had the helpless captain locked-up in the coal cellar. However, Bligh was later able to reveal his mission in secret to the magistrate, and they subsequently became friends, carrying on a correspondence for many years.

The Helford River is a beautiful estuary, with scenery much like that of the Fal, albeit on a smaller scale. Many pleasure craft use Helford waters in the summer months, and the Duchy of Cornwall Oyster farm — one of the finest of such farms in Britain — is worked in this river, its headquarters at Port Navas. With its many small creeks, the Helford River was an ideal place for smugglers and **Helford Village** was their natural

►

haunt. Situated in a wooded combe, there are many rose-covered cottages and palm trees in this lovely village, with swans and boats on its narrow creek. A pedestrian ferry now runs on request daily (40p) across the river to the small hamlet of **Helford Passage.**

At nearby Dennis Head, the **Church of St Anthony** can be found hidden among trees. According to tradition this church was erected as a votive offering by certain Normans of rank. Having been storm-driven along the coast, they were more than thankful to land safely at Gillan Creek. Sadly there are no Norman remains, but there is an interesting 13th century in-scribed font, and a holy water stoup of the same period.

How to Get There

Manaccan is a very difficult place to get to by public transport. By rail to Falmouth Station, where there is a bus service to Helston. The connecting bus service to Manaccan only operates once a week so plan your trip carefully! An alternative would be to take the ferry from Falmouth to Frenchman's Creek.

By road, from Helston, take the A3083 due south, and then turn left onto the B3293. Turn left to Newton and proceed along a series of minor roads for Manaccan.

The Manaccan/Helford Walk

This is a long walk, some 7-8 miles, but not very hilly.

We begin at **The New Inn** in Manaccan a few yards from the entrance to the mine where Manaccite was discovered. After

enjoying some Cornish Bitter and perhaps a game of shove-halfpenny in this charm-ing pub, go the road to Church Lane on the right past the Church on the left. There is a signposted footpath to St Anthony. Walk down the concrete lane past some greenhouses on the left and carry on down into the Durra — a delightful glade with a brook that runs alongside the footpath on the left. Reaching a metalled lane, turn left and carry along beside Gillan Creek until you arrive at the church of St Anthony above Gillan harbour.

Follow the path along the right-hand side of the church on to the road. 20 yards up the road, turn right and climb up till the path arrives at a gate and a signposted footpath to Dennis Head. The view from the Head,

which was fortified during the Civil War is worth stopping to drink in, before continu-ing around the coastal path. From here to Helford the path is clearly marked, although it leaves the edge occasionally, and ends in a pleasant walk through woods into the village. Turn right at the Post Office up to **The Shipwrights Arms** which is pleasantly situated by the river.

After sampling some Devenish Beers in this old smuggling haunt, turn left out of the pub and take the road to the right. This ascends past some quaint cottages. At the top of the hill bear right for a few hundred yards, past a field on the right and a hedge on the left, until descending to Penarvon Point. Here there is a National Trust signpost marking the footpath to French-man's Creek on the left. Go over the stile and follow the well-worn path down the east side of the creek through trees and gorse.

At the top of the creek the path veers uphill to the left. Follow it and go through the gate and along the path through Kestle farmyard to a surfaced road. Turn right down this country lane, go straight over the crossroads and carry on back into the pleasant village of Manaccan. Turning right will return us to **The New Inn,** which is in fact some 300 years old.

The New Inn, Manaccan

About the Inn: Built at the time when Elizabeth the First decreed that pubs need no longer be the sole prerogative of the monks, The New Inn has always played a part in the life of Manaccan. The bar displays the tiller of a boat dredged up at the turn of the century, when the pub was a favourite haunt for the crews of the corn and coal barges which used to sail from Carne Quay. The inglenook fireplace combines with the cobwalls, oak beams and thatched roof in providing a charming atmosphere. Beer garden in rear with flower beds.

Beers and Food: Cornish Best Bitter hand drawn and Devenish Bitter, plus other keg beers and lager. Hot meals in the winter and salads during the summer months. Delicious home-made food.

The Shipwrights Arms, Helford Passage

About the Inn: Built in the 17th century and has many secret hiding-places, undoubtedly because this was once a favourite smugglers' haunt. Inside there is an open fire and beamed ceiling, outside, a terraced patio down to the river, where a quiet drink can be enjoyed under the shade of a palm tree. Dominoes are played.

Beers and Food: Devenish Beers, draught and bottled. At lunchtime there is a buffet with continental salads and local shellfish or delicious Cornish pasties. In the evenings there is soup, salads and hot meals.

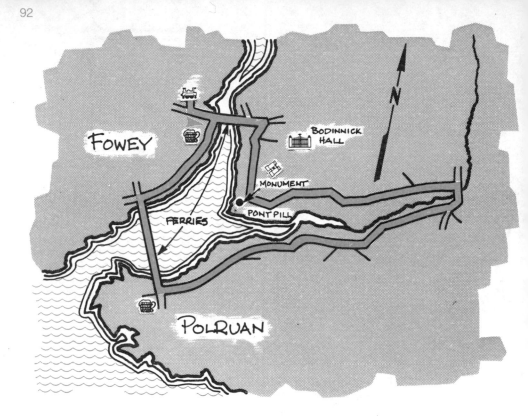

2g Fowey

The District

This delightful town at the mouth of the River Fowey is still a functioning port. Indeed it is the principal port for the Cornish China Clay industry. It has an exciting sea-faring past, for Edward III dispatched a sizeable fleet from Fowey to the seige of Calais. After the 100 years war, the Fowey 'Gallants', as the intrepid sailors were known, continued to wage war against France and, in 1457, Fowey was burnt by the French as a reprisal for the Cornishmen's daring pirate raids. After the burning of the town, two forts on either side of the rivermouth were constructed (their ruins remain) with a chain between to snap the enemies' masts.

The Parish church of **St Fimbarrus** was built around 400 AD and rebuilt in 1336. It has a fine Jacobean pulpit made from the panelling of a Spanish galleon.

Both **Bodinnick** and **Polruan** are much beloved of artists, with their almost vertical streets and their views of Fowey and the harbour.

The **Hall Walk** goes from Bodinnick and **Pont Pill Creek** towards Polruan. It is said that in 1644 Charles I, observing the Roundhead army trapped in Fowey valley, narrowly missed death from a Roundhead bullet. There is also a monument to **Sir Arthur Quiller Couch**, author and critic.

Present-day Fowey is a centre for sailing (there is anchorage for a hundred or so small craft), swimming (at Readymoney Cove) and fishing.

2½ miles north of Fowey is **Castle Dore**, an Iron Age hillfort.

How to Get There

By train to St Austell, on the Paddington to Truro line. A Western National bus takes you from St Austell to Fowey, and costs approximately £1. By road take the A390 east out of St Austell and then turn right onto A3082 for Fowey.

The Inns

The Fowey Walk

The instructions for this walk are very simple and short, as this is a very popular route, along clearly-defined and signposted paths.

Starting at **The King of Prussia Inn**, on the Town Quay, walk round the harbour, inland, to the Bodinnick Ferry. Take the ferry across the estuary (approximately a five minute journey) to Bodinnick and walk up the main road through the village. At the top of the hill a sign indicates a track to the right – 'The Hall Walk to Polruan'. Follow this path across the wooded cliffs to the head of Pont Pill Creek where, with the Quiller Couch monument away to your right, you follow the path up to a stile.

The path continues through thick woodland to the head of the creek, where you turn right into the road. Walk along the road as far as the sign pointing the way to Polruan. From here the well-marked path follows the southern cliffs of the creek to cross a farm track and a stile to the steps leading down to Polruan. After visiting **The Lugger Inn** on the harbourside, take the ferry across the estuary back to Fowey, and hence the start of the walk.

King of Prussia, Fowey

About the Inn: The original pub, dating back to 1500 or before, was a notorious smuggling headquarters and was actually named after John Carter, a big-shot in the smuggling league, who liked to call himself the King of Prussia. The pub also has a ghost, who is apparently no trouble, apart from the odd broken glass. The inn was altered in 1850, it is a tall building with a flight of steps leading directly to the waters' edge. It is a popular, comfortable and pretty establishment, decked with window boxes and hanging baskets.

Beers and Food: Best Bitter and Hick Special from St Austell brewery, both served from the wood. The lunchtime menu is very comprehensive, all the food is home-made and includes cottage pie, pizzas, lasagne and various sea-food dishes.

The Lugger Inn, Polruan

About the Inn: This interesting grey stone pub, tucked into the harbourside, is believed to be in excess of 300 years old. Like The King of Prussia, it is very much the fishing town pub, with its low and beamed ceilings and the commanding views over the Fowey estuary.

Beers and Food: Three types of bitter from St Austell brewery, including Hick Special on handpump. Varied cold bar snacks, including sea-food sandwiches and salads.

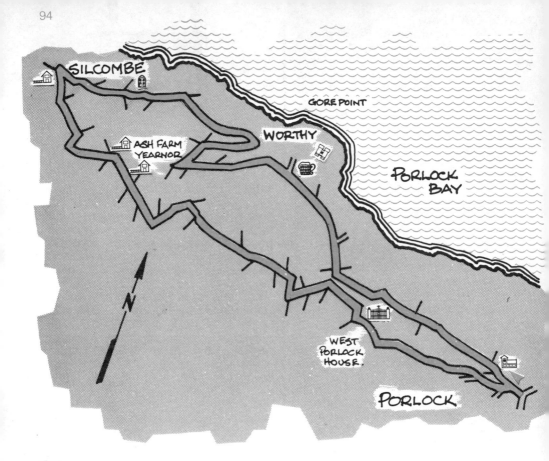

2h Porlock

The District

Porlock is a beautiful village of thatched cottages on a hillside (the A39 climbs here at a gradient of 1 in 4). It overlooks a fertile valley on the coastline of the Exmoor National Park which, to this day, is still renowned for its fine barley crop. The parish church of **St Pubrieus** (a Welsh saint, said to have crowned King Arthur) houses a fascinating collection of unusual tombs and memorials. The fifteenth century manor house — **Doverhay Court** — is now a tourist information centre. The steep road into town is said to be haunted by ghostly grey horses, after a runaway team were once killed on this perilous stretch of road.

Porlock was once a thriving and busy port, but over the centuries the sea receded and a new port was created at **Porlock Weir**. This is a tiny, hidden quay surrounded by attractive whitewashed cottages, now used as a base for fishing trips and boating, but which was at one time a delivery point for coal, woollen yarn and limestone. From here small boats would pick up timber from the nearby woods, to use the bark for tanning and in the manufacture of bricks. Porlock Weir is stalked by the ghosts of three sailors who were once washed ashore here. Their graves in Marsh Field have recently been disturbed.

Culbone Church, a little to the west along the Somerset and North Devon Coast Path, is the smallest parish church in England, measuring only 35 feet by 12 feet. Its congregation once included many of the lepers from the colony in **Yearnor Woods,**

who would participate in services via the church's 'lepers' windows'. Culbone also contains a few cottages (the sole survivors of the many that stood in its wooded combe in the 18th century) and a pottery where stoneware and sculpture is still crafted.

How to Get There
By car take the A39 from Minehead or Barnstaple to Porlock, then the B3225 to Porlock Weir. By rail to Taunton Station and then the 218 bus to Minehead. From here the 267 bus runs to Porlock.

The Porlock Weir / Culbone Walk
This is a fairly short walk, about 3-4 miles, with some steep parts but generally fairly gentle.

The Ship Inn at Porlock Weir provides an excellent place to start with a choice of draught Bass, Ind Coope Bitter and real 'Scrumpy' cider, all hand-drawn. The poet Robert Southey and Sir Richard Blackmore — author of *Lorna Doone* — have sat here and sampled the brew before you and, after following their example, leave the pub and go back out of the car park. There is a signpost pointing to Culbone and follow this by crossing the road and proceeding along the path on the right behind the hotel. The path goes over fields to the left of the harbour, which can be seen down below. After going through three gates, join the road which leads to Worthy Combe Toll. Before going into the woods cast a look over your shoulder and admire the view across the bay to Hurlstone Point.

The path into Yearnor Woods is through the gate straight ahead at the toll. The path here is part of the Somerset and North Devon Coast path, and is marked periodically with acorn signs. The path goes through a mixture of conifers, hard-

▶

The Inn

The Ship Inn, Porlock

About the Inn: A 13th century coaching inn, where the stage-coach used to change horses before climbing the hill. The stables are now used as a bottle store. Robert Southey used to come here often, and would occasionally pen a poem while sitting by the open fire in the bar. The thatched exterior has been unchanged for centuries, and the inside has a fine collection of ships' lamps, brass and copper. There is a sheltered beer garden, overnight accommodation for twenty, and darts, crib and shove-halfpenny, as well as skittle in the long alley.

Beers and Food: Bass, Ind Coope Best Bitter and 'Scrumpy' cider all hand drawn. Keg Courage, Trophy, IPA, Lager, Mild and Guinness. Bottled beers include Worthington White Shield. Large range of hot and cold snacks (the home-made pies and pasties are delicious) and four-course meals are served in the evenings (reservations necessary).

woods and rhododendron, along a tunnel and under a bridge. The leper colony was in these parts. The lepers survived by living off the land and through limited trade with the outside world. The path climbs (from where some spectacular views are to be had) and then turns inland and descends to Culbone.

After looking at the Church, and perhaps visiting the pottery (an appointment is necessary to watch the potters at work) follow the path beside the stream going through the arch at the pottery. Silcombe Farm is reached after a steady climb, then a right turn away from the stream, through a gate and left onto a farm track. Turn left again just before the farm and back down the road, leaving the Coast Path. The road goes through Parsonage Farm and then over Culbone Combe. Soon there is a track to the left which leads to Ash Farm. It was here that Samuel Taylor Coleridge wrote his famous *Khubla Khan* while in a drug-induced stupor. Coleridge was a good friend of Southey's and both of them used to frequent this area.

left. Follow it, crossing a small stream and presently Porlock Weir comes into sight below. There is a sharp left turn down a narrow path which winds down to the road above the village. Turn right, then left, to arrive back at **The Ship Inn**.

Carry on down past the turning to Ash Farm and, at Yearnor Farm, continue straight on over to the crossroads. At the entrance to Pitt Farm turn left. A path leaves the road to the right near the Worthy Combe Toll notice (to continue here would bring us back to the point where we entered Yearnor Woods). After going over the bridge, the path forks. Take the right-hand one, which leads round the edge of the woods, where it levels out. Here a narrow path signposted to Porlock turns off to the

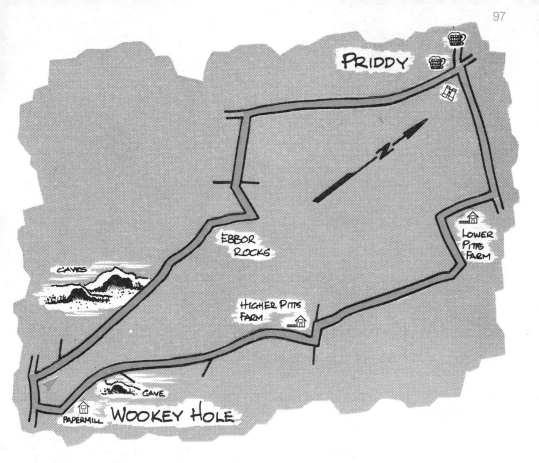

2i Wookey Hole

The District

Wookey Hole village lies under the Mendip hills that are warm and breezy in summer and bleak and windswept in winter. For reasons unknown, man's early ancestors seemed to like these cold and hostile places (while wrapped only in a skin) and Wookey Hole is the earliest known home of men in Great Britain. It seems that they shared the lease of this desirable property (?) with various rough and ready animals of the prehistoric kind, as the bones of mammoths, woolly rhinoceroses, sabre-toothed tigers and more alternate in layers with the bones and flint instruments of Stone Age cavemen.

The limestone Mendips are riddled with complex cave systems and dramatic steep sided gorges — the most famous and most visited of these is obviously Cheddar Gorge and its caves. But **Ebbor Gorge** though smaller, is more wooded and due to its status as a National Nature Reserve, is a lot less spoiled by coach parties and souvenir shops. Consequently it is rich in wildlife, having a wide variety of trees clinging to its sides, notably the oak, fir, ash, elder, hazel and hawthorn, all providing first-class accommodation for squirrels and many different birds. The peace and quiet of this area is emphasized by the presence of badgers — notoriously shy and furtive animals.

How to Get There

By bus, take the 172 (7 times daily) from Wells, which is accessible by bus from Bristol. By car take the A371 or A39 to

►

Wells and then follow signs to Wookey Hole (as distinct from Wookey). There is a car park in the village.

The Wookey Hole/Priddy Walk

Start the walk from the west side of Wookey Hole Village, ie not the Wells side and, to locate the path, walk from the centre of the village with the Mendips on your right. Pass Titlands Lane on the left and take the second path on the right (signposted Priddy). Follow the yellow arrows on the gate posts. At the first field keep middle left; at the second field keep to the centre as you ascend. At the last gate before Lammas Wood, continue straight to the top through the gate, go straight across the track and down, to the bottom of a small gorge.

You can detour here to Ebbor Rocks by turning to your right for a fifth of a mile. As mentioned above, this is a National Nature Reserve and is a natural habitat for many woodland birds — the nuthatch, redwing, fieldfare and willow warbler amongst others.

Retrace your steps to the bottom of the small gorge and follow it right up to the top and out of the woods. Go through the gate and into a field with the fence on your right, across a second field and through the gate on the far side. Turn immediately right and go through a second gate. After about 100 yards, go through a third gate (you are counting, aren't you?) then follow the path north on the right-hand side of the wall. After 300 yards turn left through yet another gate onto a track. At the T-junction turn right and walk for ¾ mile into Priddy. Incidentally, you may have noticed the views from up here — Glastonbury Tor with its tower is very prominent.

At 850 feet, Priddy is the highest village on the Mendips, and though plain it is pleasant with its rough stone walls and good walks. It is surrounded by stone circles, barrows, tumuli and other earthworks, all evidence of long lost settlements here. In the years soon after the BC/AD date change, the area was supposedly visited by large numbers of traders from the eastern Mediterranean, who were dealing in Cornish tin and Mendip lead. Many local inhabitants, in what could be regarded as somewhat blatant opportunism, believe that Jesus visited Priddy during this time with Joseph of Arimathea, who as well as perhaps being the Virgin Mary's uncle, was supposedly a tin-trader.

This divine visit would tie in nicely with those years unaccounted for in Jesus life between the age of 12 and 30. Naturally, there is no evidence to suggest any of this — could He not just as easily have been a hard working apprentice carpenter back in Nazareth? Perhaps it is evidence of the potency of draught cider more than anything else.

At any rate, turning to matters a little less spiritual, what is known is that there has been an annual sheep auction here since 1400 when remote Priddy was chosen as its site as a caution against the Black Death.

Beam us back to the present, Scotty. **The Victoria Inn** is a stone pub with a very wide variety of real ales and other beers and, of course, cider. I especially recommend the local brews — Mendip Special and Butcombe Bitter. An excellent bill of fare includes many and varied hot meals and tasty cold snacks.

After sustenance, continue on past The Victoria to the junction, where you turn right. Half a mile along the lane turn right by Lower Pitts Farm, on a track to Higher Pitts Farm and pass a barn after two 90° corners. At Higher Pitts Farm, continue straight out the back (ignoring a left turn) up over a stile and into a field. Continue to the second stile and just after it turn immediately left, heading across the fields to a third stile. When you reach it, don't climb it, but climb the adjacent stile on your right and follow the path steeply downhill towards the bottom, ignoring a left turning 400 yards down. Go through the farm on your right and out onto a lane (just to the left of the path you took up to Priddy). So turn left back to Wookey Hole.

Do not forget to visit both Wookey Hole Caves and the old Paper Mill. The caves were carved in the soft limestone by the River Axe, 'slow and blue green', as it forced its way through the rock. With aqualungs etc, experienced cavers have found 20 caves in this particular complex, though the visitor can visit only three. These three however are worth a look as they are rich with remarkable stalagmites and stalactites (which take as long as 1000 years to grow a cubic inch!).

In the Great Cave, there's a huge stalagmite known as the Witch of Wookey — she was reputedly turned to stone either by the blessings of an exorcising monk or by his curses after a love-affair of his had been blighted by her spells. Of course, all legends vary. It depends who tells them, but credibility has been added to the story by a Mendip archaeologist whose investigations revealed a deep hole in her/its chest area, inside which were the remains of a stake. So that makes 3 different endings to her life. So, at most the caves have supernatural connections and at least they are atmospheric.

The Paper Mill dates back to 1610 when paper was hand-made here. Nowadays, though, the building houses two exhibitions of note. Lady Bangor's Fairground Collection is both unique and interesting, and Madame Tussaud's Storeroom has at least 2000 moulds as well as arms, legs, torsos and heads of the famous and infamous who have been immortalized in effigy. Both the caves and the mill are open from 10 to dark in summer and 10 to 4 in the winter.

The Inn

The Queen Victoria Inn, Priddy

About the Inn: This stonewalled free house is between 250 and 350 years old and has retained its traditional charm inside and out. With a courtyard in front and two open log fires, church pew seating and the collection of old tools (used by farmers, coopers etc) this is a pub that generally reflects traditional village life and work. And the wide selection of drinks and food reflects traditional village merry-making. There is a play-garden for kids with slides, swings and a see-saw. And outside seating for many people.

Beers and Food: Wadworths 6X, Mendip Special and Butcombe Bitter (all gravity fed), Theakston's Old Peculiar, three other bitters, Guinness, two lagers and cider, plus the usual range of wines and spirits.

Pies, pasties, plaice, chicken, sausages, gammon and rump steaks — all with peas, tomatoes and chips. Pizzas, Ploughman's and hot and cold sandwiches.

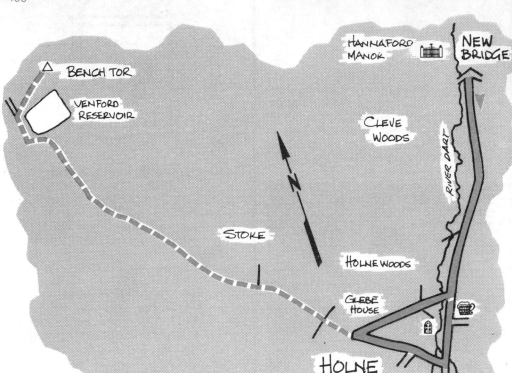

2j Holne

The District

Holne village lies above the west bank of the River Dart in a thickly wooded area on the south-east edge of Dartmoor. This part of Dartmoor is noted for its old oak trees (particularly at Holne Wood and Holne Chase), the picturesque reservoirs lying in the valleys, and the views offered by the rocky outcrops, known as 'tors'. Breeding birds include red grouse, buzzard, curlew and the wood warbler.

The village has been in existence for over nine centuries and is listed in the Domesday Book. Originally it was a community for farming and tin mining; and various relics from the latter occupation are scattered around Holne today. The inhabitants of this quiet, rural village apparently have a spendid feast on Midsummer's Day; to mark the event of a sacrificial rite that used to be carried out in the village, when a ram was sacrificed, then roasted whole and devoured. The fifteenth century church has a fine screen, and well-preserved paintings, as well as connections with Charles Kingsley, writer and theologian, who was born at the nearby vicarage.

New Bridge, the starting point of the walk, is a 15th century stone bridge spanning the River Dart as it meanders through the woods, bordering the fringe of **Holne Moor**.

How to Get There

By road, take the A38 as far as Ashburton and turn right at the sign marked 'Dartmoor', along the B3357. New Bridge is just over 4 miles along this road, and is well-signposted. By rail to Newton Abbot Station, from where special bus services run to Dartmoor (summer only).

The Holne Walk

This is an easy, shortish walk through woodland, incorporating the charming old village of Holne. However, walkers can add four miles (bearing in mind that the pub is at the end of our route) by following the suggested detour to Bench Tor.

Start at New Bridge on the Ashburton to Dartmoor Road. New Bridge is a picturesque grey stone bridge over the River Dart with three arches and pointed buttresses, dating back to the 15th century.

Cross over the bridge and look for a footpath on the right, leading to the woods. The path initially follows the winding course of the River Dart through Cleve Woods, nowadays the property of the National Trust. The path then leaves the side of the river and proceeds in a south-westerly direction, to eventually come out in a meadow. Cross the meadow to the road above and turn right, walking away from Holne village towards the moor. To your right, half-hidden amongst the trees is 'Glebe House' which, prior to 1832, was the Georgian Vicarage in which Charles Kingsley, who wrote *The Water Babies,* was born.

This road cames out onto the lower road leading back into Holne, and walkers are faced with the moral dilemma of either continuing north-west along the road over the moor to Vendford Reservoir, and beyond to Bench Tor; or heading straight for the pub in Holne. Bench Tor is an easy climb and offers fine views over the valley of the Dart. However, those in dire need of liquid refreshment should turn left, onto the road leading into Holne Village and then left again to find **The Church House Inn,** opposite the small, grey church. Incidentally, check out the village store beside the church, as their freshly-baked cakes have quite a reputation. After visiting the inn, turn right and continue along the road north through the village. At the road junction turn right and pick up the original footpath through the field to Cleve Woods and hence back to New Bridge.

The Inn

The Church House Inn, Holne

About the Inn: The inn was built in 1329 and there has been speculation that it was originally designed as an extension of the church, providing a wee drop for the clergy and parishioners who had to travel from afar to attend the service. Until the 19th century, the inn brewed its own distinctive potion, known as 'White Ale', which could well have fortified Cromwell who stayed here during the battles at Totnes. It is a part timbered building with walls on an average of three to four feet thick, which protect it from the worst of the Dartmoor winds. The bar enjoys a lively trade with both villagers and visitors, and its old world character (wooden beams, inglenook fireplace) ensures an enjoyable rest for the walker.

Beers and Food: An extensive range of beers including local Blackawton Bitter and Headstrong (made by Blackawton, a one-man private enterprise, which has been going for three years) and bass, all on handpump. Ansells Bitter, Whitbread Tankard, draught Guinness and Skol lager are also available.

The country fruit wines, such as Peach, Damson and Elderberry are a definite must, as is their special Church House mead. A comprehensive menu serving everything from roast duckling to hot cornish pasties is available seven days a week, both lunchtimes and evenings.

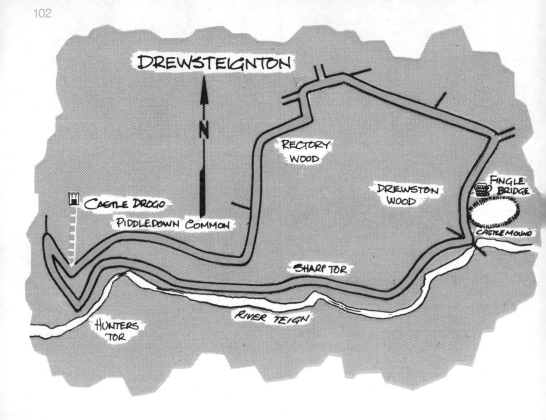

2k Drewsteignton

The District

This is rich Dartmoor country, broken by small coombes and by the **River Teign,** which runs between the steep tree-clad slopes of the Teign gorge.

Drewsteignton. A picturesque village, one mile to the north of the Teign, comprised of a cluster of thatched granite cottages and a neat yellow lichened church. There is apparently a bloody legend attached to this idyllic rural spot; namely that a dreadful murder took place here and the blood still seeps from under the door of the cottage where the deed took place. There is also a field about a mile away, which is said to scare even the local livestock.

A three arched granite bridge spanning the Teign, **Fingle Bridge** at one time carri-ed an old pack horse track. Brown trout may occasionally be spied from the bridge, as well as the most common riverside bird, the water ouzel.

Hidden amongst pine trees above the Teign, is the brooding sight of **Castle Drogo,** constructed of solid granite and resembling the most romantic of medieval castles. It is in fact very much twentieth century, finished by Sir Edward Lutyens around 1930, and now the property of the National Trust. The house and terraced gardens are now open to the public from April to October.

How to Get There

By car take the A30, the old Okehampton road to Chagford, from where the way is signposted to Drewsteignton. By rail to

Exeter Station and then bus to Moreton-hampstead, from where the 708 and the 106 bus will take you to Drewsteignton.

The Drewsteignton Walk

A walk of about 6 miles through woodland, along both riverside and ridge paths, affording dramatic views of the Teign gorge.

Start at Drewsteignton and take the Dunsford Road out of the village, following it downhill for about a mile, in a south-easterly direction to Fingle Bridge. Just beside Fingle Bridge is **The Anglers' Rest** with its adjacent terraces overlooking the river.

'Fisherman's Path' is signposted to the left, alongside the banks of the Teign. Follow this for about 1½ miles, across the rocky boulders and through overhanging trees. At a footbridge, turn right and follow the path uphill to a gate and a concrete road leading to Coombe Farm. Go through the gate and follow the road, before turning right through another gate, along a bridleway signposted 'Hunter's Path'.

The path emerges on the bracken-covered summit of Hunter's Tor and from here, by turning sharply left along a narrow path, Castle Drogo can be visited. It is supposedly the last castle to be built on such a grand scale in England, although its medieval outlines belie this; looking every inch the scene of Drogo-ian carryings-on.

Retrace your steps to Hunter's Tor and follow the high-level path round to the left. A little way along the path, a track runs off uphill to the left. Follow this northwards, across fields to the edge of the Rectory Wood. Eventually it leads onto a well-defined footpath sandwiched between hedges, which emerges by The Drewe Arms Inn, in Drewsteignton village.

The Inn

The Angler's Rest, Fingle Bridge

About the Inn: The site of this pub has built up quite a reputation for accommodating travellers over the years. Originally an old mill stood on the site and the gregarious miller opened his kitchen to those wishing to prepare their own provisions. The mill was demolished and replaced by a tea parlour, run by two genteel Victorian ladies, providing sustenance to those who came from far and wide. Although comparatively modern (25 years old) the pub's granite and timbered exterior blends into the countryside and uses its superb location, overlooking the river, to great advantage. The haunt of anglers, walkers and country lovers, it is a friendly and comfortable place, providing excellent refreshments.

Beers and Food: Courage Directors, Draught Bass and Best Bitter, all on hand-pump, with Wadworth's 6X and a draught local farm cider on gravity. The bar menu offers various light snacks as well as several hot dishes, with more elaborate fare available in the separate restaurant, both at lunchtime and in the evenings.

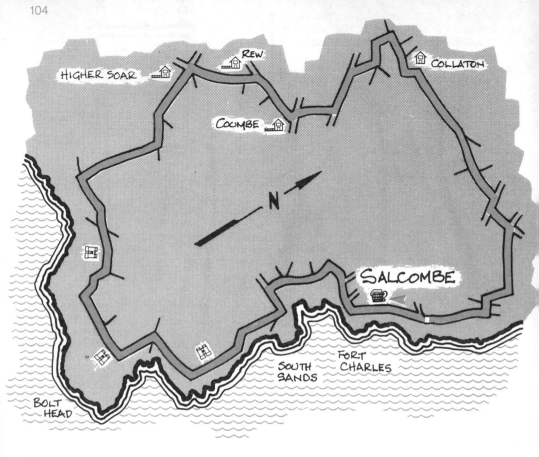

21 Salcombe

The District

Salcombe is Devon's most southerly resort. With it's mild climate — evidenced by all manner of vegetation unusual for England: palms, orange and lemon trees mixed in with pines and cypresses — and its white houses, the town is reminiscent of the Mediterranean. Indeed Dr James Huxham, a noted physician during George II's reign, was wont to compare it with Montpelier in the South of France.

The estuary is nowadays crammed with pleasure-boats, but Salcombe was once a busy port with ships unloading spices and rum from the West Indies. Nowadays there are fishing-boats after crab and lobster as well as yachts. The harbour is safe, except for the sunken rocks and **The Bar** at the mouth which can make it dangerous at night.

Salcombe Castle stands on a rock engulfed by the sea. It was built by Henry VIII to defend this part of the coastline. During the English Civil War this was the last fortress in England to resist the Parliamentarians. It was taken by General Fairfax in the third and final seige of the castle in 1646. Sir Edmund Fortesque had garrisoned the fortress (renaming it Fort Charles — still its official name) and had spent over £3,999 on repairs only to have the place reduced to rubble by Roundhead artillery. Little remains today.

At Overbecks there are 6 acres of gardens in the care of the National Trust. Laid out in the early part of this century, there are many exotic trees and shrubbery, palms and huge pink magnolias. The Botanical Gardens and Museum are open April — September, 10.00 — 6.00 on Wednesday and Friday, 10.00 — 12.00 and 2.30 — 4.30 on Sundays.

How to Get There
By rail, catch a train to Totnes or Plymouth and then get a bus to Salcombe. By road, take the A379 from Plymouth and then straight at the crossroads, after Bridge End, onto the B3197. Turn right onto the A381 to Salcombe. From Exeter take the A38 south-west. Turn right onto A384 to Totnes where you turn right again onto A381 for Salcombe.

The Salcombe Walk
Lasting as it does for some 7½ miles, this walk might be too much for granny, but the rest of the family should enjoy this beautiful stroll around spectacular clifftops and gentle Devon countryside.

After having drunk enough to get you on your way, leave **The Kings Arms** on Fore Street in Salcombe and walk south down to the water's edge. After the pier, continue on to Cliff Road and then fork left on to Undercliffe Rd. Passing Fort Charles on the left, follow the road down to North Sands and round the edge of this fine beach, before crossing over the small, wooded but steep peninsula down to the equally fine South Sands. Where the road comes to a T-junction, turn left and follow the road round on to a track. From here we are on the South Devon Coast Path which drops down a slope and over the stream which runs into Starehole Bay, before climbing up towards Bolt Head. Turn back, from time to time, and take in the view down the estuary back to Salcombe Harbour. Down on the left lies The Bar, a sandbank which runs across the mouth of the estuary. In rough weather the seas can be seen breaking across it. Tennyson's poem *Crossing the Bar* was inspired by this sandbank when he was staying in Salcombe.

Dog violets, wall pepper and sorrel grow along the path as it ascends to Bolt Head. From here there is a spectacular view across to Prawle Point and Gammon Head in the east. The path continues west above the grotesque rock formations which form these cliffs, a result of the intense heat and pressure which created metamorphic rocks in the Devonian Period, some 300-400 million years ago.

►

Kings Arms, Salcombe

About the Inn: About 400 years old, there are 3 bars. The Whitestrand (connected to the beer garden) is open in the summer only. The old bar has a tiled floor and an open fire. There is a beer garden on the quay from where the weary traveller can relax and watch the boats in the harbour. A very friendly inn.

Beers and Food: Plymouth Best Bitter hand drawn, also range of Courage Keg beers, two lagers and draught cider. At lunchtime a huge range of bar snacks and meals — local pasties, curries, steak and kidney pies, country pâté. Try the home-cooked ham platter with granary bread and salad.

Many ships have been wrecked along this rugged coastline. In 1588 a Spanish Galleon was wrecked one stormy Sunday morning below Portlemouth Down. The crew were left to drown while the congregation of East Portlemouth church scampered straight from communion to loot the cargo. Nowadays the locals are a mite more friendly!

After about ¾ of a mile, turn right along the path which leaves the coast passing a building on the left. Turn left where it meets a farm track and walk along to the small hamlet of Soar. Just after a track on the right, a footpath leads across fields meeting a lane at Rew. At the end of the lane, turn right and walk down the hill into the tiny farm hamlet of Combe. Opposite the end of the road you have just come down, a track leads off from the other side of the road (diagonally to the left).

this tiny village.

Walk through Collaton, past two turnings on the left, and along the path at the end of the road. Go down, over the stream and up to the farm on the far side. Go through the farm buildings and along the track. After about ¼ of a mile, a path leads off to the right. Follow it across fields with Salcombe now below on the right. Where it meets the road (the A381) cross over and go down the steep hill with the cemetery on the right. Turn right at the crossroads and follow the road as it winds back down into Salcombe sea front. Now in much need of liquid refreshment, make your way back to **The Kings Arms** and enjoy a few pints of local Plymouth Best Bitter in the beer garden which overlooks the estuary.

Climb the path uphill, until it meets a road; and here turn left. After about ¼ of a mile, turn right up the track which leads up to Collaton. Where it meets another track turn left, then right and right again, and into

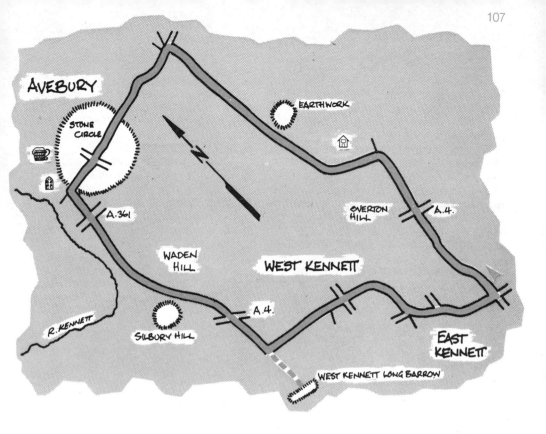

2m Avebury

The District

While Stonehenge has achieved world fame and is an essential stopping point on the Canterbury / London / Bath / Stratford / Oxford / London whistlestop tour of South England, **Avebury** has been unjustifiably overshadowed and indeed sometimes completely overlooked. Many people however, rate Avebury not merely as equal to Stonehenge, but superior — in terms of archaeological interest, of the sheer size of the Avebury, **Silbury Hill, Windmill Hill** and **West Kennet Long Barrow** complex and, perhaps most importantly for non-experts, simply in terms of atmosphere, especially in the evening. It has been said that Avebury is a cathedral, Stonehenge only a parish-church.

The walk itself is not difficult — the slopes of the Marlborough Downs being gentle rather than steep — and it incorporates the 'Ridgeway Path' for a mile or so. A small torch in your pocket is recommended.

Despite its name, the walk begins in **East Kennet**.

How to Get There

By car, East Kennet is ½ mile south of A4 (Marlborough — Chippenham road) and 3 miles east of the junction of A4 and A361 (Devizes — Swindon road). By bus from Marlborough or Calne, ask to be put off at East Kennet. The nearest British Rail Station is Swindon and then by bus to Avebury.

►

The Avebury Walk

Start in East Kennet at the West Overton end of the village and, with the telephone box on your right, walk along the village street and take the first left turning, down a narrow walled alley onto a lane. Turn left and continue straight on, on a track, leaving the metalled road as it veers right. Once you have crossed the bridge, follow the track as it continues through a gate and along the left-hand side of the field. On your right you can see 'tumuli' — ancient mounds of earth, now grassed over, which were probably burial grounds long ago.

Cross the A4 and continue straight over on the bridlepath opposite. This is a part of the ancient 'Ridgeway Path'. Again you can see tumuli to your right, but keep an eye on the sky as well, for amongst the birds that breed in the area you may be lucky enough to spot stonecurlews, wheaters, quail or the hawks and buzzards. 200 yards further up, there is a single tumulus — walk another 200 yards past it and turn left by the fence, keeping on its right-hand side. Head for a clump of trees — another tumulus. The track veers right here, heading gently downhill towards a farm for ¾ mile. At the farm, turn left at the T-junction and walk into Avebury. To see the Stone Circle which surrounds the village, go through the gate on your right.

Avebury Stone Circle is the largest 'henge' monument in Great Britain and the largest Stone circle in Europe, possibly the world. It was built sometime between 2000 and 1600 BC by the Beaker Folk. Their name derives from their odd practice of being buried with, of all things, bell-shaped drinking beakers beside them. What Avebury, bigger than Stonehenge, was built for, nobody really knows (perhaps an open temple?) but, as with Stonehenge, the feat of construction and its precision cannot be underestimated. There were about 100 local sandstone megaliths, hewn from the Marlborough Downs, though only 4 survive from 30 in the Central Circle and 5 from 32 in the South Circle. The stones are not worked as they are at Stonehenge, but there are two basic shapes — male and female - I leave it to you to decide which is which.

By now you may feel it is necessary to re-enter the 20th century — and so, to **The Red Lion**, where you can rest your aching brain for a while and concentrate on your palate.

After refreshment it's worth wandering about in Avebury for a while. A very interesting little village, there is the Alexander Keiller Museum which houses excavated remains from this whole prehistoric complex — well worth a quick browse. The Church of St James was mentioned in the Domesday Book — some of the nave and the windows are Anglo-Saxon, the aisles and font are Norman and the tower and rood - screen are 15th century. Avebury Manor is an Elizabethan house with good panelling and plasterwork and a beautiful garden with fine examples of topiary (tree and hedge-shaping, if you didn't know) and a lovely circular dovecot. Supposedly, the manor has a ghost who wears a white hood — someone to avoid when or if you visit. The house is open to the public. And so, back to the walk.

Continue past The Red Lion on the lane and go past the church to take a path on the nearside of the Old Rectory on the left. Go up to and through a gate to where the path veers right through the car park and out onto the road. Turning right here, walk along the road for 20 yards alongside the River Kennett. At the fork don't continue over the footbridge, but turn left over the stile, to stay on the left bank of the Kennett. Go over stiles and through a gate to hit the main A4. Walking here, you cannot fail to miss Silbury Hill on your right — a vast conical hill looking rather like a steam-pudding. 130 feet high, it is three-quarters man-made, making it the largest artificial mound in Europe. Why and when was it built, you may ask. All the experts can say is that it's pre-Roman (their road goes round it) and that it may be the grave of the master-architect of Stonehenge (a bit far-fetched, perhaps) — it remains a mystery.

Cross the A4 by turning left along it and then very soon right at the near side of the house opposite. This is signposted to West Kennett Long Barrow. Follow the path and where it turns 90°, continue straight on uphill for ¼ mile to the Barrow. It's well worth seeing, being the largest chambered tomb in England and Wales. Built between 3000 and 2500 BC, it's 350 foot long and its largest stones weigh 20 tons. How were these moved? Yet another mystery to add to your list. Anyway, at least you know why you need a torch.

Retrace your steps to where the path turned 90° and turn right for East Kennett along the left-hand side of the field. Cross the metalled track and climb the stile on the other side. Go over a second stile by a gate. The path turns right (you can see the village now) keeping the hedge on your right to where the path widens until the path veers right uphill. Turn left here along a track to meet a lane, Turn right along this lane into the village or left along it to the A4 to catch your bus home.

The Red Lion, Avebury

About the Inn: Within the Avebury ring of stones and known mainly to sheep, is a 17th century thatched inn, known as The Red Lion. Reputedly spooked by a female ghost and her attendant dog, this pub was once the stopping-off point for Royalty, on their way to the nearby manor house. In the bar is the somewhat unusual sight of an 80 foot deep well; well, actually it is perhaps more accurately described as a fathomless pit, covered by glass and lit by spotlights. Old beams and wooden seats (with extra seating outside in the summer) make this an attractive and interesting place in which to while away a lunchtime.

Beers and Food: Tankard, Trophy, Heineken, Stella, draught Guinness and Traditional West Country ale from the wood. At lunchtime various salads and sandwiches are available as well as hot meals such as chicken in the basket.

East Anglia

A countryside usually characterised as flat and featureless, East Anglia actually contains many secret and unexpected parts. The salt flats and marshes of the Norfolk coast have a windswept beauty known mainly to the local birdlife. Further inland, sleepy villages remain entrenched in former times.

The paintings of Constable and Gainsborough have highlighted the Englishness of Suffolk; with its calm and leafy backwater atmosphere where windmills stare out across the fertile landscape.

Historically important, East Anglia has many fine churches and old market towns to explore.

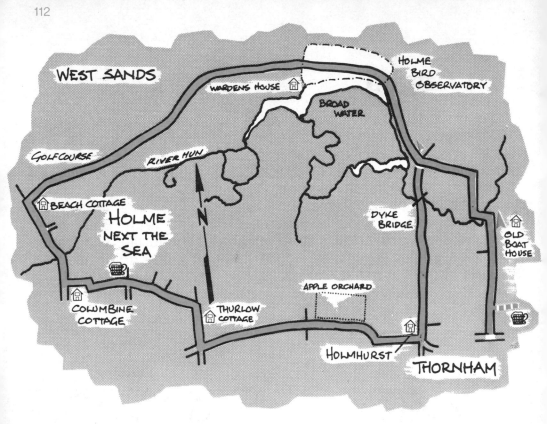

3a Holme-next-the-Sea

The District

Holme-next-the-Sea marks the end of the Wash coast and has 'a broken, sandy, windswept beauty quite unsurpassed'. It lies on the edge of a chalk ridge; its cottages are made from local chalk and feature many old apple trees which are common in the area. Holme Church, between the village and the marshland, boasts a good tower, built by Henry of Nottingham in the reign of Richard II. The church, which was partly rebuilt in 1771 and damaged in 1887, features a memorial brass to Henry.

East of the village, a bird observatory and nature reserve is open daily in summer and on weekends in winter (permits available from the warden on site). It is home to 234 species of bird.

Both Holme and **Thornham,** about a mile and a half south-east, have a strong linear appearance, possibly due to Roman alignments. The old Roman road called Peddar's Way stretches from near Ixmouth in Suffolk, to the coast between Holme and Hunstanton. The remains of a Roman signal station were discovered in Thornham. Separated from the sea by a mile of marshland, this attractive town is famous for its wrought ironwork and a 15th century church.

How to Get There

By car, A149 (King's Lynn Ring Road) passes through Thornham. Train to the stations at either Hunstanton or Wells-Next-Sea, then an East Counties bus (frequent runs) to Thornham.

The Thornham / Holme Walk

A long (about 6½ miles) though flat and gentle stroll behind the sands along the Norfolk coast. Liable to be muddy much of the year because of the marshland and waterways in the area.

Begin on the A149 at Thornham. Take the first turning on the right leading towards Holme past Thornham church and the Kingshead Hotel. Follow this road to an old boathouse on your right (cars can be left here). Take the footpath on the left, passing over dykes and beside a tidal lock gate and parallel bars.

Follow a clearly defined path towards the Holme Bird Observatory which lies just on the West Sands. The warden will issue a permit if you wish to visit the observatory.

Continue past the warden's house on a path following the sands towards a golf course. Turn left onto a path that leads through a gate, passing a beach cottage on your left, then onto a metalled road. Turn left at Columbine Cottage (you can buy local honey here) into Holme village. Continue down the road, past an inn and Thurlow cottage onto the main road, at which you should turn left. Continue past an orchard, along to Holmhurst, a small red-brick cottage on your left. Turn left onto a footpath and back onto the main dyke. Cross the dyke bridge and turn right at the dyke, back towards where the walk began. As you return, turn left at Oswald Waterfield's seat on the right towards **The Lifeboat Inn**, 100 yards down on the right.

A smallish but very charming 16th century tavern that has been hosted by members of the same family for over 200 years, The Lifeboat is lit by paraffin lanterns and gaslights. It is the site of what is believed to be the last remaining, regular game of pitch penny in the country. The game consists of tossing 13 'pennies' from a set distance — in this case the bar's open

▶

The Inn

Lifeboat Inn, Thornham

About the Inn: In Ship Lane, only 100 yards from the sea, a compact tavern about 400 years old and kept in the same family for almost half of its life. Low-ceilinged, lit by lanterns and gaslights, the bar is small but very well decorated, with genuine antique guns, brasses, an open fire at each end, wooden refectory tables and chairs. The dining room has olde worlde charm with lace table cloths and seats about 30. A concreted square at the back looks onto the sea and is used in summer. Darts and pitch penny. No music whatsoever (a blessing?), children welcome. Overnight accommodation.

Beers and Food: Hand-drawn Greene King, Adnams and Samuel Smiths plus three draught lagers. Excellent range of food from bar snacks to Norfolk Roast Duckling in the restaurant — has to be seen to be believed!

fire — into a box with a hole on the top — built into the seat! When Oswald Waterfield owned the inn, he set up a prize of a bottle of Scotch for the player who filled the box with all 13 pennies. One day, fifteen years ago, the feat was finally achieved, and a bottle of Scotch duly handed over — a miniature! Since then, Oswald has been unable to shake the reputation of being a skinflint and they say that his ghost still hovers around the doors at closing time, to prevent patrons getting drinks after time.

The new owner is some what more generous; he has put up a gallon bottle of Scotch to the second person to achieve the next-to-impossible.

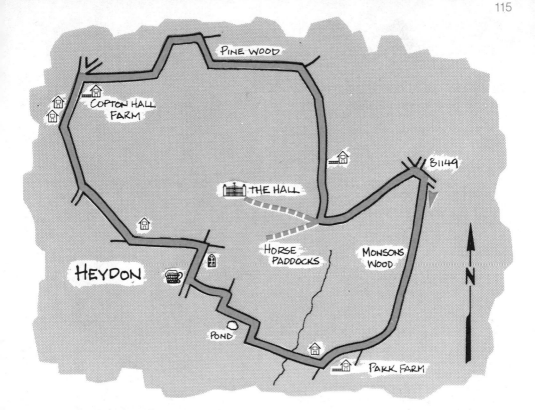

3b Heydon

The District

One of the most attractive of Norfolk villages, **Heydon**, with its rural setting, is frequently used as a backdrop to TV series and plays. Its houses and cottages are gathered around the pretty village green, with its Gothic-style pump in the middle. Heydon's church is of late 14th century or early 15th century vintage, and is rather unusual with its Perpendicular pulpit, quaint font and family pews and memorials. Here, as throughout the village, the Bulwer family seem to predominate — they were Lords of the Manor in the 15th century.

A secret tunnel leads to **Heydon Hall**, built in 1581, a classical Elizabethan mansion, with 18th century additions, which reinforces the feudal atmosphere that permeates the village. Bulwer Long is the present owner of the Hall and does his best to maintain the feudal traditions of his family, exacting a certain amount of deference from locals and 'tithes' from his tenants. Lord Lytton wrote many of his novels in the Hall.

The village park is a Victorian creation with Gothic lodges at the entrances. Mighty beeches, limes and oaks populate the park, providing the so-called Cromwell's Oak — said to have saved Oliver from the horns of an enraged bull — with company.

How to Get There

By car, A140 north from Norwich. Fork left onto B1149. Cross B1145, a well-defined road by a red-brick building opposite the turning to Oulton. Train to Norwich, then, if possible, take the 'workers' bus' to Holt.

►

This runs about 5 times a day; there are no stops as such, but the driver is very co-operative and will arrange a convenient pick-up point and time for your return journey.

The Heydon Walk

If arriving by train, the bus will drop you at the junction of the B149, the third road left over a humpbacked bridge coming from Norwich. Turn left onto the well-defined track by the red-brick building, opposite the turning to Oulton. If arriving by car, leave your car at this point. Walk along the edge of Morrison's Wood past a large barn on the right into Park Farm. Bear right, through the farmyard, and turn right at the cottage with two coach lamps on the porch. Cross a stream via the pretty red-brick bridge and go through a gate. Continue over the ploughed field to an iron cross gate (this leads to private property). Turn right at the gate and follow the edge of the field down to a stile, passing a small pond in the private field.

Over the stile you turn right along the edge of the woods. After 50 yards, iron steps lead left into a rhododendron garden; follow the path over several wooden footbridges, past a summer house, into romantic gardens with a sleeping tree, which lead onto the village green at Heydon. The village won a best-kept village competition twice in a row in the mid-Sixties. **The Earle Arms Inn** faces you as you enter Heydon. This halfway stage in a 5¾ mile stroll is a good time to revive aching legs with a glass of Adnams direct from the barrel, and to pit your aim or wits against local enthusiasts of dart, pool, draughts or chess.

Leaving the inn, if you can, turn left and pass through the gate houses just beyond the church. Turn left again and follow the path. At the fork just past the small house to your right, bear right through a white fence and then straight out onto a metalled road through two more gatehouses. After about a half mile, past tiled cottages, you arrive at Cropton Hall farm. Turn sharp right alongside the farm till you reach a pine wood, at which you should fork right. As the

The Inn

path bears left, almost at the end of the wood, take the grass strip between the fields (to the right) to the gate opposite. Pass through the gate and alongside some farm buildings to a crossing. To return to the start of the walk turn left, and at the main road turn right. To view Heydon Hall turn right; alternatively, the Hall's horse paddocks are straight ahead into the park.

Earle Arms Inn, Heydon

About the Inn: Lying beside Heydon's beautiful village green with the church in view and an old water well, erected to mark Queen Victoria's Jubilee, blocking the entrance (not really!), the inn is hosted by Paul Easton. Its white-painted brickwork features an impressive ship's figurehead, though no one is quite sure how it got there. Very homely atmosphere in three bars, served by a central area where the real ale is contained in barrels. Pool room with juke box is separate at the back of the inn. Darts, pool, draughts, chess (the inn supports two darts teams). Small car park at rear, drinks taken on the village green in fine weather. Overnight accommodation on a bed-and-breakfast basis.

Beers and Food: Adnams Suffolk ales direct from the barrel. Adnams, Tolly Cobbold, Greene King and Newcastle Brown bottled. Simple, reasonably priced bar food.

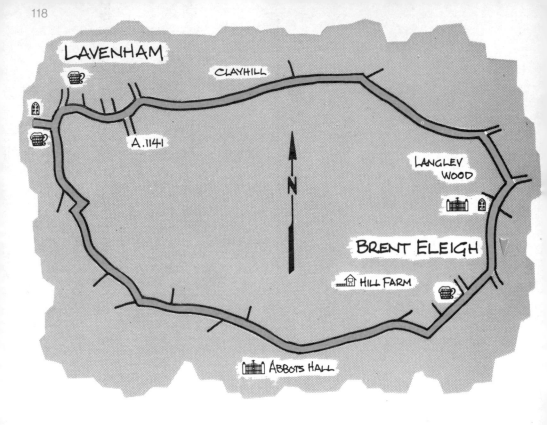

3c Brent Eleigh

The District

Lavenham is an unspoilt, medieval town in one of the loveliest parts of Suffolk, near to Kersey and Long Melford. One of the great weaving towns of the Middle Ages, its irregular streets of half-timbered cottages have changed little since Flemish weavers settled here in the 16th century. The Guildhall and the Perpendicular Church, famous for its peal of bells and priceless carvings and decorations, are well worth a visit. Built to magnificent proportions, the church is a Gothic masterpiece and has been described as 'the most splendid Wool Church in East Anglia'.

Within easy reach are villages of historical interest like **Long Melford,** with its Elizabethan halls of Melford and Kentwell: **Hengrave Hall,** just outside Bury St Edmunds; and Sudbury, site of Gainsborough's house. In **Bury St Edmunds,** visit the Abbey, the Corn Exchange, the Norman Tower, and the Moyses Hall.

Brent Eleigh is a tiny village full of 14th century charm; its Church of St Mary contains many fine carvings and recently discovered wall paintings dating back 600 years. Racing at nearby Newmarket.

How to Get There

By car, A134 south-east from Bury St Edmunds. Left onto A1141 through Lavenham to Brent Eleigh. By BR, to Sudbury, Ipswich or Colchester, with bus connections from the stations to Brent Eleigh.

The Brent Eleigh Walk

In the heart of the East Anglian apple

country, the walk lies amid the patchwork of ploughed fields that once were home to Gainsborough and Constable, and echoed to the prosperous sound of weaving mills at full tilt. It is a gentle, 5 mile stroll through farm and partly wooded land.

The Swan Hotel, in Lavenham High Street, dated back to the 14th century and was very fashionable during the wool trade boom; rather more recently, it was a popular meeting place for American servicemen stationed in the area during the last war,. and retains many servicemen memorabilia from those days. A glass of Greene King or Abbot Ale taken by a blazing log fire in winter, or in one of the inn's two beer gardens, will set you up nicely for the task ahead.

Take the A1141 from Lavenham to the small village of Brent Eleigh; **The Cock Inn** is immediately on your right as you enter the village. Just behind the pub sign is a wide tarmac track leading off to the right. Follow this to the top of the hill. Follow the telegraph poles (taking care *not* to turn off onto a path to the left) until you can see Brent Eleigh Hall, a green-pillared mansion, in the distance behind you.

Follow this track down the other side of the hill, over a silty stream in the floor of the valley and up another hill. The path turns sharply to the right and, as you climb, the Hall and the church at Brent Eleigh become

The Inns

Swan Hotel, Lavenham

About the Inn: One of the area's enduring landmarks and a picture postcard example of Tudor building, the Swan is in Lavenham High Street. It features a delightful enclosed garden and two magnificent bars with an authentic, heavy-timbered Elizabethan atmosphere. Its vast fireplaces keep up a warm glow in winter. There are also showcases of American service memorabilia and a row of hand-bells used by Lavenham's famous bellringers. It offers a programme of winter concerts. Accommodation for 74, including one fourposter bedroom!

Beers and Food: Greene King IPA and Abbot Ale handpumped, Tartan Bitter, Double Diamond and a variety of lagers. A selection of hot and cold bar food, with restaurant offering extensive à la carte and table d'hôte menus at lunchtimes.

Angel Hotel, Lavenham

About the Inn: In 1450, the licence to this popular Market Square tavern was granted to one Susan Braithwaite for the rent of 1s 11d a year Susan was only four years old at the time! The centuries have added to its traditions while keeping its history intact. Landlord Cyril Cheshire welcomes children

visible in the distance to your right. The path turns left almost immediately, then, with Lavenham church tower visible in the far distance, follow the path until you reach a track on you right which leads down to a farm. Take this track until you reach a cluster of oak trees at the end of a field. Turn left down a narrow track lined by a hedge, which brings you into an open field. Follow the field to the right keeping close to a ditch and a stream.

At the end of the field turn left, then almost immediately sharp right through a hedgerow, then right again, bringing you back close to the stream. When you reach the stream turn left. The path you are now on meets a hedge, to the right, after about 100 yards. Follow the hedge round to the left until a gap flanked by iron posts appears. Take the opening through the hedge and follow the stream until a track crosses it. Take the crossing and then turn, keeping the stream now on your left. The stream divides after about 20 yards; take the right fork and follow it up to an iron gate. Turn left through the gate and approach the farm buildings dead ahead. Passing the farm by a duck pond on your right, Lavenham church tower will loom before you about half a mile away.

By now, the track has become a small tarmac road. Follow it past a modern house and farm buildings as it bears to the right, then past a pink thatched cottage. Wider now, the path passes a small estate of houses and continues into Lavenham. At the end of the road turn left towards Lavenham church or right into the centre of the village.

The church boasts an imposing, ornate exterior with beautiful stained glass windows; its chancel is over 600 years old, most of the rest of the church being built at the turn of the 16th century.

The Cock Inn is in Church Street (opposite the church) and is 100 yards towards the village centre from a quaint tea shop. A modern pub, with an open fire, it serves Greene King Suffolk ales. **The Angel Hotel,** in the Market Square, is a traditional tavern which has offered accommodation and hospitality since before Columbus discovered America, and before William Caxton introduced the first printing press to England.

Follow Lavenham High Street, turning right at a pink cottage into Market Lane. This brings you to the Market Square and the site of the Guildhall as well as The Angel Hotel. Cross the square into Prentice Street, following the street down to a stream and a bridge. A telegraph pole points towards a public footpath which you should take, bearing left beside the stream and skirting a field. Having turned in a semi-circle, follow the field to the left onto a track which meets another track after about 50 yards.

Turn right, keeping the farm on your left, and follow the track through a field and over into a second field. Step over, rather than into, the ditch and turn right, placing the ditch on your right. The path meets a hedge at the top of the field; turn left, following the hedge for just a few feet before turning right through a gap (which is liable to be partly over-grown in summer). Cross through the field then pass through a gap in the far hedge, which brings you out onto a narrow road. Turn right towards the farm house, taking the path between the farm house and outbuilding into another field. Lavenham church tower, in the distance to your right, is again the major landmark.

At the end of the field turn left, between trees, towards an orchard, cross over a track and follow the route between the trees. After a mile the path meets a single lane road; turn towards Brent Eleigh, the Hall (private) and the church of St Mary, a

14th century Jacobean building with many interesting memorial stones worked into the floor. Follow the road through the village to **The Cock Inn** (not to be confused with the inn of the same name in Lavenham). Here landlord Stephen Potter will let you soothe your aching feet and serve you with Abbots Ale, a local favourite.

and offers good innkeeping at reasonable prices. Overnight accommodation.

Beers and Food: Variety of real ales drawn by hand from the wood. Excellent value in meals, with three-course lunches a speciality. Evening meals by arrangement.

Cock Inn, Lavenham

About the Inn: In Church Street, opposite the Perpendicular Church. Modern pub with thatched roof, front garden, open fire and bench seating.

Beers and Food: Greene King Suffolk ales; off sales. Good range of fresh bar meals, hot and cold.

Cock Inn, Brent Eleigh

About the Inn: Jacobean interior; popular with locals, children very welcome. Olde worlde bench seating with one giant round table taking up most of the space in one of its two bars. Not-so-olde-worlde darts and fruit machine.

Beers and Food: Good, simple pub grub can be taken outside in the garden during fine weather. Abbot's Ale.

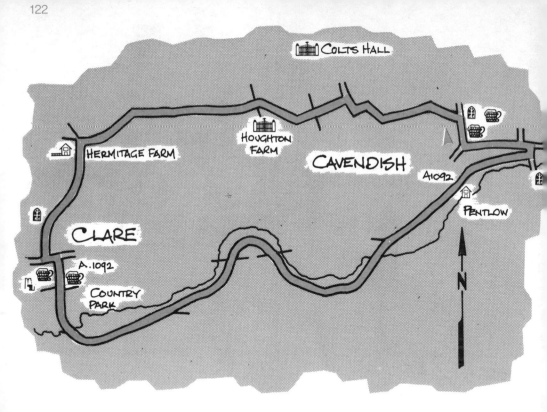

3d Cavendish

The District

This charming Suffolk walk encompasses two quaint villages sited in the heart of Constable country, well off the beaten tourist track. **Cavendish,** with its population of 800 (at the last count) is a beautiful village of thatched cottages and two fine inns clustered around the sloping village green. The ancestral village of the Dukes of Devonshire, it features an elegant 14th century church, a Rectory and, in Wether Hall, a farmhouse that dates back to Tudor times, and the Regency splendour of Cavendish Hall.

Two miles to the south-west is the village of **Clare;** somewhat larger, with half-timbered houses sporting the ornamental plaster coating — called pargetry — which is a feature of the region. Clare is well-known for its interesting antique shops; its country park encloses the ruins of Clare Castle and a disused railway station, as well as a special butterfly garden and many breeds of wildfowl. The castle is of Norman origin.

The 15th century Priest's House in Clare is the home of the local ghost story. On the advice of an eery, dark stranger, a dishonest local merchant began to sell off half-burnt candles to generate the income to settle his debts. All was working smoothly when the merchant broke one of the terms of the arrangement. He was brutally murdered by the cowled stranger, and his ghost still stalks the house.

How to Get There

By car, A134 from Sudbury towards Bury St Edmunds. Turn west (left from Sudbury) at the north end of Long Melford onto A1092 to Cavendish. By rail, Sudbury (not always open) or Bury St Edmunds station, then bus from outside either station to Cavendish.

The Cavendish/Clare Walk

A fairly easy, 4½ mile walk, which should take about three hours. The walk begins at **The Five Bells**, on Cavendish green.

Walk past the church towards a 'cul de sac' sign and turn left at the pink beamed house, following the route towards Colt's Hall. Keep straight on this path, ignoring two offshoots on the left, past the blue-painted house. About 20 yards past this house turn left and follow the footpath banked by a hedgerow along a field. At the end of the field take the wooden bridge and turn right into a second field.

After about 200 yards, turn left up a track heading towards a hillside farmhouse. This track is flanked by a hedgerow, firstly on your right, later to your left as the track passes through the hedge. As you pass the farm the hedge is once again on your right, the track bears right and leads through a field. The path may be poorly-defined in summer as it crosses the field, in which case skirt the field, keeping the hedge to your right. At the end of the field, cut through a gap in the hedge on your right onto a track which leads towards some farm buildings. Turn left in front of the black

The Inns

The George, Cavendish

About the Inn: On the green in Cavendish, this imposing open-beamed inn, proudly run by John and Joyce Harris, is thought to have accommodated the masons and workmen who constructed the village church nearby. Although a great attraction for visitors (the pub apparently has an international reputation as the archetypal village inn) it is a homely, no frills establishment that relies on good fare and a friendly atmosphere. According to John Harris, pub games will NEVER find their ways across his threshold! Comfortable accommodation.

Beers and Food: Draught Truman beers, Guinness and range of ciders. Bar snacks and a large selection of home-prepared hot dishes.

Bell Hotel, Clare

About the Inn: A large free house, popular as an accommodation centre for exploring the district, yet retaining its 16th century character. Boasts a fine collection of sporting paraphernalia and an imposing open-beamed restaurant with an excellent menu. 'Absolutely no music!'.

barn onto a concrete road which bends gradually right, past the farmhouse.

Following this road will bring you into Clare. When you reach the main road, turn left into the centre of the village. Walk towards the church, passing the library and **The Cock Inn** on your right. The route takes you past the church and **The Bell Hotel** into the village market-place. It curls to the right past the Post Office. Turn left down a lane, past the ruins of Clare Castle and over a footbridge. The path now veers left onto a riverside track, through a gate with the Old Priory to the right.

Keeping the river on your left, follow the track over a bridge and then over two stiles and across the sluice gates. It hugs a stream for about a quarter mile, until the stream turns away to the left at a junction at the end of a field. At this junction turn right, across a metal bridge and over a field onto the road. Turning left onto the road will lead you toward Cavendish. After 300 yards turn left onto a bridlepath, which twists for almost two miles past a farmhouse. Walking between the farm buildings on your right and the stream on your left, follow the path that runs alongside the stream for about a mile.

The path eventually leaves the stream, doubling back for 25 yards to meet another path. Once on this new path, turn left and follow the track which leads back towards the stream. At a junction about 200 yards further, turn left.

After a quarter mile the path meets some farm buildings; turn left down between two sets of railings and over a bridge. Pass two houses on the left and follow the track until it reaches a road. Turn right onto the road and follow it into the centre of Cavendish, stopping off at **The George**, a beautiful early 14th century hostelry looking out onto the village green.

Beers and Food: Adnams and Bass handpumped; a range of draught lagers and Tartan keg. Bar snacks, wine bar-type home-prepared meals and full table d'hote restaurant.

The Cock, Clare

About the Inn: A charming period tavern, with a separate small restaurant, ideal for those who want their pub games. In the centre of the village just behind the church, it offers pool, darts, fruit machines and jukebox.

Beers and Food: Draught Charrington's Bitters (IPA and Crown). Pizzas, salads, good Ploughman's and sarnies.

The Five Bells, Cavendish

About the Inn: A small, friendly inn with stone bar, open fire and beamed ceilings. A nice garden used in summer.

Beers and Food: Draught Anglican Strong Bitter, Carlsberg lager and Watney's Norwich Bitter. Pizzas, basket meals, sarnies and Ploughman's.

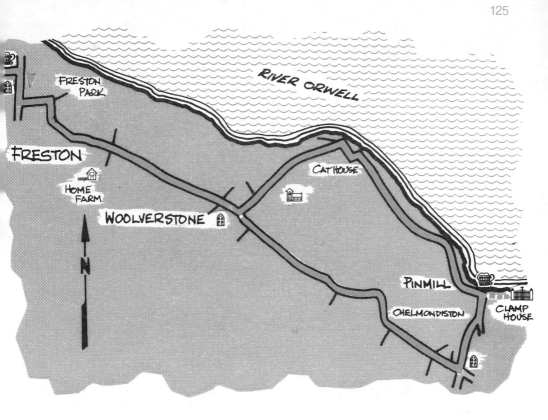

3e Freston

The District

Set near attractive parkland beside the River Orwell in south-east Suffolk, **Freston** boasts an elegant Elizabethan tower nestling on the river bank. Built originally as a lookout for homecoming ships, it was rebuilt two centuries ago by an Ipswich builder as a place of education for his daughter. It features six small rooms stacked one on top of the other. The church tower of **Chelmondiston** has an unlucky history: destroyed by a German flying bomb in the last war, it had previously been cursed by a local witch and caught fire inexplicably in the 15th century. Having been rebuilt, it was then struck by lightning.

Pin Mill, on the banks of the river near Chelmondiston, takes its name, according to legend, from the fact that a local land-owner in the 18th century gave the profits from the operation of the windmill to his daughter — this income represented only 'pin money' to this industrialist (well, that's the story they gave our researcher!).

The area was once a notorious smuggling den, Pin Mill, with its sheltered beaches and woodlands, being deeply implicated. Dutchmen used to smuggle gin in on local fishing boats and, on more than one occasion, the **Butt and Oyster** was raided by irate officers from HM Customs and Excise. Smugglers were given the all clear by the placing of a cat in the window on the local cathouse, a Gothic cottage on the banks of the river.

►

How to Get There

By car from Ipswich, A137 south. Left onto B1456, then right at crossroads to Freston. From Colchester, A137 north. Cross the River Stour and after Brantham turn right onto B1080. Through Holbrook and then left at crossroads to Freston. By rail, to Ipswich station then bus to Freston.

The Freston/Chelmondiston Walk

Approximately 6 miles through parkland alongside the River Orwell. An easy walk requiring no special footwear.

A pint of Tolly's Original and a plate of scampi at **The Boot Inn** in Freston herald the start of this excellent, well-marked walk offering good views of the surrounding countryside. A footpath leaves the inn (marked for Woolverstone and Pin Mill) and proceeding from the end of the first field, turn right along the track and then continue straight towards Woolverstone Church. Take the footpath down towards the Cat House and follow the path across pastures and saltings to a lane.

Walk through a boatyard and past the marina clubhouse to take a public footpath pointing along the river bank. This passes between trees, turning inshore for 25 yards and then back along the river. Parts of this path may be boggy after wet weather. The track leads through several fields and onto a fir lined path towards Pin Mill. Where it forks take the right fork as it bears to the left, then turn right under a telegraph pole. Turn left in front of a pink stone cottage and head towards **The Butt and Oyster**. This inn is in a superb location beside the river, and serves a mean glass of Tolly's straight from the barrel.

A short distance up the road take the path which crosses the field on the right to Chelmondiston Church, then follow the lane to the end and cross a meadow in front of Woolverstone Park to the church returning on the same route to the start.

You may make a pleasant extension to this walk by continuing up the road from The Butt and Oyster, past houses on the left-hand side of the road, until some steps are reached which lead to the top of the cliff. Returning along the top towards the river there is a path along the edge of the cliff and through woodland to Clamp House. Return by the same route or by a lane from Clamp House into Chelmondiston village.

The Inns

Boot Inn, Freston

About the Inn: A small, friendly tavern with a low, beamed ceiling and wooden bar, and a music room off the bar with a piano. Landlord Ted Mainwaring welcomes children in the rear garden. Darts, piped background music.

Beers and Food: Tolly Cobbold Bitter and Mild handpumped, Guinness and Tuborg lager on tap. Cold bar snacks and selection of tasty seafood dishes — scampi, plaice, haddock, cod — as well as home-prepared beefburgers and chicken basket lunches.

Butt and Oyster, Woolverstone

About the Inn: An excellent inn, located right on the estuary, with a strong seafaring atmosphere. A pink exterior and a beamed ceiling, and a flagstone floored interior project a hearty welcome. The bar boasts a blazing open fire in winter and a smoke room. Car park, garden that opens onto the river and a special room for kids. Pool, dominoes and fruit machines. Live music at weekends.

Beers and Food: Tolly Cobbold Bitter and Mild (Old Strong in winter) hand drawn from the barrel. Draught bass. Good range of hot and cold bar snacks, and full lunches in the separate dining-room.

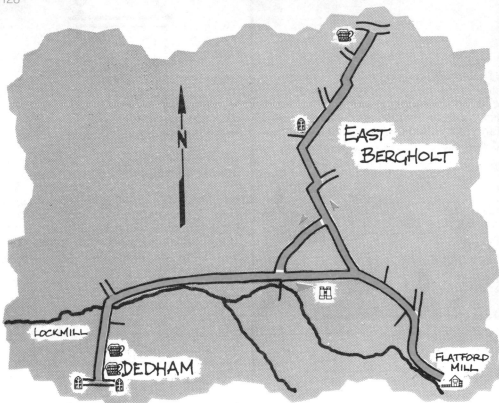

3f Dedham

The District

The Valley of the River Stour, in which this walk lies, has changed little since Constable's day, except perhaps in ways that reflect the area's growing popularity with visitors. Born in nearby **East Bergholt**, in 1776, the artist has immortalised this pocket of central England in his much-admired canvasses. The village was also the home of Sir Winston Churchill's son Randolph. Its early Tudor church is well worth a visit, boasting an unfinished tower and a memorial glass to Constable.

Flatford Mill, featured in several of Constable's paintings, stands beside the tranquil Stour, bordered by swaying ash and willow trees. Many of the local buildings captured in the artist's landscapes still stand: **Valley Farm**, painted in 1835, and **Willy Lott's Cottage**, painted in 1814, all still keep the old mill company.

Just a mile or so to the west of the walk, hugging the A12 (formerly a Roman road) lies the quaint village of **Stratford St Mary**. The site of an ancient Roman settlement and a splendid Elizabethan yeoman house, its beauty and charm have been only slightly marred by the main road and the monstrous pumping station that unfortunately dominates the horizon.

How to Get There

By car, A12 Colchester (Ring Road) to Ipswich, then off at Stratford St Mary towards Dedham. By train, to Ipswich or Colchester stations, then bus to Dedham.

The Dedham/East Bergholt Walk

Quite an easy, gentle stroll, about 6 miles through the Stour valley. Some parts may be muddy after rainfall.

Dedham itself is a pretty village, and our walk begins at **The Marlborough Head** in the village centre. The church opposite was built in 1492 to replace a Saxon church; its magnificent stained glass is worth a look. Walk out of the pub towards the War Memorial beside the church. Walk down Mill Lane and past Lock Mill, continuing over the bridge. Immediately after the bridge, climb the stile on the right onto a footpath that follows the river bank. Dogs should be kept on a lead as the surrounding fields are often populated by grazing sheep. At the end of the field cross stile (being careful to keep your tweeds off the barbed wire) and follow the river bank.

After a mile the river turns away to the right, while the footpath continues towards a hill and over a broad wooden bridge. The path forks left and right on the other side of the bridge, but take *neither* of these forks; instead cross a stile straight ahead and towards the top right-hand corner of the field, over a ditch and up to a barbed wire fence. There are often cattle in this field, so try to keep flapping red scarves under control — or be prepared to take on the world 100 metres record!

The top of the hill affords sweeping views

The Inns

The Sun, Dedham

About the Inn: On the High Street opposite Dedham church, this early 16th century coaching inn is believed to be the site of one of the last witch burnings in East Anglia in 1976 (or was it 1769?). A heavily timbered interior with open fires in both bars and in the restaurant, it offers a warm atmosphere. Several local festivals are held near the inn throughout the summer months. Children welcomed in the restaurant and on the terrace outside.

Beers and Food: Tolly Cobbold draught bitter and mild. Worthington E, draught lagers and Guinness. Soup, pâté, Ploughman's, salads, sarnies and hot specialities of the day served over the bar. Restaurant with full à la carte and table d'hôte menus. Dinner dances held occasionally.

Marlborough Head, Dedham

About the Inn: A pleasant Ind Coope house, with a white and timbered exterior and cosy open-beamed interior. Open fire in the main bar. Children welcomed in the restaurant and the garden outside. Not enthusiastic about canine patrons.

down to Dedham, with its church tower in the distance, and the river. Continue along the fence until you reach a stile at the end of the field. Crossing the stile brings you out onto a road. Across the road a stile leads onto the path to Flatford Mill. The path turns right, following the road, then forks to the right at the car park. After visiting the mill, retrace your steps to the stile and this time continue up the hill towards East Bergholt. The path passes a wooden seat at a junction with a track returning to Dedham. Continuing straight ahead for another 300 yards brings you out in East Bergholt, in front of the church. Turn left at the church for the village centre.

Call in **The Red Lion** for lunch and a wide variety of pub games — fans of 'Space Invaders', this is home from home for you! — then continue the walk by turning back to the church. Turn right, past the War Memorial and retrace your steps back to the wooden seat at the junction with the path signposted for Dedham and Stratford. Take the path, ignoring the first fork but taking the right fork at a second junction over a bridge and back towards Dedham. The route leads towards the river bank and along to the bridge you took at the beginning of the walk. Turn left here onto Mill Lane and walk past the mill back into the centre of Dedham. It is (almost) impossible to get lost. A glass of Tolly Cobbold at **The Sun,** opposite Dedham church, will soothe away any blisters.

Beers and Food: Draught Ind Coope beers (Bitter & Mild). Wide selection of bar snacks and speciality hot dishes, together with full menu in the separate small restaurant.

Red Lion Inn, East Bergholt

About the Inn: Off the road leading to the village centre, this small, friendly inn is able to squeeze a dazzling array of bar games into its low-ceilinged lounge, including darts, fruit machine and the habit-forming 'Space Invaders'. Children's garden, piped music.

Beers and Food: Tolly Cobbold Original Bitter handpumped; draught Guinness and Tuborg lager. Hot and cold bar snacks and a separate restaurant with table d'hôte menu.

The Midlands

There is nothing uniform about the Midlands; the scarred and smouldering landscapes of the black country and the hustle and bustle of Birmingham are as characteristic as the trim cottages and neat hedgerows of Warwickshire. In this amorphous region the steep-sided Malvern Hills tower above the lush Vale of Evesham and, to the north the wooded wilderness of Cannock Chase leads onto the bare ridges of the Long Mynd.

Indeed the North Midlands is magnificent walking country, from the medieval forestlands of Leicestershire and Nottinghamshire, to the limestone uplands of the Peaks.

It is also architecturally rich, with a castle at Beeston, a palace at Chatsworth and the first iron bridge to be built at Coalbrookdale.

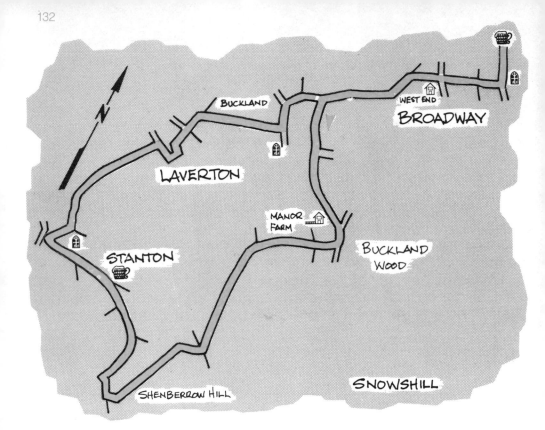

4a Broadway

The District

Broadway is a peaceful village at the foot of the Cotswolds built mainly of golden Cotswold stone. Its old cottages and gabled houses date in the main from the 16th and 17th centuries. The main street, lined with trees, rises to a height of 800 feet at The Fish Inn, offering a fine view out across the Vale of Evesham to the long blue ridge of the Malvern Hills. The locals claim this is the most beautiful village in England. As a visitor you will be hard pushed to disagree.

The 12th century church of **St Edburgha** has a square tower and many Norman features. During the Reformation the bells of Broadway were hidden in Middle Hill Wood, to prevent them from falling into the hands of the Puritans. Legend has it, that ever since their ghostly chimes can be heard at night, and they were even tolling during World War II when the ringing of bells was prohibited. Opposite the church is the former home of the 19th century eccentric, Sir Thomas Phillips. The pre-Raphaelite painter, Millais also lived here.

Nearby **Buckland** has an interesting early English Church. The stained-glass, east window which once depicted the seven sacraments (only three are now discernible) is said to have been much admired by William Morris. The church is also famous for its Bridal Bowl — made in 1507 of maple and silver — which can be seen in its case. See also the painted fragments of stone on the sill at the rear of the nave, and the beautifully embroidered altar frontal.

Stanton, a little further to the south-west, is another archetypal Cotswold village built of local stone. Surrounded by folds in the hills, with its panoramic view of the Vale of Evesham, this village is also claimed by the locals to be the most beautiful in England. Certainly, it is one of the most picturesque of all the small Cotswold villages. The manor house of Stanton dates back to Saxon times. It was given by the Saxon Kenulf to Winchcombe Abbey, then at the Dissolution it passed to Katherine Parr, a present from Henry VIII. The old church of **St Michael** has a tiny room containing many old relics. It is worth climbing the crumbling stone steps at the back of the nave to visit it.

How to Get There
Take the A44 from Evesham if travelling by car. Train to Evesham or Moreton-in-Marsh (direct line from London Paddington) and then a Midland Red bus to Broadway.

The Broadway Walk
About 8 miles long involving some steep gradients, so it's best to limit the expedition to able-bodied adults.

The **Lygon Arms** in Broadway provides a suitable starting point. This is the inn where Cromwell stayed the night before the battle of Worcester, and to this day it provides refreshment for travellers. After a drink, follow the road south towards Snowshill. Opposite St Edburgha's Church, a footpath goes off to the right, signposted to Buckland. Follow the path over meadows and across a stream by a wooden bridge. Cross West End Lane and follow the right-hand sign into a field and up through the woods. Near the end of the wood the path forks. Take the left-hand path which leads out across a field, and meets a convergence of tracks at a stile. Turn left along the ▶

The Inns

Lygon Arms, Broadway

About the Inn: A 16th century tavern whose famous customers have included Oliver Cromwell and Charles the First, as well as, more recently, Prince Philip, Edward Heath, Robert Mitchum and William 'James T Kirk' Shatner, who boldy came where all these had been before. It has a gabled frontage and interior which boasts a collection of antiques, early glass and porcelain in oak-panelled rooms with open fires. The Great Chamber has a four-poster bed with the date 1620 carved upon the oak bedhead. Outside there is a large lawn with formal gardens.

Beers and Food: Whitbread Tankard and Newcastle Exhibition on draught. Sandwiches on sale, as well as hot and cold snacks in the Goblets wine bar. Full meals for around £3 a head.

Mount Inn, Stanton

About the Inn: Originally a farm house dating from the early 17th century. Built of Cotswold stone with a fine old yew tree outside, the interior has original flagstone flooring and an open inglenook fireplace. ▶

track past the farm, and when it joins with other tracks at the edge of Buckland Wood, turn right and follow the footpath signposted to Shenberrow Hill.

From here there is a well-worn bridleway running over the hills capped with beeches and dry-stone walling. Its worth pausing from time to time to enjoy the excellent views that are to be had on this stretch. Where the track is crossed by another, take the path that leads up the edge of the woods on the right to Shenberrow Hill Fort. This is a large iron-age settlement that covers nearly 5 acres. Passing the fort, bear right to pick up the track which drops, through woods, down to **Stanton**. Finally, a steep (and sometime muddy) track leads, conveniently, directly to **The Mount Inn.**

By all means enjoy the panoramic view from the beer garden and certainly try some of the hand-drawn Donnington Ales; but unless you enjoy being beaten continually, avoid the temptation to challenge the locals at the old game of 'Spoof' which is played here.

Take the path through the churchyard of St Michael's to follow a high yew hedge on the left, emerging, at last, via a steel gate onto meadows. Go across the fields, picking up the path which drops diagonally down towards Laverton. Where the path meets a lane, turn right and left at the top to follow the road through this tiny village to the Post Office.

At Laverton go up past the Post Office, and where the road comes to a dead-end, a footpath leads off it. This continues out on to the lane to Buckland. Go right here to see St Michael's Church or left to pick up the narrow lane opposite, which leads back to West End. It goes over a brook and through a gate, then up steep meadows joining the initial part of the walk. Retrace the first part of the walk back into Broadway.

Unusual collection of match-boxes. Furnished veranda and large lawn with extensive view.

Games, darts, dominoes and 'spoof'.

Beers and Food: Donnington's Ales all hand-drawn. A range of hot and cold snacks are served. Excellent toasted sandwiches or try the Ploughman's lunch served with a hot cottage loaf.

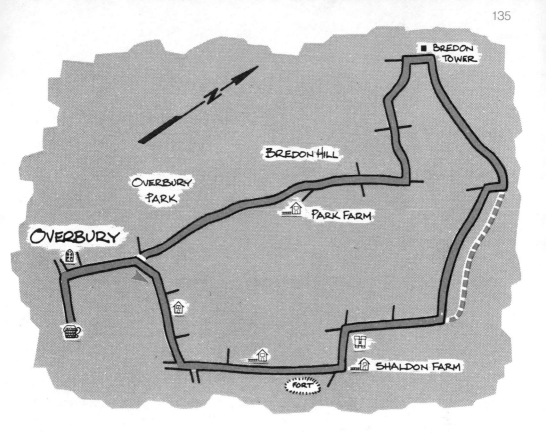

4b Overbury

The District

The main attraction of this walk is Bredon Hill, which commands extensive views over the rolling countryside of the Cotswolds and the lush Vale of Evesham.

On the north side of the hill, near the summit, is an iron-age settlement, the inner ramparts of which cover eleven acres. This was the scene of some fierce fighting in the first century as the remains of many mutilated bodies were discovered here. Within the camp is the Banbury Stone, a great slab of oolitic rock thought to have borne the brunt of human sacrifices in Druid rituals. Nowadays all you are likely to witness is the less-sinister activity of badgers (provided it is the dead of night, and you are equipped with infra-red lighting!).

Parson's Folly, also just inside the sett-

lement is a square stone tower which, when originally erected in the 18th century, had two rooms. Bredon Hill has been the inspiration for literary works, notably Housman's *Summer on Bredon* and William Cobbett's *Rural Rides,* in which he described the hill as one of the 'very richest spots in England'.

The well-preserved village of **Overbury** is owned by the Holland-Martin family, who live in 18th century Overbury Court. Look out too, for the parish church of St Faiths, parts of which date back to the 11th century.

How to Get There

By road, follow the A435 north from Cheltenham towards Evesham. At Teddington Hands roundabout, take the second left for

►

Overbury. By rail to Cheltenham station and then bus to Overbury.

The Overbury Walk

This a fine walk, if fairly strenuous (about 6 miles) over hilly terrain.

The bus takes you to **The Star Inn** in Overbury and from here you walk down the road, into the village, towards the Post Office. Turn right and walk up past the church and the Red House School to a T-junction. Here take the path to the right, which is bounded on either side by a stone wall.

This, incidentally, is the first of many stone-walled paths which you have to follow on this walk, and whilst they may not have the rugged splendour of Hadrians Wall, they do serve a purpose (if only to way-mark our route!).

Continue along the path, ignoring the turnings to the left, past an old derelict stone house. The stone wall now only runs along the right-hand side of the path, and, as it descends, you should turn off to the left. Keep walking along the path until you reach a sign indicating Bridle Farm, where you should pass through a wooden gate and continue until you see the farm and an adjoining stream. With a stone wall now running alongside to the left, the path continues past a hill-fort (hardly discernible) to the remains of Shaldon Farm. Turn left by passing through a metal gate and the path continues between (you've guessed it) stone walls, behind which, to the right, is a field of sheep (not stone).

Turn right following a path which runs via four wooden gates and continue until you pass the radio mast to your left. The path is now bounded by a wire fence to the right, and you should go through another gate before turning left along a track running parallel to the wood on the right-hand side.

The path continues via another gate before bending left in the direction of Bredon Hill summit which gives unobstructed views across the neat squares of the market gardening lands of the Vale of Evesham. Pass through two more gates and follow the stone-walled path to the 18th century Bredon Tower (otherwise knows as Parson's Folly). The path is now less discernible. Consequently you must bear with the stone wall (which is now on your right) and at the top of the hill, bear sharply left. Look out for Kemerton Camp, at first you will see a crater, at the bottom of which are messages made from fragments of the Banbury Stone. The settlement itself consists of 2 earth mounds, circumscribed at the base by a dry moat.

The path continues past the settlement, with a wire fence running alongside to the right and stone wall to the left. Eventually, having passed through two wooden gates, you arrive at Lalu Farm. At this point take the open path bearing sharply to the right, away from the farm (Incidentally, you should then see the radio mast away on your left). This leads down to Overbury Park, with trees on both sides, and at a fork you will see a sign telling you to bear left for Park Farm. However ignore the sign, and take the path up to the right, which leads

down to a cluster of small buildings. Pass through yet another gate, in front of a pool and a stream, to eventually emerge triumphant at a lane, whereupon you turn right for Overbury village.

The Star Inn, Overbury

About the Inn: Prior to 1837, four houses for the poor used to occupy this site. The land was then acquired by a brewery and The Star Inn erected; built from local Cotswold stone. The snug interior has two open fires and features the landlord's collection of mugs (over 100) and of corn dollies. There is limited accommodation available, plus a garden with swings to keep the kids amused, and no less than three car parks.

Beers and Food: It is a Whitbread house and they stock a real ale on handpump. The lunchtime menu includes Ploughman's, Scampi, beefburgers and soups, along with the ubiquitous sandwich.

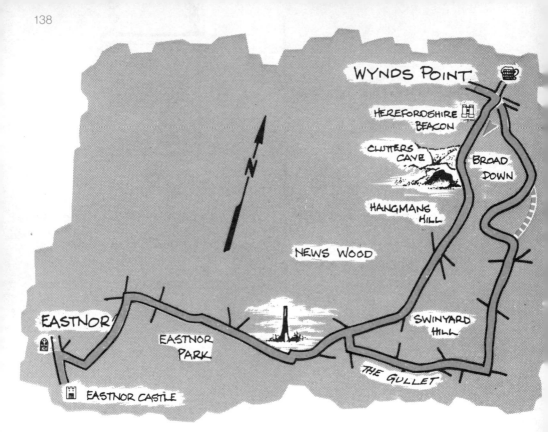

4c   The Malverns

The District

The Malvern Hills are a chain of pre-Cambrian peaks, fortunately as tough as old boots, which run for nine miles along the old county boundary of Worcestershire. The lower hills were part of the medieval hunting ground of Malvern Chase, whereas the rough commonland of the higher regions is good walking terrain. And for the naturalist the main attraction is the profusion of butterflies in summer.

The hills have been the inspiration for many artists' works including the 14th century poem, *Piers Plowman* by William Langland and Elgar's *Enigma Variations* and *Dream of Gerontius.*

The Herefordshire Beacon is the second highest of the Malverns' twenty distinct summits, and is the site of the British Camp, an impressive ancient hill fortress where, it is estimated, about 20,000 men were once stationed. Nearby, the village of Little Malvern harbours the remains of a Benedictine Priory and several wells containing excellent mineral water.

Do not be fooled by **Eastnor Castle,** although it looks every inch a Norman fortification, it is in fact a 19th century castle, set in parkland (where you might catch glimpses of deer).

How to Get There

By road take the A499 south from Worcester, through Great Malvern and on to Wynds Point. By rail to Great Malvern Station, where a bus takes you direct to the Malvern Hills Hotel, on Wynds Point.

The Malvern Hills Walk

A walk of about 5 miles, along well-trodden paths, incorporating some fine views of the Herefordshire Hills, the Vale of Avon and even the Welsh uplands (on a clear day), as well as some interesting historical remains.

Opposite **The Malvern Hills Hotel**, take the path signposted 'The British Camp'. This steep ascent is made somewhat easier by stone steps. Eventually you reach the Herefordshire Beacon and the site of the old British Camp, recognizable by a series of earthworks. Walking past the settlement you will come to a circular white slab set in the ground; for the technically-minded this is a directional indicator pointing towards Hangman's Hill.

Continuing on the same path you will see **Clutter's Cave** below to your right. The cave is 6 foot high, 6 foot wide and 10 foot deep and, depending on your source, was either inhabited by a particularly small shepherd or was used for some particularly small religious festival.

Past the cave, the descending path widens and comes to a fork. Bear left here and then follow the path round to the right and through the wood, as far as the park entrance. The path through Eastnor Park winds towards an obelisk; a landmark for miles around, erected in memory of a flag-bearer killed in battle in 1758. The path continues past the obelisk and through a wooden gate. At this point the path is not very clear, so stick to the edge of the ridge to your left. A little further on the path is more discernible, and bends left towards the castle, which at this point, suddenly hoves into view.

The path leads to a lane which you follow to the main road. Turn right if you wish to visit the castle. Then retrace your steps back to the entrance of Eastnor Park, where you will see two paths. Take the one going downhill, with a stream on your left. This path leads to Gullet Quarry, which you will now see on your left. Further on you come to a T-junction where you should turn left. After a while you will see a wooden gate on the right; go through the gate and across the stream, ignoring two paths bearing left. The path then takes you through Castlemorton Common. By a letter box, attached to a post, you turn left and continue on the path as it bears left. This path skirts the wood and eventually comes out at the car park at Wynds Point.

The Malvern Hills Hotel, Wynds Point

About the Inn: The present white Georgian building dates back to the 19th century but there has been a hostelry on this site for over 500 years. Although very much a country hotel, with its spacious oak-panelled reception, lounge bar and 15 bedrooms; the inn offers a warm welcome to walkers, and has indeed just opened a special hiker's bar.

Beers and Food: Bass, Worthington 'E' and Traditional Brew XI on gravity, provide liquid strength for the intrepid hill-walker. For those more substantially minded, the inn offers a wide selection of food at most times, either in the bar or the restaurant. Traditional roast lunches are available on Sundays.

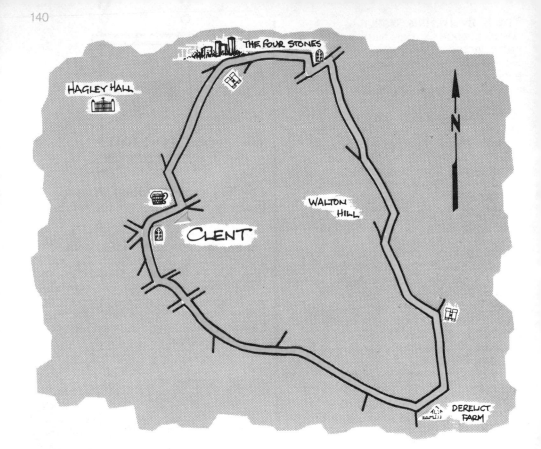

4d Clent

The District

Only a short distance from the heart of Birmingham, the Clent Hills are a surprising break in an otherwise industrial landscape.

The walk covers the two chief heights of the **Clent and Walton Hills**, as well as part of the commonland, farmland and woods of the Clatterbach valley.

The walk begins at **The Vine Hotel** tucked into the foot of Adam's Hill and only a few hundred yards from Clent Village. Comprised of little more than a church, Ye Olde Cafe and a telephone box, the village has a quiet, perhaps even forlorn air. However Lower Clent, on the other side of the hill, has more markedly moved with the times, and is well-equipped with an amusement arcade, ice-cream and pop-corn stalls and ponies for hire.

Only 1 mile to the north of Clent is the **Hagley estate**, containing a classic example of the first kind of English landscape garden. Hagley Hall, a Palladin mansion, is open to the public in the summer, and at least one hour should be allotted to completing the picturesque trail around the grounds.

How to Get There

By rail to Birmingham New Street. From Birmingham city centre, a Midland Red bus (302) runs hourly to Clent.

By road, take the A456 south-west from Birmingham, passing under M5 and crossing two roundabouts. Turn left onto minor road, and right at the T-junction for Clent.

The Clent Walk

One of the delights of this walk is that it encompasses a surprising range of terrain. The gently rolling hills give way to unexpected climbs and drops, as well as patches of dark, dense woodland. In fact, the steepness of a couple of the hills should stand as a warning to those prone to pegging out.

However, do stock up at **The Vine Inn**, where on a fine day it is very pleasant to while away a lunchtime sitting out on the large open courtyard with a couple of their crusty cottge loaf rolls and a pint (or two). But before you feel that even walking as far as the car is too much effort, you should head off down Vine Lane, which is to your right on leaving the pub. Continue past a row of pretty blue and white cottages to the main crossroads, which form the centre of Clent village. Turn left and walk up signposted Walton Pool lane, noting Clent House peeping above the shubbery to your left. After approximately a quarter of a mile you will see a footpath to your left, leading diagonally across a field to an iron kissing gate. Go through and cross the lane into another field. Head for a stile in the middle of the field (to the right of a cluster of buildings) and you will see a driveway. This leads out into another field, by some black and white posts, and you should continue across to a lane and stile on the far side. Clamber over the stile into a field where you should make for a gate to the left of a barn. A diagonal course downhill, through a field belonging to a herd of cows, leads to a farm track, onto which you turn left.

The next part of the walk simply follows this well-defined rough track, edged with blackberry brambles, around the base of Calcot Hill. The track starts climbing, you will see a pine forest to your left, and eventually comes out on the top of Calcot Hill by a derelict farm-house. Turn left and walk around to the back of the farm, past the outhouses to the field, in which there is the shell of a gutted barn. Keep to the edge of the field, past the barn and you'll see a stile on your right. Scramble over this and you will be confronted with a breathtaking view over a valley with a solitary white house clearly discernible on the facing wooded hillslope. Turn left and follow the path along the side of the hill, the hill dropping away to your right. Follow this path around to the left; in effect you are walking the perimeter of the field and

➤

The Inn

The Vine Inn, Clent

About the Inn: In Vine lane, just outside Clent Village, The Vine has the charming backdrop of ivy-clad hillside. The black and white timbered building has been restored in recent years but the bar still retains a cosy atmosphere with its low ceiling and wooden seats. Chicken and geese are kept outside in the courtyard in wooden pens.

Beers and Food: A Mitchell and Butler House. The Vine offers a wide range of bar snacks, including scampi in the basket and Ploughman's lunch with crusty bread.

should now see the gutted barn to your left.

The path begins to narrow and follows the ridge of the hill through a forest of baby oaks and hawthorns. Suddenly the path descends steeply into a sheltered hollow and then almost immediately climbs back up again. The path then veers to the left, over a stile, and continues along the ridge, through undulating pasture on which sheep and horses graze. This is probably the most dangerous part of the walk as it was here that the editor had her backside nipped by a nervous nag, presumably bored with the vegetarian diet.

The footpath comes out by a modern white house and you should cross the adjacent field and turn left along a track leading to the top of Walton Hill. Bear right on the hill summit, making for a clump of distant trees where you will find an Ordnance Survey triangulation pillar.

Legend has it that almost 2000 years ago Caractacus, an Ancient Briton, suffered defeat at the hands of the Romans on Walton Hill. However he reappeared three year later, no doubt filled with Dutch courage, to seek his revenge in the nearby Clatterbach Valley.

The walk continues over the brow of the hill, along an exceedingly well-trodden path. At the hill's edge take the path straight in front of you to descend, and not the one to your left which leads down to the car park. Scramble down the rough grass and bracken to a road at the bottom, where a signpost indicates a path across a field leading to St Kenelm's Road. Having crossed the field, turn left at the road and walk downhill to the next turning on your left, which is Chapel Lane. St Kenelm's church is a little way up this lane to your right.

The boy-king to whom this church is dedicated, supposedly had his head chopped off on the instruction of his jealous sister. She got her come-uppance when a tell-tale dove flew to Rome with the news, and the Pope made Kenelm a saint, causing the wicked sisters' eyes to fall out. (Well it's a good story isn't it?).

After exploring the church, continue up Chapel Lane and take the first turning to your right, signposted to Hayley Green. After a third of a mile you will see a car park and the beginning of a footpath up a steep hill through beeches and firs. Force those legs up to the top and onto the blustery summit, where there are excellent views, apparently as far as Wales on a clear day. Hopefully the more myopic, might just make out Hagley Hall and its adjacent folly, a mile beneath.

Eventually a wide open track takes you to the Four Standing Stones; sadly these are not prehistoric remains, but were erected in the 18th century by Lord Lyttleton of Hagley Hall, a man whose jealousy of Stonehenge seemingly knew no bounds.

However continue past the Stones in the same direction, ignoring the first left-hand track, but following the next left-hand fork round through woodland. The wide track narrows to a gate, leading to a conifer forest. Follow this track for a little while, until a stile and the end of the woods. Once over the stile you can begin your descent over the rough grassland, or continue along the path to double back in a zig-zag fashion. Either way leads to the wooded slopes behind The Vine Inn, and hence the start of the walk.

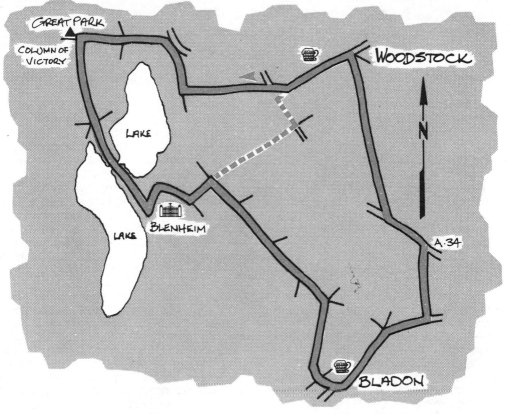

4e Woodstock

The District

Woodstock is situated on the banks of the River Glyme, 8 miles north of Oxford. With its wide streets and well-maintained period buildings, it proudly reflects its royal heritage. The Royal Manor house was occupied by Henry I, who established a deer park in the grounds. During his residence here, Henry II made Woodstock the scene for one of the best-known romances in English history, when he built a bower for his devoted companion Rosamund Clifford. The Black Prince, son of Edward III was born here and Princess Elizabeth was imprisoned in the Royal Manor by her sister Mary.

The town has for centuries been one of the glove-making centres in the country, an industry which is still thriving today. However, its main attraction is **Blenheim Palace**. The Royal Manor of Woodstock was conferred upon the Duke of Marlborough by Queen Anne for his crushing defeat of the French at Blenheim in August 1704. £500,000 was voted by Parliament to build the palace and the foundation stone was laid in 1705. Sir John Vanbrugh designed the building and the grounds were originally laid by Henry Wise. These were later modified by Capability Brown in the 'natural' style. Brown was also responsible for the damming of the River Glyme, thereby creating a vast lake.

In nearby **Bladon**, Sir Winston Churchill is buried in the churchyard at the head of his mother's grave.

How to Get There

By car, the A34 from Oxford straight to Woodstock. Alternatively the 421 bus from Oxford stops outside the Bear Hotel in Woodstock.

The Woodstock Walk

Set primarily in the grounds of Blenheim Palace this is a gentle stroll with lots to see and therefore has potential to be very time-consuming. However, there are plenty of opportunities to cut the walk short, so press on and leave the decisions until later.

The walks begin at the City and County museum on Park Street opposite **The Bear Hotel**. Assuming that your thirst for knowledge has been satisfied by this convenient starting-point, turn right outside the museum (left if you have been in The Bear Hotel) and follow the road to the park gates. At this early stage officialdom intrudes and demands the following tariffs:

Entry to Park: 10p per person
Entry to Palace: Adults £1.50 children and old-age pensioners £1.00.

Having lightened your pocket you may leave your worries behind and turn sharp right through the gates following the path downhill. Keeping the lake to your left, follow this path until you cross a small bridge across the River Glyme. The path then bends round to the left. At the top of the lake turn left by the side of a cottage. After the cottage, you will see, on your right, the Column of Victory. Leave the path and walk across the grass to this impressive monument. In the distance you will see Blenheim Palace. Walk directly across the grass to the palace. Should you choose to visit the palace you will need an hour or two in order to savour the fine paintings and memorabilia of a bygone age.

With your back to the palace gates, turn right to the refreshment area, public conveniences and car park. From here you take the main path through the car park until you come to a crossroads. At this point you can cut the walk short by continuing straight on the main road and turning left to re-enter Woodstock. Should you decide to continue the walk, turn right at the crossroads (signposted Garden Centre and Walled Garden), go across a cattle grid

and follow the road to the Garden Centre. The Centre is open daily and is well worth a visit. From the Garden Centre follow the road signposted to **Bladon**; cross another cattle grid and follow the road round to the left. This road comes to an end at Bladon Lodge where you exit via a kissing gate. Walk down to a T-junction where you will see The White Horse public house on your left. By this time, licensing hours permitting, a cool pint of the foaming ale will doubtless slip down a treat.

For those hardy souls who care to stroll around this quaint village, the Old Malthouse with its fifteenth century chimneys and mullioned windows will not go amiss. However, if you are now ready to head home, then turn left outside the White Horse and walk along the main road for about ½ mile to Bladon Chains caravan park. Turn left here and, 100 yards down, you reach the A34 where you turn left. Approximately 150 yards on, on the right-hand side of the road, you will see a faded public footpath sign leading you to a modern housing estate. At the end of this footpath turn left, then immediately right, to find yourself in Crecy Walk. At the end of this road you come to a T-junction and, directly opposite, the public footpath continues under the name of Willoughby Way. This narrow path, sandwiched between private property, leads out to Recreation Road. As you leave the footpath there is a telephone kiosk on a corner and you bear left here. Continue down this road and you will meet Oxford Street and The Crown Inn. A narrow road, by the side of The Crown Inn, leads you back to The Bear Hotel and the City and County Museum.

The Bear Hotel, Woodstock

About the Inn: Located in the older part of Woodstock, legend has it that the inn was once the lodging house of one of Henry II's courtiers. First licensed in 1237, the building was reconstructed during Tudor times, but the cobbles of medieval Woodstock still lie under one of the bars. The large open fireplace of Cotswold stone also dates back to this period. The walls are adorned with a fine brass collection and a rather intriguing collection of bear-baiting equipment.

Traditionally this has always been a popular meeting place, in fact, the Town councillors used to meet here after the presentation of their accounts. On this joyous occasion a hogshead of ale was given to the townsmen. What a pity this custom has been discontinued. The hotel boasts 33 individually furnished rooms each with a colour TV and a private bathroom.

As an optional extra, room 16 comes fully equipped with its own poltergeist. However, this rather bashful, if noisy, spook only appears to the select few.

Beers and Food: The bar is well-stocked with aperitifs and liqueurs, but has a rather limited selection of Bass Charrington beers. In the restaurant there is a wide choice of food from the à la carte menu, and a good selection of wines.

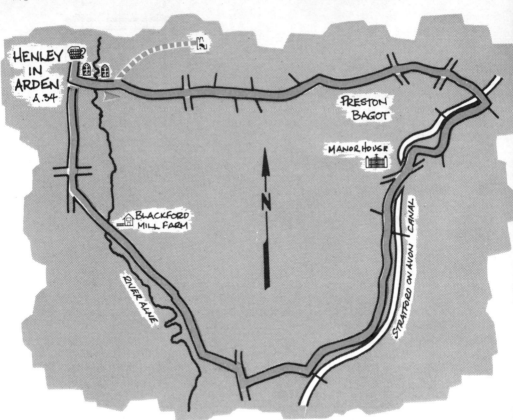

4f   Henley-in-Arden

The District

Although within easy motoring distance of the great Midlands metropolis of Birmingham, Henley-in-Arden offers a taste of Warwickshire rurality that Shakespeare knew and loved. Indeed the fertile countryside and the slow rivers give one the feeling that man has been tilling the land in the this area for centuries.

Henley itself consists of a High Street, a mile in length, containing many examples of different types of English domestic architecture. This ancient market town was once the seat of Plantagenet power, owned by the de Montfort family; but was actually burnt to a cinder after Simon de Montfort's defeat at the nearby Battle of Evesham. Phoenix-like it rose from the ashes (well, with a little help from local architects); but

the de Montfort's castle at **Beaudesert**, just outside Henley, remains a sorry sight, consisting of a flattened hilltop and a surrounding ditch.

Scour the High Street for shops selling ice-cream, it is a local industry with a truly world-wide appeal.

How to Get There

Henley-in-Arden is on the A34 between Stratford and Birmingham. It can be reached by train (or bus) from both Stratford and Birmingham (although there are no trains on Sunday).

The Henley-in-Arden Walk

This walk is not for outward bounders as its features (three churches, the remains of an ancient castle, a river, a canal and a manor house) are to be appreciated, not conquered. That being said, the pubs outnumber the churches two to one, so you won't be short of excuses to sit down and be idle for a while.

The bus stops outside **The Three Tuns Inn** and from here continue down the main road (the A34) to Beaudesert Lane, which turns off to the left. Walk past the Church of St John the Baptist and soon you will see another church, namely the church of St Nicholas. The path runs alongside the base of the old castle site (although you can actually reach it via the churchyard — and then rejoin your original course). This path is flanked by a fence, and eventually leads to a road, which you should cross over.

Keep heading in the same direction, passing through a wooden gate. The path is now less well-defined and is also quite steep. Pass through two gates to eventually arrive at Edge Lane. In front of you is Whitley, a large red-brick house, with a lane running alongside it. Cross over the facing stile and then turn right until you come to another stile, where the path disappears. Here you should walk across the field, passing Church Farm on your left, to the old rectory and the signposted path to Preston Bagot.

The Inns

The White Swan, Henley-in-Arden

About the Inn: Directly opposite the Church, The White Swan is one of several pubs in Henley which claim to be the oldest in the village. However it does date from the 1660s and the evidence suggests it could have been an old coaching inn, which places it firmly amongst the fore-runners. The low-ceilinged, timbered bar is particularly inviting, or you can sit outside and enjoy watching a game of bowls on the adjacent bowling green.

Beers and Food: For a fine taste of the Midlands, succumb to a pint of Ansells. There is a separate Cavalier steak bar as well as a comprehensive bar menu; including soups, salads, pâtés and plaice and chips.

The Three Tuns, Henley-in-Arden

About the Inn: A picturesque brick and timbered inn; inside which part of the plaster has been pulled away to reveal the original wattle and daub walls. Enjoy a quiet pint in the intimate bar, with its low ceiling and quiet corners.

Beers and Food: Another Ansells pub, with traditional Mild and Bitter on tap. Catering is a speciality of this pub, and the present Spanish landlord offers traditional Spanish cooking in the restaurant (evenings only). The lunchtime bar food was highly praised by Egon Ronay this year and includes steak and kidney pie, stuffed pancakes and apple pie, all home-made on the premises.

Climb the hill to the church and cross over the lane directly in front of you. The way continues over a stile and along an almost invisible path leading across a field to a stream, next to which is the Stratford Canal. Cross the stream and turn right along the canal towpath, passing alongside a road bridge and several locks to a manor house (away to the right).

Here you should cross over the bridge and continue along the towpath on the other side of the canal. At the next bridge turn right, following the path to a sign indicating the Flood Alleviation Scheme office. Turn right along the lane for about 200 yards, before turning left into a field. The path runs along the right-hand side of the small River Alne, via a number of stiles and wooden gates.

Eventually you come to Blackford Mill Farm, where you turn left and pass in front of the farm buildings. Cross over a small wooden bridge and walk past school play-ing fields to the A34. Turn right for Henley; you will pass Henley-in-Arden High School on your right.

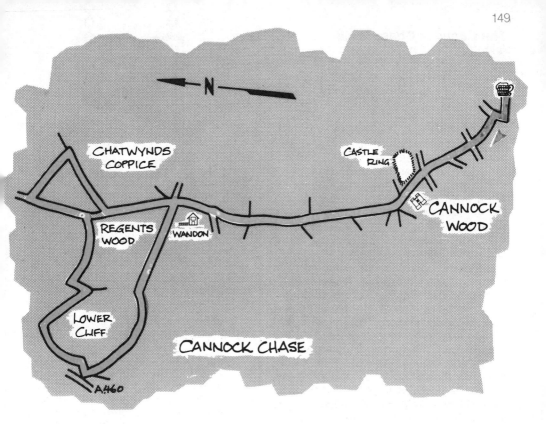

4g Cannock Chase

The District

In the heart of the industrial Midlands, **Cannock Chase** is a 28 square mile haven of gentle hills, tranquil valleys and abundant natural life. Designated as an Area of Outstanding Beauty, it was probably used as a hunting ground by the rulers of Mercia, the kingdom that covered most of the Midlands before the Norman Conquest. In the Domesday Book, the Chase is recorded as belonging to the king. In 1281 Edward I ordered all wolves on the Chase to be hunted down and killed. Nine years later the area ceased to be a royal forest, and passed to the Bishop of Lichfield. In the middle of the 16th century, after the Dissolution of the Monasteries, the Chase was give to the Paget family, ancestors of the present Marquess of Anglesey.

The soil is gravelly and considered too poor for agriculture, but supports a species of grey-faced sheep peculiar to the Chase. Near **Cannock**, a thriving industrial town whose life centres around its market place, the woodlands of the Chase rise to their loftiest point — just over 800 feet above sea level — at **Castle Ring**, the site of an elaborate hill-fort and earthworks constructed by the early Britons about 2,000 years ago.

How to Get There

By car, A461 Birmingham (Walsall), north-east to Lichfield. Left onto A51 then left at Longdon onto minor road for Cannock Wood. Nearest BR station is Lichfield (on the line from Birmingham), then a bus which stops opposite the station (No 308) to Cannock Wood. ▶

The Cannock Chase Walk

A long (about 4 miles) though fairly gentle walk across real away-from-it-all terrain rich with natural life. Much of the route passes eerily through a dark forest, making this a must for those that insist they are unscareable.

Fallow deer roam the Chase, and dogs should be kept under control. The Chase is also home to weasels, stoats, badgers, foxes, lizards, grass snakes and adders.

The walk begins in Cannock Wood, at **The Park Gate Inn.** About 300 years old, the inn looks much like an unprepossessing old farmhouse from the outside, but this is deception. Within, there is a strong 'olde worlde' atmosphere with a perfect gastronomic complement, ranging from haute cuisine restaurant fare to fresh, appetizing pub food and a cold buffet in summer. Some Ansells ale, handpumped, washes down landlord Sidney Brearley's home-prepared foods a treat.

Outside the inn, turn right towards Castle Ring (signposted). To the left of Castle Ring, the highest point on the Chase (offering a fine view of the forest and patchwork landscape) take a whitish sand path. Much of the route is along Forestry Commission tracks, which are easy to follow. The triangulation point, close to Castle Ring, allows a view over nine counties — Stafford, Flint, Cheshire, Derby, Nottingham, Leicester, Warwickshire, Shropshire and Northampton. When the sand path brings you out onto the main Rugeley road, cross a small stream and descend through the trees to a lower road, Marquis Drive. Turn left. At the T-junction, follow the road around to the right, past the nursery marked by a wooden gate with a notice reading 'Forest Garden'. The track climbs, passing a stream, a pump-house and cottage to the left, before reaching the A460. Follow the track round to the right, through a golf course, passing the clubhouse on the left.

Turn sharp left at the end of Lower Cliff woods and continue around the edge of Regent's Wood. When you reach the main road, turn right and return to Wandon. At the crossroads take the right turning and rejoin the forest path back to Castle Ring (this is marked by a small white pole with a yellow cap, actually a gas line marker).

Park Gate Inn, Cannock Wood

About the Inn: Opposite Castle Ring at the highest point on Cannock Chase, this fine inn hides great period atmosphere within a modest exterior. A stone fireplace, large collection of copper and brassware and antique furniture provide an interesting and homely environment. Well-known in the area for good English food. Large garden, no bar games. Background music only.

Beers and Food: Sid and Trudi Brearley took over the inn in 1963, and have established a reputation for providing good English cooking. A range of bar snacks and pub grub, with a comprehensive, reasonably-priced menu in the busy restaurant. Cold buffet served in the bar throughout summer. Ansells beers handpumped, several lagers on tap. Range of wines available by the glass.

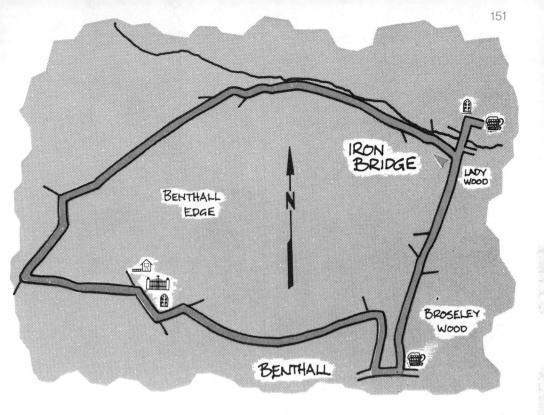

4h Ironbridge

The District

The village of **Ironbridge** stands on the River Severn in Telford Shropshire and takes its name from the bridge across the Severn Gorge which, two centuries ago, made industrial history. The first iron bridge in the world, cast at **Coalbrookdale** in 1779, it heralded the dawn of the industrial revolution. In Coalbrookdale's blast furnace, Abraham Darby perfected the technique of smelting iron ore, using coke as a fuel.

The entire area has been turned into a living museum dedicated to the great age of industry. The Ironbridge Gorge Museum Trust has preserved Coalbrookdale as an authentic iron-making community — Abraham Darby's original furnace site can be visited; the Seven Warehouse and ad-

jacent wharf are reminders of the era in which the Coalbrookdale Company dominated the lives and livings of the local population. At **Blists Hill Open Air Museum** a 42-acre woodland site has been devoted to recreating the historic Shropshire industries of iron, coal and clay, together with early transport systems, and the **Coalport China Works**, the site of a famous bone china pottery that moved to Staffordshire in 1926, after 150 years as the hub of the small village of Coalport.

The museums are open all year round and can be comfortably visited as part of a day's visit.

How to Get There

By car, A458 from Shrewsbury to Bridgnorth, turn off at Much Wenlock onto B4378 and right onto B4380 for Ironbridge. From Telford A4169 south to Ironbridge. By rail, to Wellington station then bus from station to Ironbridge.

The Ironbridge Walk

A 4½ mile walk through the Ironbridge Gorge passing many places of interest for the entire family. Ironbridge itself is particularly well-stocked with fine watering-holes.

The walk begins at **The Tontine Hotel** in the village square. The Tontine offers reasonably priced overnight accommodation, an interesting selection of beers and fortifying grub, and a ghost. The Square hosts a market every Friday.

Cross the bridge from the Tontine, past the Tourist Information centre on your right. You can pick up free leaflets on the local places of interest at the centre. Turn right and pass through a wooden gate marked 'Picnic Area and Nature Trail'. Turn left after the bridge and follow the path down as it bears right, keeping more or less to the edge of Lady Wood. The footpath joins a wider track with a dilapidated stone wall and a clearing to the left. Cross the stile by the wide gate ahead of you.

Passing an arched bridge to the right and a small waterfall to the left, follow the path which keeps the river on your right. It forks just before some electricity towers. Take the lower track, past the massive cooling towers on your right. The path is easy to follow for the next couple of miles,

▶

The Inns

The Robin Hood, Ironbridge

About the Inn: A two-century old inn in Waterloo Street, this is a sailor's pub which was originally a stopping-off point for the cargo boats working the River Severn. An old Georgian house divided into two lounges, it is decorated with many unusual antiques. Children welcomed in the garden (seating provided in summer).

Beers and Food: A wide range of real ale, including Ansells Bitter, M&B Springfield Bitter, Bank's Bitter, Courage and Marston, and Stella Artois and Carling Black Label lagers. Hot snacks.

The Bird in Hand, Ironbridge

About the Inn: Beside the Robin Hood, this inn was built in 1774 and sports a heartwarming open fire. Darts and dominoes. Children welcomed. Seating outside in summer.

Beers and Food: Bank's hand drawn; draught Harp lager. Hot and cold snacks.

New Inn, Benthall

About the Inn: The oldest inn in the area, on Bridge Road leading towards Ironbridge. A small cosy place with a friendly atmosphere, highly regarded by locals, Taped music, dominoes.

Beers and Food: Greenhall Whitley Best Bitter and Mild — both very distinctive ales — hand-drawn; Gruhalle lager and Guinness on tap. Bar snacks, basket meals in summer.

▶

eventually opening out onto a clearing of shale and broken brick. Follow the path marked by wooden posts at the edge of the clearing, keeping the perimeter of Bentall Edge about 15 yards away.

Take the track which cuts down left through fields, keeping a hedgerow to your right. Walk through (Wonderwomen can jump over) the metal gate and head towards a red-brick farmhouse to your left. Turn right at the lane and past the farmhouse. To your left is St Bartholomew's Parish Church, a charming, early Victorian yellow brick church, and Benthall Hall.

From here the path is fairly well signposted. Turn left just past the church, taking two stiles and keeping straight ahead towards the village of Benthall. In the village take the upper road to the right, which joins the main road returning to Ironbridge. At the junction to the village is **The New Inn**. It is older than pubs in Ironbridge, a small but friendly inn offering a range of fine real ales. From The New Inn follow the road downhill to Ironbridge.

Tontine Hotel, Ironbridge

About the Inn: A haunted, mid-18th century inn in the village square. A large lounge bar features a collection of brasses and copperware. This small family run hostelry offers accommodation. Children welcomed, but muddy-booted hikers frowned upon.

Beers and Food: Mitchell & Butlers Mild, Springfield Bitter, Worthington E, Carling Black Label and Hemeling lagers on tap. Snacks and sandwiches served in the bar; à la carte restaurant.

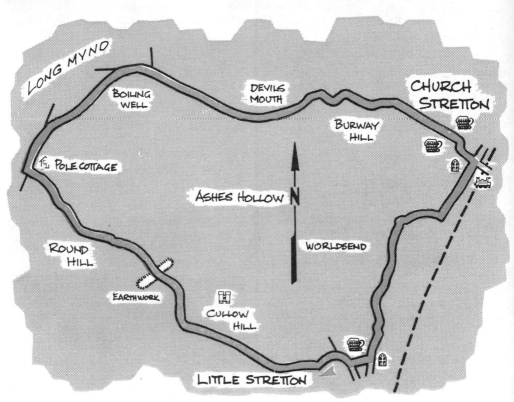

4i   Little Stretton

The District

One of the great tracts of upland sweeping eastwards from the Welsh border into Shropshire, the **Long Mynd** has a very particular character. That undulating moorland plateau offers wide open views and creates a sense of wilderness, while the deeply incised valleys, locally called hollows or batches, seem to penetrate into the heart of the hills. The story of the Long Mynd began 700 million years ago on an ocean floor, with the accumulation of layer upon layer of silt, sand and gravel. Increased restlessness in the earth's crust pushed up these sedimentary layers, now turned into rock, into a great 'U' shaped fold. Over hundreds of millions of years the forces of erosion have worn away the folded rocks, first to give a plateau, then

streams have dissected the plateau into the rounded blocks which give the hill its present distinctive shape.

From the top of the Mynd the vista is of rolling hills, extending to the horizon on every side, some wooded, some too steep for trees. The Mynd is beset by legends. The **Devil's Chair**, an outcrop of rock shaped like a huge armchair , is so-called because on Hallowe'en and Christmas Eve the devil supposedly settles on that eerily quiet hunk of stone. The 'funeral way', is the local name for a path across the brow of the Mynd, on which on some nights a funeral procession has been spotted, complete with horse-drawn hearse and pallbearers, all floating slowly by about six inches off the ground! In sharp contrast, the Mynd has also been one of the richest sources of UFO spottings in the country; locals swear that strange alien craft have *not* been confused with the odd errant ball from the nearby golf course, one of the highest in the land, or the wide-winged property of the Midlands Gliding Club.

Little Stretton and **Church Stretton** are full of charming 17th century brick and timber cottages and barns, and the more modern buildings have retained the original character.

How to Get There
By car, the A49 from Shrewsbury to Ludlow, the B4370 (north section) for Little Stretton. By rail, to Church Stretton station, then a bus that stops beside the station to Little Stretton.

The Little Stretton/Long Mynd Walk
A lovely if chunky walk, about 7½ miles, over the Long Mynd involves a fair bit of climbing and ridge walking, so it is best appreciated by sadists, masochists and those watching their weight.

After rolling a little Ansells Bitter or Bass Worthington around the tongue, in the quiet 17th century **Ragleth Inn** on Ludlow Road in Little Stretton, follow the side lane at the junction and turn right at the end of the lane. Turn left before the bridge and the camping site and follow the track uphill towards a sheep track. From here the path is easy to follow — a solitary sheep track cutting through the hills.

Climbing Cullow Hill offers a spectacular view of the Ashes Hollow, and a stiff back. The path leads out onto a plain, covered in heather, as you approach the main track. Pole Cottage, now demolished and marked only by a corrugated tin shack, is slightly to your right. Turn right at the main track and head up to Boiling Well, the site of a natural

The Inns

Ragleth Inn, Little Stretton

About the Inn: Built in 1620, this single storey inn used to be a rope works, and numbers the late Rupert Davies (the actor who played Maigret) and the Headmaster of Eton among its celebrated customers. Hikers are welcome at the open fires of both bars. Cosy, with low ceilings and timbered interior, and comfortable. Favoured by local farmers. Seating available in summer in the small garden. Children welcomed, background taped music. Fruit machines and pinball.

Beers and Food: Ansells Bitters and Bass Worthington real ale on draught. Draught Guinness and Black Label lager. Wide range of bar snacks, morning coffee served till 12.30.

Circa 1600

Buck's Head, Church Stretton

About the Inn: A 17th century manor house, of stone masonry, in the High Street. Bed and breakfast accommodation for eight. Seating outside in the small paved garden. Children are welcomed at lunchtime, and by arrangement with landlord Ray Mellor, hikers may bring their own food providing they buy a drink. Darts, pool, fruit machines, dominoes and video games available.

spring which 'boils' out of the ground to form a stream and marshland area. Follow the sign pointing to Church Stretton.

It's downhill from here, folks! Devil's Mouth, just in front of Burway Hill, gives you a view of Church Stretton as you descend. To your left is Cow Ridge, Haddon Hill, Cardingmill Valley and Bodbury Hill.

Leaving the National Trust land through a gate over a cattle grid is easier for humans than cattle. Continue down to the village. Pass the crossroads and turn right at the bottom of Burway Road into the High Street. Here looms a difficult choice of temptations. **The Buck's Head**, a 17th century manor, on your left, **The King's Arms** on your right. The close-mouthed will strut straight past both on their way back along the B4370 to Little Stretton, and the comforts of **The Green Dragon Inn**, an attractive free house with a wide range of real ales and beers and a welcoming open hearth.

Beers and Food: M&B (Mitchells & Butlers) Bitter and Mild, Bass Worthington, Guinness and Hemeling lager on Draught. Black label lager and Worthington E. A wide range of bar snacks, hot and cold lunches and morning coffee.

Green Dragon Inn, Little Stretton

About the Inn: Situated on the old Ludlow Road just after it peels off the A49, this charming inn stands looking up at Ragleth Hill. An attractive bar with part-beamed ceiling and an open fireplace, modern dining room with restored wooden beams. Lawn at the rear with umbrella-tables. Bed and breakfast. Children welcomed.

Beers and Food: This free house offers M&B Mild and Springfield Bitter on draught, M&B Brew X1, Worthington, Youngers Tartan, Carling Black label lager. Range of bar snacks.

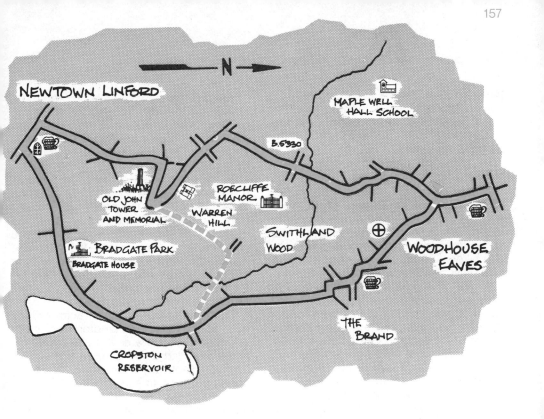

4j Woodhouse Eaves

The District

Woodhouse Eaves, the epicentre of earth tremors in 1839 and 1893, is a charming village of rough stone buildings set in the hilly countryside between Loughborough and Leicester. **Loughborough,** about 2½ miles to the north-east, was just a hamlet before both the Romans and the Danes settled there. It is famous for its bell-foundry — the biggest ringing bell in the country (the Great Paul in St Paul's, London) — was made there.

Though some consider it oppressively red-brick, **Leicester** is one of England's most historic cities. First a Celt, then a Roman settlement, it boasts a fine Norman castle and church, St Mary de Caestro, a Guildhall on which work was commenced nearly 600 years ago, the Jewry Wall and a fine Gothic cathedral.

The walk's main attraction is **Charnwood Forest,** a broken upland of pre-Cambrian rock to the north-west of Leicester. It resembles Scottish scenery, and was volcanic at the time when mammals first began to appear. **Ulverscroft Nature Reserve** is set within the forest. The nearby ruins of the Norman priory, and **Bradgate Park,** one of the first country houses built in England, are worth a visit. The forest is the natural home of many hardwoods, especially oak and beech, and the undergrowth — broad fern, furze, crowberry and whortleberry — is the habitat of pheasants, redstarts, treepippits and both red and fallow deer.

►

How to Get There

By car, A6 Leicester to Loughborough Ring Road, west onto B591. From Loughborough left onto a minor road for Woodhouse Eaves. By rail, to Loughborough station, then bus which stops just by the station in Woodhouse Eaves.

The Woodhouse Eaves Walk

A long (8-9 miles), fairly arduous walk — though with a short cut (see map) — best suited to experienced, dedicated ramblers and hikers. Strong shoes or boots adviseable (essential after wet weather).

A pint of Ansells Mild or Bitter and an excellent cold buffet at **Ye Olde Bulle's Head**, at the junction of the main road in Woodhouse Eaves and the forest road, is just what the doctor ordered before setting out on this calorie-burning hike. Turn left outside the inn and walk through the village along Main Street. Turn right at Maplewell Road and continue up the hill.

Beyond the village you reach a footpath marked 'to Newton Linford', just before a Tudor farmhouse. Take the path down between fields, bearing right and then taking a right fork through a gate and into a cornfield. Walk through the field towards the golf course, with Maplewell Farm and schoolhouse to your right (about 300 yards away). Cross a stile onto the golf course. Keeping the hedgerow on your right and the pond on your left, continue up the hill to a large tree and a fence. Head down to the B5330, crossing the stream via a flat stone bridge (golfers will put you on the right track if you stray).

The path continues uphill over the road, fenced on the left, wooded on the right, opening out onto a field at the top. Cross the field onto Benscliffe Road. On your left you will see the War Memorial in Bradgate Park, an obelisk dominating the skyline from the crest of a hill. Heading towards this you will reach the Hunt's Hill entrance to Bradgate Park. The path leads into the park, up to Old John's Tower and the memorial. The climb is steep but rewarded with a spectacular view of the park and surrounding landscape; it is quite windy at the peak, an excellent spot for gliding or, for those pilots who prefer to keep their feet firmly on the ground, kite-flyers.

From the tower several tracks radiate out; the one to Newton Lindford is more or less due south, towards the War Memorial, and a mounted compass by the tower will help you dispel any uncertainty. The track brings you out at the village of Newton Lindford beside All Saints' Church. Any thirst or hunger (or just the need of a few minutes sit-down) can be satisfied most agreeably at **The Bradgate**. To return to Woodhouse Eaves, re-enter the park and take the footpath running eastwards, roughly parallel to the main road.

A weir runs alongside the path, sheltered by trees and ferns. It runs through to the deer sanctuary. Further along on your left are the ruins of Lady Jane Grey's former home; where she spent 16 happy years before being married off to Lord Dudley, with whom she was subsequently beheaded in the Tower. The screeches emanating from within are from peacocks to whom the estate is now home.

Continue along this path, past the reservoir until you reach the Hallgates exit. A steep ladder takes you over the gates and into a car park. Walk past the exit towards the main road; 30 yards to your left is a green sign indicating the footpath to Swithland Wood. The path bears diagonally across a field, over a bridge, and across a stream and a stile leading into the woodland.

Bear left towards a bridlepath and continue up the hill. The path eventually forks into three; take the lowest path, on your

right, which leads to a clearing at the forest's edge. There is a low dry-stone wall at the clearing; take the gate (or walk around the wall) and continue along the bridlepath as it bears left.

Keeping alongside the wall, with the woods to your left, until you will reach a grey gate. Turn right here and follow the road down to the triangle. Take the path (signposted) towards Woodhouse Eaves, then turn left up Brand Hill. About 200 yards up the hill stands the **Wheatsheaf**, an Elizabethan-style coaching inn. The central coachway leads through to the car park and onto Brand Lane, which rejoins Main Street at the other end of the village from Ye Olde Bulle's Head.

The Inns

Ye Olde Bulle's Head, Woodhouse Eaves

About the Inn: At the junction of Forest Road and Main Street, this fine stone and slate tavern offers a cosy interior with hand-made mahogany furniture and a large open fire, with a unique bar constructed by hand of stone. A small, well-kept garden is used in summer. Darts, billiards, background music on tape or jukebox. Children welcomed.

Beers and Food: Ansells Bitter and Mild handpumped, Skol lager on tap. Cold buffet, hot snacks and a full restaurant menu.

The Bradgate, Newtown Lindford

About the Inn: A small, friendly inn situated about 200 yards from the exit of Bradgate Park. A two-storey, late 19th century tavern built of stone and bricks, it offers a small paved area with benches and tables for drinking outside in summer. Darts and jukebox music.

Beers and Food: Everards Old Original and Beacon Bitters on tap. Hot snacks in the bar and a grill room (3-course meals around £3.50 a head).

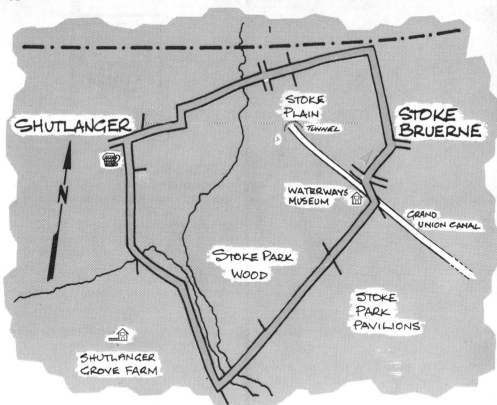

4k Stoke Bruerne

The District

Stoke Bruerne is a quiet 19th century village which rests by the side of the Grand Union canal. It lies at the southern end of the Blisworth Tunnel which, at two miles long, is the longest tunnel on the British waterways. There is an attractive humpback bridge which dates from about 1835, but the village is perhaps best-known these days as home to **The Waterways Museum.** The visitor can browse around a wide range of exhibits, housed in the three floors of a converted 19th century grain warehouse, and gain an insight into some two centuries of thriving canal life. The museum shop sells literature, posters, illustrations, models and badges, so if you're hard up, don't tell the kids that it's there.

South of the village there is Stoke Park Pavilions, a house set in 400 acres, of which only the twin 1630 pavilions remain. It's open most of the summer.

East of Stoke Bruerne lies Easton Neston Park, the old home of the Fermors and the Earls of Pomfrel. Designed by Nicolas Hawksmoor in the early 18th century and built of local Helmdon Stone, it is a dignified and noble edifice. There are some beautiful 18th century gardens with a good ornamental pond and a 17th century temple.

How to Get There

By car from London, M1 to junction 15 then A508 through Roade turning left at Stokegap for Stoke Bruerne. Train to Bletchley then bus no 330 (no Sunday service) to Stoke Bruerne.

The Stoke Bruerne Walk

About 3½ miles long and flat, most of the family should be able to haul themselves around this one without too much effort.

We begin at the Waterways Museum. Take a look inside — its only 50p and 25p for baby Jim and granny — then go back through the car park to the road and turn left. Keep on the road through the outskirts of the village and go through the iron gate with the Public Footpath sign to Blisworth. Take this track until you reach a belt of woodland — an old railway embankment — then turn left, go over the gate and straight on following the edge of the field. Veer right at the end of the field through some scrubby woodland. Cross the lane and go through the iron gate opposite. If you can stop Rover chasing all the rabbits there are around here, walk diagonally across this field and through a gate on to the Blisworth road. Go over the road, into another field and walk along by the left-hand hedge.

Halfway along by a water trough, there's a gap in the hedge. Go through it and continue with the hedge now on your right. Walk right round the edge of this field and turn right when you reach the road. This will lead you straight to **The Plough** at Shutlanger, where children can play on the swings outside, while you down some Charlie Wells' ales within. Spare a few minutes to listen to the record landlord Edward Worr and some of the locals have made; its very funny!

The Inns

Boat Inn, Stoke Bruerne

About the Inn: A beautiful thatched building by the canal side built in the 17th century and run by the Woodward family since 1827. The bars feature murals of canal life and have beamed ceilings and stone floors. The lounge bar has a central chimney and a spiral roof. All have open fires. There is also a restaurant, tea room and an outdoor drinking area by the canalside. Try throwing the 'cheese' in the Northamptonshire skittle room.

Beers and Food: Ruddles country, Marston's Pedigree, Sam Smiths and Bass all hand-drawn, plus 14 other beers and lagers. Apart from a huge selection of bar meals, you can have afternoon tea or an 'à la carte' meal in the restaurant for around £7 a head. There is also a huge wine list.

On leaving the pub, retrace your steps a hundred yards and turn right down Water Lane, past a farm on the right and down the lane which continues straight on from the end of the surface road. At the bottom of the lane go through the gate and down the field which, in the summer, is covered with Butterbur and Marsh Marigold, until you reach a stream. Here Rover will probably rush off after a duck or a water-rat. When you've got him back, cross over the footbridge and turn left, following the stream. The stream goes off to the left after a while, but keep following the track until you reach a stile marked with a white arrow. From here on there are a lot of these arrows — follow them, they mark your route. The arrows take you across two brick culverts over streams and up to a lane. If you wish to visit Stoke Park Pavilion (open June, July, August weekends from 2.00 to 6.00) turn right here.

Retrace your steps back to the arrows and follow them through an avenue of poplar trees back to the canal and up it to **The Boat Inn,** where your can finish the day with a choice of four real ales, all hand-drawn, plus fourteen other keg beers and lagers. You can sit outside by the canal or play Northamptonshire skittles indoors.

The Plough, Shutlanger

About the Inn: This friendly village pub where people traditionally stop on the way to Towchester races, has a beamed interior and a large collection of mugs and guns. There's a play area for the kids and seats outside as well as a pet goat in the garden. Room for caravans and tents. Skittles, darts and dominoes inside. Sometimes Morris dancers come here to perform.

Beers and Food: Charlie Well's Bombadier and Eagle beers, also bottled beers, wines and spirits. Selection of bar snacks.

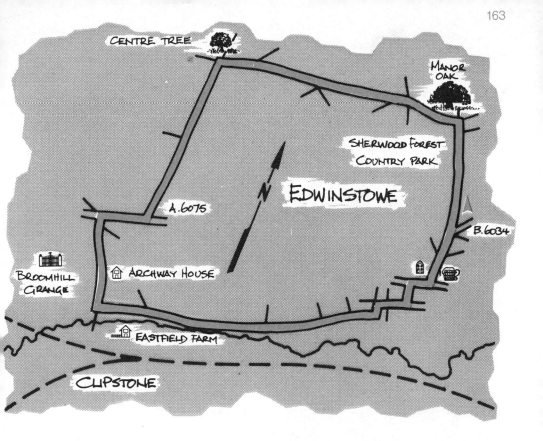

CENTRE TREE

MANOR OAK

SHERWOOD FOREST COUNTRY PARK

EDWINSTOWE

A.6075

B.6034

BROOMHILL GRANGE

ARCHWAY HOUSE

EASTFIELD FARM

CLIPSTONE

41   Edwinstowe

The District

The village of **Edwinstowe** takes its name from the Saxon king Edwin. A Christian, this king of Northumbria often visited the spot and, after he was killed in battle in 633 AD, his body is said to have been brought to the village. St Mary's Church, which is mentioned in the Domesday Book, is the legendary site of Robin Hood's marriage to Maid Marian. **Thoresby Hall**, the home of Lady Manvers, boasts an elaborate ornamental fireplace that represents the entire efforts of one man's working life.

The village is set in the heart of **Sherwood Forest**, a complex of woodlands that covers 156 square miles. Deer still roam the greenwood in the shade of mighty oaks that were young when the Robin Hood legends were born, though the forest has been much encroached upon by farming, collieries and military training areas over the centuries. The Major Oak, the forest's largest tree, is believed to be 1000 years old and, according to legend, was used as a meeting place by the Merrie Men. One of the attractions of the Sherwood Forest country park is the man-made lake, originally constructed about 200 years ago and used as a source of power for the mill. The lake is rich in natural life: local fish include carp, perch, tench, bream; many water birds are attracted by the marshes, temporary pools and the slow-moving streams.

How to Get There
By car, A60 from Nottingham to Warsop, turn right onto A6075 to Edwinstowe. From Lincoln, A57 towards Worksop, turning left onto A6075 to Edwinstowe. From Sheffield, A616 to Edwinstowe. By rail to Mansfield, then bus (Nos 13 or 15) to Edwinstowe.

The Sherwood Forest Walk
An easy walk in the romantic, legendary footsteps of Robin Hood and the dastardly capers of the Sheriff of Nottingham. About 5½ miles across level woodland, prone to muddiness in parts.

A leisurely tankard at **The Royal Oak** and you're off, answering the call of adventure — if Errol Flynn can do it, so can you! From the crossroads, walk up the B6034 past the church. Taking care not to trip over your lincoln green tights, take a half-left turning onto a track that leads through a small wooden fence at the corner of Sherwood Forest country park. Pass a cricket field on your left and follow the signs directing you to the Visitors' Centre and

Major Oak. The path meanders through a picnic area and car park (which are not thought to have existed in Robin's day).

Walk through the Visitor's Centre, avoiding assorted pamphlets, souvenirs and absolutely genuine Friar Tuck artifacts like the plague, and follow signs for the Major Oak. Several areas will be fenced off to protect saplings and some of the wildlife — which includes tawny owls, kestrels, woodpigeons, wrens, shrews, badgers and voles. As the path circles round to the left you will see the Major Oak. Before walking around to the front of the tree (the front is marked by benches) turn right along a straight, wide broken-up track. You will probably find it easier to walk along the grass path beside the track. The route is skirted by a thick coniferous forest.

Continue along this track until you reach a gate across your path. Walk around this track and take the first, similarly surfaced track on the left, which runs off at right angles. The path cuts through forest, emerging into a small car park by A6075. Walk up to the main road, cross it and turn right. About 20 yards further, turn left onto

a road, which descends gradually towards Archway House. This early Victorian extravagance boasts an elaborate neo-Gothic style. Walking past the House downhill to the river, turn left just before the river, down a narrow track fenced on either side. Continue along this path, not deviating to cross the river. You will emerge into a field with school buildings and playing fields away to your left.

Walk across the field and out into the children's playground, through a gap in the iron railings. Turn half-left and walk up to the road. Turn right, straight onto the end of the path; then turn left into First Avenue. Take the first right into Fourth Avenue, turn left at the first T-junction then right at a second junction back to The Royal Oak. Standing on the corner, this attractive Tudor-style inn was previously one of the oldest buildings in Nottinghamshire.

The Inn

Royal Oak, Edwinstowe

About the Inn: In the High Street, about 5 minutes walk from the cricket ground and forest, this large, well-furnished inn was rebuilt in the early 1930s in a Tudor style. The diamond-shaped windows in the cottage opposite were taken from the original tavern that stood on this site, which was one of the oldest buildings in the county. The Royal Oak's long tradition of warm hospitality is maintained by landlord Leslie Aldred. Photos and prints depicting the area's history line the walls of the lounge bar. Darts, pool, dominoes. Background music in the lounge, jukebox in the bar. Children welcomed in the outside area.

Beers and Food: John Smith's and Courage real ales and Blackthorn Cider on draught. Good range of pub grub, including scampi, home-made beefburgers, shepherd's pie, steak sandwich, Ploughman's and sarnies.

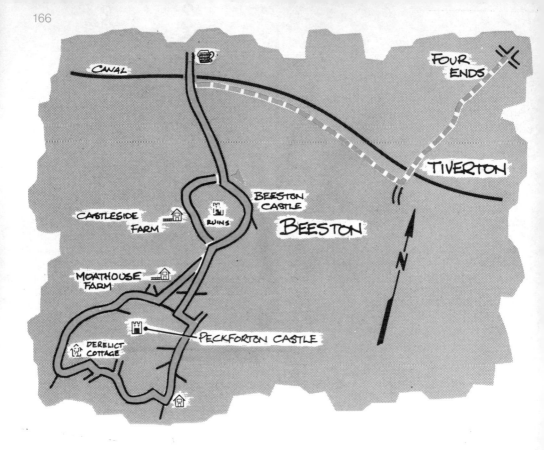

4m Beeston

The District

Two castles perched on the red-sandstone hills of the Cheshire plain (see **Alderley Edge** walk for further district details) are the features of this walk. **Beeston Castle** dates from the 13th century, the Domesday Book crediting possession to the Baron of Malpas, Robert Fitz-Hugh. At the outbreak of the Civil War, the castle was garrisoned by the Parliamentarians, but surrendered to the Royalists after nine months. After the Battle of Rowton Moor (4 miles north-west of Beeston), the closing stages of which were watched by Charles I from the castle's tower, Beeston Castle fell to the Parliamentarians and was destroyed by Cromwell. This, and the ravages of time, account for the castle's current dilapidated condition.

There are a number of legends attached to Beeston. It is rumoured that Richard II cast his treasure into the castle's well before it fell to Bolingbroke (later Henry IV). However fanciful this story might be, it is true that Richard had special ties with the castle and the district; his personal bodyguard consisted of 2,000 Chesire bowmen, renowned throughout the country for their unrivalled archery.

The fertile plain that surrounds the castle is typical of the county, its rolling farmland thick with Friesian cattle. **Peckforton Castle**, a mock-medieval mansion built by the wealthy landowner Lord Tollemache in the mid 19th century, was used as a hospital during the last war, but has remained largely empty ever since. It is not open to the public.

How to Get There

Beeston Castle lies 3 miles south of Taporley, which is on the A49. Turn off at junction of A49, A51 and B5152, driving down A49 towards Tiverton. Take the turn off for Tiverton Village and Hall, follow road for 2 miles and take next left, signposted for Beeston Castle. Nearest BR station is in Chester, with infrequent buses to Four Ends Lane outside Tiverton. This would add about 2 miles to the main walk (see dotted route on map).

The Beeston Walk

Not too long (about 3½ miles) but a fairly arduous ramble across rolling Cheshire countryside, featuring a visit to Beeston Castle. The route follows quiet lanes, bridleways and a woodland footpath, sections of which may be muddy after rain. Not recommended for idle strollers!

Though a car is not essential, it is recommended that you drive to **Beeston Castle,** leaving the car in the castle's car park. Those in need of pre-expedition sustenance can double back across the canal bridge to **The Shady Oak,** to sample home-prepared bar food and a glass of Boddington's at this free house.

Walk back across the humpbacked bridge towards Beeston Castle; when you reach the road, running round the base of the castle hill, turn left and follow the signpost to the castle entrance. At the next road junction turn right and walk past the entrance. Enter the right-hand car park, where you will see a narrow path running parallel to the castle walls on the right and a hedge of holly bushes on the left. Follow the path for about 100 yards until you reach a signposted junction. Turn left here and follow the path towards Buckley Hill until you reach a lane; cross the lane, and take

▶

The Inn

Shady Oak, Tiverton

About the Inn: Formerly The Royal Oak, this inn stands in Mill Lane on the bank of the Shropshire Union Canal. It was built during the construction of the canal, and was originally a coal wharf. The inn is in the process of modification and renovation by new landlord John Dook. Its gardens overlook the canal and its forecourt, beside the foot of a humpbacked bridge, offers tables and benches for enthusiasts of imbibing al fresco. Music provided by a jukebox; darts, dominoes and pool.

Beers and Food: This free house offers a varied and changing selection of real ales, drawn by electric pump, as well as key lager on tap and a standard range of bottled beers and lagers. Boddington's is always available on tap. Hot and cold home-made pub grub and usual bar snacks.

the track to the left of the 'magpie' house immediately before you. Follow this track, crossing a ditch by a wooden footbridge and subsequently a stile onto a ploughed field, until you arrive at a narrow lane between a moat farmhouse on the right and the 'main' road on the left. Turn left and walk down to the main road, then turn right onto the road (Stonehouse Lane).

Follow Stonehouse Lane for about a quarter mile until you reach a red-brick cottage on your left, and a gateway onto a private road on your right. Beyond this gateway you will see a double wooden gate about 50 yards straight ahead, while to the left is a second gateway into a field. Take the latter, into the field. There is no footpath through the field, but a public right of way exists close to the wire fence and you should follow the line of the fence, right the way round, until you reach a gate onto a cobbled road. Turn left down this road, then right about 30 yards later up a steep hill.

Follow this road through woodlands thick with sweet-chestnut trees. Native to the Mediterranean, these trees were introduced to Britain by the Romans. The road passes farm buildings and continues for almost a mile and a half before meeting a junction, on which stands the now derelict Rock Cottage. Turn right here and follow the signposts to Beeston. The route veers to the right and meets two staggered gates; take the furthest and cross into a field by a stile. Leave the field by a gate.

Following signposts for Beeston, descend the hill. At the next junction turn right onto a stoned path. At the foot of the hill you leave the woodland via a gate and turn right. This track leads you back past the moat farmhouse; turn left over a stile and back onto the path that brought you from Beeston. The end of this trail brings you back to Beeston Castle; you turn left and follow the path round the castle walls and back onto the road.

About 200 yards past The Shady Oak take a footpath to the left, signposted for **Delamere Forest**, cross the fields towards **Wharton's Lock**, walking under a railway bridge. At the canal bank turn left over a stile and follow the bank towards The Shady Oak. Its gardens overlook the Shropshire Union Canal, and children are welcome in the gardens and in the forecourt drinking area. Landlord John Dook is in the process of renovating the inn inside and out, and is unlikely to be thrilled by hikers tramping across his new lounge in muddy boots!

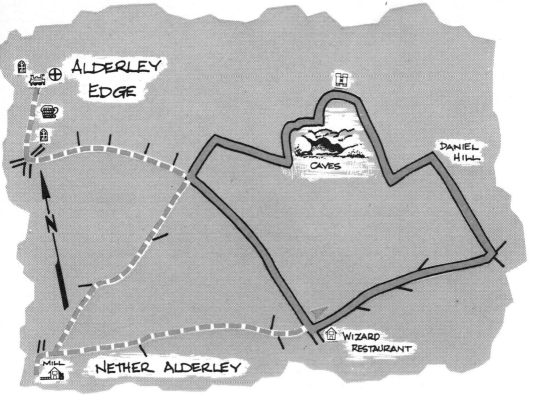

4n   Alderley Edge

The District

The county of Cheshire — non-metro-politan, diverse in its landscape and famed for its characteristic black and white 'mag-pie' architecture — is the setting for this village ramble. **Alderley Edge** itself offers fine views down onto the rolling countryside and the Cheshire plain. **Chester**, the county town and former Roman city on the River Dee, is the only walled city in the country whose walls are preserved intact. The city offers many places of interest, including a beautiful 14th century cathedral notable for its monastic remains, impressive half-timbered houses and mansions, and some very fine inns like **The Falcon** and **The Bear and Billet.** Building of the castle was begun shortly after the Norman Conquest.

31 miles from Chester, **Alderley Edge** is a residential village bordered by woods. A wooded sandstone escarpment rising steeply from the Cheshire plain, it is an outstandingly beautiful area protected by the National Trust. An old mill at **Nether Alderley**, to the south of the village, dates from the 15th century, and Chorley Hall from the 16th. The walk passes old mine workings, caves and the foundations of a castle which was never completed because it was decided that **Beeston**, 22 miles further south-west (q.v.), would be a better site for fortifications.

Jodrell Bank, 8 miles south-west of Alderley Edge, is noted for its massive radio telescope.

►

How to Get There

By car, Alderley Edge lies on the junction between the A535 (from Manchester), B5085 (from Knutsford), B5087 (from Macclesfield) and A34. A National Trust car park is located just outside the village on the B5087. By rail, from Manchester to Alderley Edge station. The walk begins about 200 yards from the station.

The Alderley Edge Walk

An excellent though quite strenuous ramble along good paths of gravel, stone or compacted mud. Prone to muddiness in a few spots after wet weather. About 3½ miles, though sadists can add another couple of miles by negotiating the Nether Alderley extension, described briefly at the end of the talk-round, and shown as a dotted route on the map.

The fields of Cheshire are generally divided by hedges rather than fences, these hedges providing a rich tapestry of plant and animal life, Hawthorn bushes dominate these hedgerows, but oak, beech and hazel trees and holly, dogrose and honeysuckle bushes intrude. The hedgerows provide homes for many birds, insects and rabbits, and some ground nesting birds are able to pitch their tents in the undergrowth.

The walk begins with fortification at **The Moss Rose,** a charming 17th century inn known to locals as the 'Drum and Monkey' because many years ago an organ-grinder used to take his lunch in the tap room, leaving his organ and his apish companion outside. Sit beside the bowling green, where the inn's landlady, Elsie Crossfield, places chairs and umbrellas in summer.

The Moss Rose stands at the bottom of Alderley Edge, about 200 yards from the station. After a sip of its Robinson's Best Mild or Bitter climb up to the B5087 Alderley Edge/Macclesfield road, turn left and walk up to the Wizard Restaurant. The restaurant is linked with the area's most enduring legend. A farmer from Mobberley, crossing the Edge to sell a white mare at Macclesfield market, was stopped by an old man who offered to buy the horse. The farmer refused, confident he could obtain a better price at the market. The old man warned him that he would not find a buyer in Macclesfield. The prediction proved correct and the old man was waiting for the farmer on his return journey. 'Follow me', he commanded, and the farmer, now terrified by the old man's over-bearing, presence, obeyed. They stopped by a wall of rock; the old man touched it with his staff and a pair of iron gates appeared with a roll of thunder. Trembling, the farmer followed this wizard into a cave, where hundreds of warriors and milk-white horses were sleeping. A second cave was piled high with treasure. The wizard invited the farmer to take what he considered a fair price for the horse, explaining that one of the slumbering knights lacked a horse. 'There will come a day', the old man added, 'when these men and these horses, awakening from their enchanted slumber, will decide the fate of a great battle and save the country'. As the farmer left he was told that no mortal would ever see the iron gates again; and, sure enough, when he looked back they and the wizard vanished. Some say the wizard was Merlin, and the sleeping warriors King Arthur's knights waiting with their horses until England needed them again in time of trouble.

One tall story later, cross the road and turn right onto a wide trail next to the restaurant. Follow this trail to a junction, cross the junction, then follow the left fork of the narrower path on the other side. This path is fairly steep but levels off at the next junction which is marked by a large tree. Bear left and continue past several sandstone outcroppings. A few yards further turn right at a Y-junction and, at the next junction, turn sharp left to begin the climb to the top of Daniel Hill. On this stretch of the route a number of yellow painted marked posts carved with a 'U' (for 'up') show the easiest ascent.

The summit offers a sweeping view of the surrounding countryside. On the Edge itself the sandstone rock pushes right up to ground level. The caves in the middle distance are not safe for exploration, but a peek inside the entrances is possible for those wearing tread-soled shoes (water

The Inn

seepage makes the floors of these caves very wet and slippery).

Leaving the caves, return to the junction behind the Edge, turn left and follow the path as it descends. Keep on this gravelled path, ignoring turnings at several junctions that you encounter, for about 1½ miles. It will eventually bring you down the hill and out onto the main road.

Those with the stamina for the Nether Alderley extension should cross the road and follow the public footpath on the other side. This leads out onto the open heath. Turn right down towards the gravelled bridlepath, walk along the bridlepath and onto a private road. About a mile down this road a public footpath on the left is signposted for Nether Alderley. Take the path until it emerges onto a lane, turn left and after about 150 yards take the path to the right, towards Nether Alderley.

At the end of this path take the cobbled Bradford Lane (this is difficult to walk on and some will prefer to use the grass verge). The mill standing off Bradford Lane is open to the public. Walk past a row of expensive houses on your right and into the open countryside. At the fork in the road bear left towards Bradford house. Continue on this lane past the camping and caravan sites, bear left at the T-junction through woodland onto the B5087. Turn left and walk up to The Wizard restaurant.

Moss Rose, Alderley Edge

About the Inn: A 17th century tavern off Heyes Lane at the bottom of the Edge close to the station. Set beside a charming bowling green, with a homely local bar, a tap room and a gaming room. Traditional country pub atmosphere and special collection of Macclesfield silk pictures adorning the walls. Taped back-ground music, children welcomed to sit outside next to the bowling green.

Beers and Food: Handpumped Robinsons's real ales (best mild and Best Bitter); these are the product of a small Stockport family brewery. In winter, draught Old Tom from the cask. Excellent fresh sarnies and cold snacks, curry or home-made soup in winter.

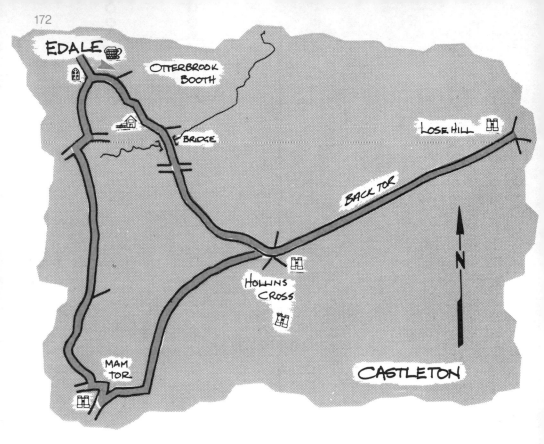

4o Edale

The District

Set amidst some of the Peak District's most majestic scenery, the walk leads to the summit of **Mam Tor**, with its hill-fort and wide views of moorland and the valley. A few miles to the north-west of Bradwell (see **Bradwell / Great Hucklow** walk), **Edale** — properly called Edale Chapel — is an unspoilt village in the delightful Vale of Edale, below the slopes of **Kinder Scout**, the most southerly of Pennine peaks.

One of the region's more curious customs is the ancient ceremony of well-dressing, a thanksgiving for water which involves decorating wells with floral religious pictures. **Tissington** is the site of one of the most colourful of the ceremonies, on Ascension Day (40 days after Easter).

The region features magnificent caves with floodlit groupings of stalactites and stalagmites. Some caverns in the **Castleton** area are open to the public. A fast-flowing stream leads to the Peak Cavern, which boasts a number of natural rock chambers, including Roger's Rain House (where water continually runs down the walls) and the Orchestral Chamber (where a continually playing orchestra drives visitors *up* the walls!). Treak Cavern is a fairy tale grotto, while within Speedwell Cavern water falls spectacularly into a bottomless pit. Queen Victoria twice visited the caverns, once as a Princess, the second time as monarch.

Castleton, about 1¼ miles from Edale, takes its name from the impressive ruins of Peveril Castle, built by William the Conqueror's illegitimate son, William Peveril.

Successive monarchs used the castle as a base for hunting expeditions in the area, until it fell into disuse in the early 15th century.

How to Get There
By car, A6 south-east from Stockport (near Manchester), left onto A625 towards Sheffield, off left onto a narrow road for Edale. From Sheffield turn right just before Hope. By rail, to Edale station (Manchester to Sheffield line).

The Edale / Mam Tor Walk
About 3½ miles over rugged, heath and moorland terrain, in parts fairly steep. As with the Bradwell walk (q.v.) proper equipment and clothing are essential, and the safety precautions associated with hikes across quite desolate country should be observed. Definitely *not* for casual walkers, though hardy, exuberant kids could have a lot of fun (under strict supervision).

The Pennine Way starts in the car park of **The Old Nags Head Inn!** And so does our walk. Enjoy some handpumped Theakston's Bitter and one of landlord Denis Liston's 'Hikers' Specials' (after which you'll be fit for anything... or nothing), then set off down the road, leaving the inn on your left. About 40 yards past the parish church take the footpath to Otterbrook Booth.

Turn right at a gateway and walk along the ridge overlooking a stream. As you approach the farm building in the midst of a wall at the top of the field, cross by a stile on your left, into a second field. With the wall you have just crossed to your left, walk

The Inns

Old Nags Head, Edale

About the Inn: Built in 1576 and used as a resting place for pack horses carrying wool and stone from Yorkshire to Lancashire. Three bars, including one reserved for mucky hikers, and a special children's room. Three large open fires. Darts, dominoes and cards, live folk music most nights. One of the few inns that heartily welcomes hikers.

Beers and Food: Theakston's and Tetley bitters hand drawn, Stones and John Smith Bitters together with several lagers and cider on draught. Best Mild draught Guinness. Vast range of good pub grub: 5 different salads, roast chicken, scampi, steak and kidney pud and 'Hikers' Special' (defies description!).

The Rambler Inn, Edale

About the Inn: Previously the 'Jolly Rambler', turn-of-the-century hostelry built with the railway. Typical Victorian railway architecture, with three bars (hikers in the main bar, no muddy boots in the lounge). Darts and dominoes, the inn prides itself on providing two good teams for local leagues. Two large gardens, accommodation for 20 (about £7.50 per person, bed and breakfast). TV lounge for residents.

Beers and Food: Five real ales (including Theakston's 'Old Peculiar', Tetley Bitter, Pollard's Bitter and Mild), three draught

round the field until you reach a small wooden gate. Turn right through the gate, walk under the bridge and follow the path as it bears left. Cross through a stile, then turn right and continue to the end of the field. Follow the track across a path and on its weaving way towards Hollins Cross. The landscape is sparse here, and the path is plainly visible well ahead.

Halfway up the hill a signpost marks the route to Castleton. This leads to the top of the hill and Hollins Cross (marked by a stone pillar erected by the local Ramblers' Association in memory of Tom Hyth). Turn left, taking the signposted route along Back Tor to Lose Hill. From the brow of this hill a fine view of the valley extends to the hills beyond the reservoir.

Return to Hollins Cross and follow the path straight to Mam Tor. Soil erosion caused by the elements and the volume of visitors to the area has made it necessary for the peak of Mam Tor to be wired off for its preservation. At the top of Mam Tor, follow the fence to the left and take the steps down onto the other side. At the foot of the steps, left would take you into Castleton via the caverns; turn right, and you will be heading back to Edale.

Take the route back to Edale, follow the road downhill until you reach a stile (about a mile beyond the steps). Cross the stile, then follow the path, crossing a dry stone wall by some wooden steps onto a lane below. Turn left and follow the lane down to the road, then turn right and left at the crossroads back into Edale.

The Rambler Inn, about 100 yards from Edale station and set back from the main road, will slake that thirst with a choice of five real ales and three draught lagers. Its two large gardens offer magnificent views of the surrounding countryside.

lagers. Wide range of pub grub and bar snacks, and à la carte restaurant offering a varied three-course meal with coffee for about £5 a head.

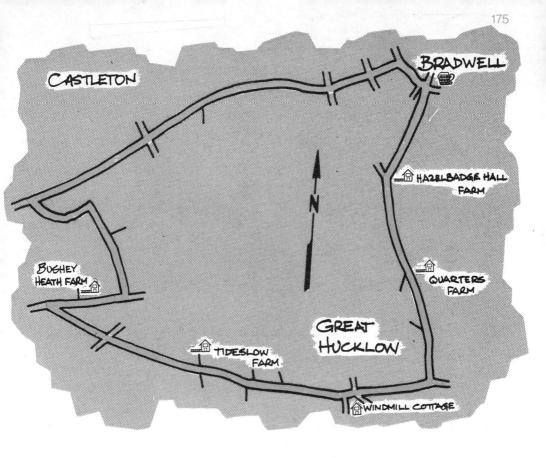

4p Bradwell

The District

Bradwell, meaning 'broad stream', nestles in a fairly remote valley in North Derbyshire's Peak District, part of the Pennine Chain which forms England's backbone and continues across the Scottish border. The Chain is the longest and most adventurous high-level route in the country.

Great cities hug the Peak District on three sides, harbouring almost a third of Britain's population within a radius of 50 miles. Yet at the same time it offers countryside of unparalleled beauty: peat moors to tramp, precipitous ridges to climb and limestone caves to explore. Beside the roads giant circles of the hard dark grey rock, called Millstone Grit, mark the boundary of the 542 square miles of the Peak District National Park. People have

lived in this district for 4,000 years — a long time to spend in any one place! — and relics of early settlers can be seen at the earthworks at **Arbor Low** ('low' is a local term meaning 'burial place'), constructed about 1,700 BC. **Hazelbadge Hall,** built by the Vernon family in 1549, is haunted by the ghost of Margaret Vernon, who rides between the hall and the village around midnight (except Christmas and bank holidays!). She was the last Vernon to live at the hall, about 300 years ago, and was jilted by her lover, whose subsequent wedding to another woman she attended.

Just above **Hucklow Edge**, near **Great Hucklow**, the Derbyshire and Lancashire Gliding Club is based, offering courses for beginners.

▶

How to Get There

By car, A6 south-east from Stockport (near Manchester), left onto A625 towards Sheffield, right off A625 at Brough, onto B6064 to Bradwell. By rail, to Thornhill station (on Manchester to Sheffield line), then bus to Bradwell.

The Bradwell / Great Hucklow Walk

The Peak District National Park operates many guided walks and conducted discovery trails throughout the area (phone Bakewell 2881 for details).

This is a tough walk for hardy, experienced hikers, and requires proper equipment: strong, comfortable, shoes (walking boots in winter) and adequate clothing. Between November and Easter the weather can change very suddenly, producing vicious, sub-arctic conditions, and the National Park's own safety leaflet warns of the dangers of exposure. A detailed map of the area, and possibly a compass, are advised.

The walk passes across moorland past earthworks and ancient burial mounds. Start at the end of the Roman Road caravan site; walk into **Bradwell**, down as far as the church on the left side of the road. Turn left a 100 yards beyond the church, continue across several junctions until, about 1½ miles later, you reach a T-junction. Turn right and walk down to the main road.

Cross over the road and walk up to the lane opposite, taking the first turning to the right. Follow this road to its end, then take the public footpath across a ridge and running parallel to the road below. The path leads eventually to a point beneath Hazelbadge Hall Farm, the haunt of our delectable lady ghost. Further down the road as it bears right, a gravelled path takes over. Follow this to Quarters Farm, where a signpost points the way across a field.

Passing over a stile, follow the line of the left-hand wall into a second field. Continue to follow the wall until it turns off to the left, when you walk straight on towards a stile barring a hole in the wall. On the brow of the hill before you, you will notice a stile leading to another field. Crossing into this

field, follow the line of the wire fence over another stile, after which the path runs parallel to the wall. A steep hill looms before you, the path carries on up and over the hill, but you may prefer to walk round its base. Bear right at the bottom on the other side of the hill; you will see a stile at the end of this track beside a junk yard (yes, even in the Peak District!).

Climb the stone steps to the footpath, follow the footpath to the end and bear right towards Windmill Cottage. Leaving this attractive thatched cottage on your left, follow the lane up a hill. At the top of the hill the lane bears right towards Little Hucklow, but you carry straight across onto a stone road crossing heathland. When you reach the junction with the Lane Head to Little Hucklow road cross the road and continue along the path, which is no longer stoned. The path leads uphill towards Tides Low broadcast beacon and down the other side of the hill. Crossing over one lane onto a footpath, you reach Tides Low Farm. Turn right here and walk for about a mile towards Bushy Heath Farm. Just beyond this second farmhouse, turn left down a narrow track. This eventually meets a lane, onto which you turn left.

This lane meets a footpath at a junction which is signposted for Bradwell. Turn right onto this footpath and follow it until it rejoins the lane, which you then continue down in the direction of Bradwell for 1½

miles, reaching a crossroads, at which the left route heads towards Castleton. Cross straight over and follow the lane for another half mile before turning left and following the road into Bradwell. **The Shoulder Of Mutton**, in Church Street (on the road from Hope to Great Hucklow), will be waiting to welcome you with a pint of Trophy Bitter or Whitbread Mild, and an excellent fixed menu three-course lunch (about £ 2.50) or dinner (about £ 3.25).

Shoulder Of Mutton, Bradwell

About the Inn: A very un-touristy establishment built of brick in the middle of the village on the Hope to Great Hucklow road. The present Shoulder Of Mutton (an original pub of that name is now a cafe across the road) was built in the 1930s. Boasts a large open fire, two bars, impressive collections of horse brasses and pistols adorning the walls. Homely decor and atmosphere enhanced by the friendliness of landlord Tom Butt and his bar staff. Inexpensive overnight accommodation, a rugged garden with outside seating and a welcome for children in the garden and the restaurant complete the inn's hospitality. Darts and dominoes, live music on weekends, back-ground jukebox sounds during the week.

Beers and Food: A Whitbread house — Trophy Bitter and Whitbread Mild, many bottled beers and lagers. Stella Artois and Heineken on tap. Wine by the glass and a wide range of cocktails. Food ranges from simple bar snacks and sandwiches (with chips and salad if desired) to a comprehensive three-course table d'hôté menu in the restaurant complemented by wide choice of wines and champagne.

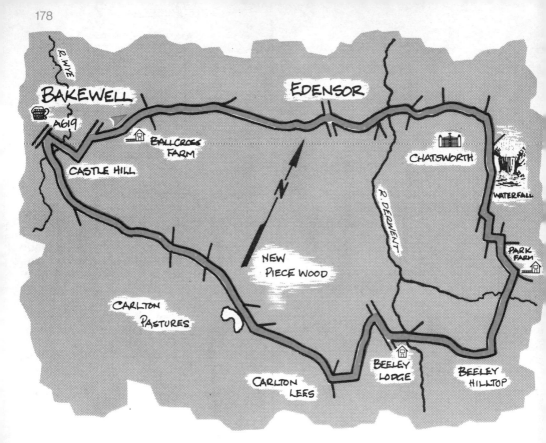

4q Bakewell

The District

The home of world-renowned tarts (!) **Bakewell**, on the banks of the Wye in Derbyshire, owes its name to the Saxon 'bad quell', meaning a bath well. The 'Bath House', built in 1697 for the Duke of Rutland, is fed by warm springs which have been prized for their recuperative properties since Roman times. Monday is market day in this peaceful country town. It is a good walking base, with many pleasant routes along the banks of the Wye (with its charming 14th and 15th century bridges) and along the River Derwent, the longest river in the Peak District. The cruciform church, dating back to the 12th century, is well worth a visit, as are **Castle Hill** and **Stanton Deer Park** on Stanton Moor. A Bronze Age Stone Circle (the Nine ladies)

stands on the moor.

Chatsworth, the so-called palace of the Peak District, is the home of the Dukes of Devonshire. Famous the world over for its State Apartments and its great art collection, it was built in the late 17th century and lies on the main Matlock to Sheffield road, B6012, 8 miles north of Matlock. The Palace and Farmyard are open to the public. In the early 19th century, the sixth Duke built a model village at **Edensor**, planned and designed by the designer of the original Crystal Palace.

Haddon Hall, on the banks of the River Wye just off the A6, is England's finest example of a medieval manor house. With a history going back before the Norman Conquest, it has been in the possession of just four families in all that time. It is a picturesque array of towers, turrets and battlements walls.

The Bakewell tart is said to have originated as the result of a cooking mistake at **The Rutland Arms**, now a hotel that still bakes the tarts freshly every day.

How to Get There

By car, A6 from Manchester to Matlock or B6012 Sheffield to Matlock, then A6 to Bakewell. Nearest BR station Matlock, with good bus connections from Matlock to Bakewell.

The Bakewell Walk

A long (about 6 miles), scenic walk across some beautiful Derbyshire countryside, taking in Chatsworth House. Unlikely to be very muddy, but the walk involves quite a lot of climbing.

Start on the main road in Bakewell leading to the bridge crossing the River Wye from the north-east bank. Walk along Station Road, noting the disused railway buildings on your left just before the bridge, continue up Castle Hill until you reach a black and white house on your left. Turn right onto the footpath. The footpath carries you up steeply through trees towards Balcross Farm, passing through an old wooden gateway. Emerging onto the road you will see the farmhouse before you.

Turn right at the farmhouse and follow the road over the brow of a hill. The path is now lined by stone walls, with New Piece Wood to your right. Leaving the woods behind you reach a fork in the road; bear right, onto a path labelled 'Unsuitable for motors'. The path descends gradually; after a while it offers a fine view down onto the village of Edensor, with its wonderful gardens and unique chimney stacks, and

▶

Queen's Arms Hotel, Bakewell

About the Inn: Homely and strong on atmosphere, the inn is popular with local people. Open fires, walls covered in brasses and a tap room for games playing add to the character. One double room for bed and breakfast. Darts, cards and dominoes; Background music and a piano for anyone who cares to try his or her hand. Children welcomed.

Beers and Food: Mansfield Bitter and Mild, Marksman lager, draught Guinness. Food ranges from simple bar snacks and usual hot and cold pub dishes, to inexpensive full meals in the separate restaurant (drinks can be taken through). Special Sunday lunch for £ 2.50.

the steeple of St Peter's Church dominating the skyline.

Walk into and through Edensor, keeping to the left, and through a large white gate. The main road is now in front of you. Directly opposite is Chatsworth Park. A bench seat surrounding a tree marks the route over the hill towards Chatsworth house. Take the path over the hill and down, crossing the River Derwent by the footbridge and then climb to the left of the house and towards Chatsworth farmyard. Fork right just as you reach the farmyard, keep to the path crossing many streams and negotiating' a stile. About a half mile along this path a man-made waterfall appears suddenly through the trees to your left. Follow a narrow track (avoiding any private land) through a series of sharp uphill bends, until you reach a crossroads just before Park Farm. Turn right.

Keeping to the left on this new path, cross a small stream and then over a gate. Beside the gate, wooden steps carved into the wall take you over onto a narrow track. Follow this for about 50 yards, then look down to your right. You will see a meandering track crossing the field below you. Take this track, cross through the field over a solid wooden gate and head towards farm buildings in front of you. At the buildings turn right onto the road that takes you down to Beeley Lodge. Turn right at the lodge onto a B road, keeping to this until you re-cross the Derwent, with the weir upstream to your right. Follow the road as it bears right until you reach a car park on your left.

Walk through the car park, following the path for nearly a mile past some farmhouses at Calton Lees until your reach a crossroads. Walk straight across, through the gate to your left (*not* the one marked 'Private') and follow this path alongside a stream and a stone wall all the way to Calton Houses. Passing through two gates by the houses, turn left and follow a stone wall until it comes to an end. When you are abruptly stopped by a fence across your path take the stile on your right, cross the grazing field (the sheep seem very tame) with New Piece Wood about 300 yards away to your right.

Walk left around a large pond and cross the fence by a stile. Stop! Over to your left you will see a wood. Head towards this until you reach a stone wall bordering the wood. Turn right at the wall and follow it along until you reach some wooden steps that climb over the wall. Use these, being prepared for a steep descent through the woods. The path through the woods is not clearly defined, but keep descending until you emerge onto a golf course. Take care (and keep your head down) as you break cover onto the course as you are liable to be standing in direct line of the golfers' fire! Leave the golf course by the disused railway bridge and follow the path down to the main road.

At the main road turn right, back towards the bridge into Bakewell. **The Queen's Arms Hotel** is in Bridge Street on your left. Enthusiastically run by landlord Derrick Pye, this cosy olde worlde inn is a favourite with locals, offers a good selection of inexpensive meals and pub grub and a tap room for the games crazy.

The North

The north is a highly diversified region, with a rich variety of life beneath its gritty surface. For up north the landscape can be uncompromisingly tough; from the vast expanses of wild moorland in North Yorkshire to the gaunt contours of Northumberland and Durham.

The sheltered Yorkshire dales, with their meandering rivers, and the prosperous farming country of the central plains, perhaps seem more obviously suited to exploring by foot. Cumbria and the Lakes really needs no further introduction, except to say that they can be best appreciated off-season.

This area contains a wealth of historic buildings and antiquities, such as the dramatic ruins of Riveaulx, the serene early Christian monastery on Holy Island, and the romantic mansion of Cragside at Rothbury in Northumberland.

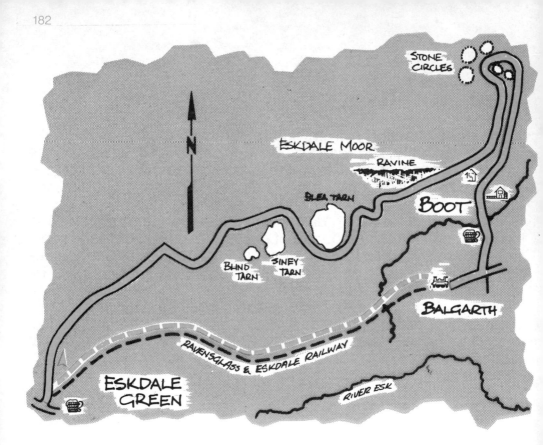

5a Boot

The District

At the end of the 18th century, touring the Lake District was the most popular summer excursion in the kingdom and today, two hundred years later, the area is still recognized as a mecca for town-dwellers and holiday-makers seeking to get away from it all, amongst some of the most beautiful countryside Britain has to offer. The Eskdale to Boot walk explores one of the loveliest Lakeland valleys, yet one that is comparatively unknown because it is cut off from other parts of the National Park by the Cumbrian fells which are the highest peaks in England.

The vale of **Eskdale** boasts some of the most dramatic and varied scenery in the region, with steep fells and fertile farmland sweeping down to fine sandy beaches against the Irish Sea. It can be reached either by the Ravenglass and Eskdale Railway (known as 'T'laal Ratty' to Cumbrians), a tiny 15-inch gauge train, or by car through Hardknot Pass, the most difficult motoring road in the Lake District. The pass is guarded by **Hardknot Castle**, one of the most spectacularly sited Roman forts in Britain and offering wonderful views of the valley and across to the Isle of Man on a clear day.

The small village of **Boot**, at the eastern end of the walk, is close to **Wastwater** and boasts an historic corn mill which has recently been restored to working order. Just beyond the village on the railway line is **Muncaster Castle**, which — though still lived in by the Pennington family (its owners for 700 years) — is open to the public and contains superb antique furniture, portraits and tapestries. Its gardens are famed throughout Europe and offer many attractions for younger members of the family.

The Rivers Esk and Mite are popular fishing grounds.

How to Get There

By car, M6 from Carlisle or Lancaster, to junction 36. Take A591, then left on A590 coastal road. Turn onto A5092 at Greenodd, then follow A595 coastal road to Ravenglass. By train, to Ravenglass station. Then take the Ravenglass and Eskdale miniature railway to Eskdale Green.

The Eskdale Green / Boot Walk

One of the most spectacular and enjoyable walks in this book, though fairly strenuous in places. The walk is *not* circular, but deliberately includes a journey back through the vale of Eskdale on the miniature railway from Boot. About 6 miles long (allow 3 hours).

Having caught the miniature railway from the sands of Ravenglass to Eskdale Green, a hearty and leisurely lunch at **the King George IV Inn** is in order before setting off, as all intrepid explorers must. For those intrepid explorers that are likely to get lost trying to find the pub, it is about 300 yards along the main road from the station. Back on the main road after imbibing, retrace your steps past enclosed conifers until you reach a signposted track directing you to Esk Moor and Wastwater. Follow the track over a bridge spanning the railway line, turning left onto a lane leading to three cottages.

Just before these cottages the track turns at right angles through two kissing gates and towards a gate which leads onto a well-defined path. Take this path up the

The Inns

King George IV Inn, Eskdale

About the Inn: Located at the junction of the roads from Eskdale Green to Broughton and to Hardknot Pass, the inn dates from the 15th century, though a building has been on the site since Roman times, as an old Roman well in the cellar bears witness. A typical old Lakeland cottage, with an interior of exposed black beams, flagged floors and an open fire, The George IV has a cosy atmosphere. Small shrub garden. Darts, pool and dominoes. Children welcomed.

Beers and Food: McEwan's Draught Ale hand drawn from the barrel and McEwan's Bright Beer. Well over 100 brands of whisky (seeing is believing!) on sale. An impressive range of nourishing pub grub, including plaice, scampi, veal chicken, venison and beef Strogonoff served with chips or rice.

Burnmoor Inn, Boot

About the Inn: Centrally located in Boot (a past winner of the 'best-kept village' contest) The Burnmoor Inn is about 340 years old. Indeed the cherry tree that stands outside is equally antique. A homely pub, where there is always a fire going (to burn more wood!) and a warm welcome extended to the weary fell-walker.

side of a hill, past ferns and granite stone on your left. As you near the top of the hill you pass a derelict cottage, then a fence which can be crossed over a stile on the right-hand side. The summit tends to resemble a bog, so try to skirt round it down the other side of hill toward Blind and Siney Tarn. Passing the northerly side of Siney Tarn, with its rushes and black-beaked gulls, turn left towards Blea Tarn, a tranquil water set in the mountains. From here you can let the kids jog down a charming hairpin green track taking them down 800 feet into the valley... and, of course, jog up again while you do something more civilised, like take a rest.

Continuing along the ravine beside Blea Tarn, you pass an old wall here, and about a half mile further, a group of derelict cottages and Blea Tarn Hill. The route leads you onto an old blue and pink granite track, which peters out into an indistinct (though still recognizable) path leading to the stone circles on the wider plateau of Esk Moor. To the left of this path the area is very marshy, with a Forestry Commission forest and an unbroken wall skirting the top ridge of the moor. To the north-east, the towering mountains of Scafell, Scafell Pike and Esk Pike — popular climbing venues — dominate the horizon.

Retracing your steps towards the derelict cottages, pass through a gate beside the last cottage on the right, and descend a rough track to a gate about 700 feet below at the entrance to Boot village. As you enter the village you will pass the corn mill on your left. Cross the bridge spanning Whillan Beck and walk on towards **The Burnmoor Inn**. After refreshments, and when feeling returns to those aching calves, catch the miniature railway back to Ravenglass.

Beers and Food: A free house serving a wide range of beers and bottled lagers. This pub does not serve food, so its a good idea to stock up at the King George IV.

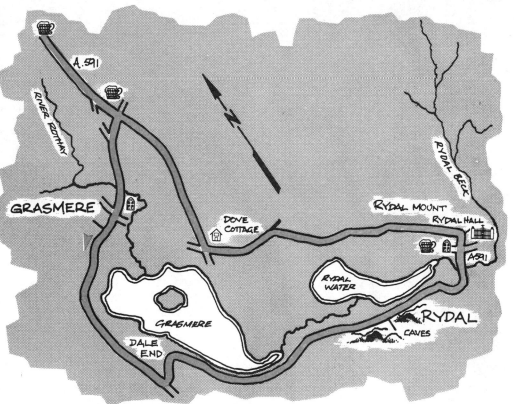

5b   Grasmere

The District

These are the fells, lakes and wooded dales that stimulated William Wordsworth's poetic genius.

Grasmere village is set back from the lake in the leafy valley of the Rothay. The lake itself has to approached on foot and the best views are from **Loughrigg Terrace** on the southern side. **St Oswald's Church** was attended by Wordsworth and his family and their gravestones lie in the yard, shaded by yew trees. The oldest part of the church dates back to the 13th century, but extensive alterations have left it something of an architectural hotch-potch. **Dove Cottage** at the east end of Grasmere is testimony to the poet's humble beginnings and its homely interior with many of the original furnishings intact, can be visited today. (Open daily in summer between 10 - 1 and 2 - 4.30. Closed mid January - 1 March).

Silvery, reedy **Rydal Water**, esconsed between the Crags of Nab Scar and Loughrigg Fell, is one of the most beautiful lakes. At the eastern end is **Wordsworth's Seat**, a tree-covered knoll on which the bard spent many an hour in peaceful contemplation. **Rydal village**, comprised of a church and a clutch of houses, is where Wordsworth retired to, having completed most of this best work. Stylish **Rydal Mount**, surrounded by flowering shrubs, was the family's last home, and is open to the public from April to December (except Mondays).

Dora's Field, through St Marys Churchyard at Rydal, given by Wordsworth

▶

to his daughter, is best seen in Spring, when covered by 'a host of golden daffodils'.

How to Get There

By road, Grasmere is 30 miles from the M6, exit at junction 36 and take the A591 into Grasmere. By rail to Windermere station (on a direct line from Euston) and then bus to Grasmere.

The Grasmere / Rydal Walk

This is an easy walk of about 6 miles along well-defined paths, or minor roads, through an area rich in birdlife (warblers, sparrowhawks, wagtails and tawny owls) and interesting vegetation (oak, beech, silver birch, wood garlic, bluebells and foxglove). Those with microscopic vision may be able to make out tiny snails and leeches wriggling in the lakes, along with the more conspicuous perch and pike.

Became part of the in(n) - crowd and start at **The Swan Hotel**, for as Wordsworth remarked in his poem *The Waggoner*... 'Who does not know the famous Swan.' A long white-washed building, this inn has weathered many alterations over the years,

which accounts for the endearing irregularity of its interior.

After sampling the Tetley's ale, cross the A591 and turn off down the road to your right, which leads to a T-junction. Turn left and walk down the road into Grasmere, heading for the church of St Oswald.

In earlier times the church used to have an earthen floor which had to be covered with reeds from Grasmere lake; a tradition still remembered today by an annual procession of villagers, headed by a brass band and bearing rush-woven emblems.

Members of the party who are not wild about the ecclesiastical wonders of this world, should sidle off to the gingerbread shop, on the north-west side of the church, to buy some of the exquisite slabs of gingerbread.

Before it gets dark, you should set out on the Conniston Road, walking southwards along the west side of Grasmere Lake. Ignore a sign indicating a footpath to Loughrigg Fell, and follow the lake-side path for about a mile. At Dale End, a sign points you in the direction of the water's edge, and you should follow this, over a stile. At the end of the lake there is a bridge and here you climb the slope to a bench, and proceed along the well-defined track in the direction of Rydal. Follow the path to the end of the lake and, when the main path swings away from the lake, fork left downhill through trees. Cross over the footbridge and turn left along the main road (A591) for the Glen Rothay, a busy and plush hotel.

Retrace your steps to the A591 and walk

up the road leading into Rydal, passing Dora's Field and the church to Rydal Mount. Just beyond the house, a path to the left takes you through the gardens and onto a signposted path. Pass through a series of gates and, after about a mile, the track joins a tarmac lane; leading to Dove Cottage. Continue to the main road and walk north to **The Swan Hotel,** and hence the start of the walk.

The Swan Hotel, Grasmere

About the Inn: This ancient 17th century coaching inn was a favourite haunt of many of the Lake Poets and Authors. Indeed there is even an armchair, vaguely resembling a rocking chair, yet without the rockers, which is said to have been frequently graced with Wordsworth's be- hind — and which nowadays occupies pride of place in the bar. The higgledy- piggledy interior, with its low oak beamed ceilings and inglenook fireplace, adds a homely touch to this historic tavern; the present landlord having done much to make this a warm and friendly place to visit. There are 31 bedrooms, many of which offer beautiful views over the fells.

Beers and Food: A well-stocked bar serv- ing, amongst others, Tetley's draught and Scottish and Newcastle bitter. A wide range of wholesome bar snacks, featuring such regional delicacies as home-made pies and pasties, Cumberland sausages and Wes- tmorland tattie-pot. If you are feeling parti- cuarly flash, try out some of the delicious traditional dishes available in the separate restaurant.

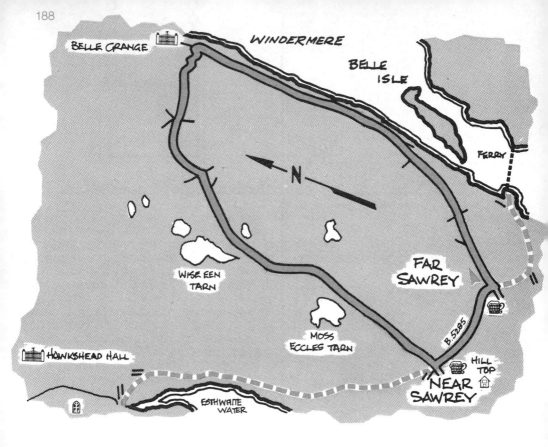

5c   Far Sawrey

The District

The Lake District in Cumbria may well be justified in boasting the best walks and scenery in England, and our third walk in the area (**Boot, qv**) is across tranquil countryside hugging Lake Windermere — the scene, together with nearby Coniston Water, of many a dramatic attempt on the world water speed record. The county claims 180 fells (ground over 750 feet above sea level), 15 lakes, ancient settlements, prehistoric stone circles, and a wide range of sporting facilities to match.

Ambleside, an historic and picturesque village north of Windermere, is probably the best base for an extended stay in the area. It is the centre of the local bus service (nicknamed 'Ribble'), which fans out in five directions throughout the Lake District, and the 'Mountain Goat' minibus which services the more inaccessible parts of the District. Ambleside offers many fine inns, including **The Golden Rule,** off the A591 at the northern end of the town, **The Unicorn,** over the bridge beside the mill, and **The Waterhead** on the quayside.

The area is still comparatively unspoilt and uncommercialised; rich in animal and plant life, it is home to wild fell ponies, red deer, buzzards, ravens, kestrels and peregrines, and a multitude of freshwater fish. Aficionados of the Lake District find the early Spring and Autumn the most rewarding times of year; Nature is at its most fascinatingly unpredictable, and the people — unharried by the droves of summer tourists — most friendly. There are a number of good Youth Hostels in the area.

How to Get There

By car, from Carlisle M6 to Exit 37, A684 to Kendal and A591 to Windermere. From Ambleside, A591 to Windermere. By public transport, train to Ambleside, then 'Ribble' bus to Windermere (Bowness Pier).

The Far and Near Sawrey (Lake Windermere) Walk

A moderate, though long lakeland walk (about 10 miles in all) which will take a good half day. Many delightful, secluded picnic spots en route, so stock up in Windermere before you set off. Features a journey by ferry across the lake. Waterproofs, sturdy walking boots and a compass essential, particularly out of the summer season.

From Bowness Pier in Windermere, a ¾ mile quayside walk brings you to the ferry on the east side of the lake. The crossing is quick and cheap, taking you to the west side of the lake. Walk up to the main road (B5285), past Sawrey Church below you, to the left, then take a steep climb to Far Sawrey. **The Sawrey Hotel**, a sunny 18th century coaching hostelry, is just on the right of the road. A fine building, a friendly landlord and a large garden make this a delightful spot to stock up with a home-cooked lunch and a glass of Theakston's Old Peculier.

Turning right out of the pub, then sharp left, a track leads along and above the hotel, through two gates and past a coppice of ash. The path leads diagonally downhill towards Windermere, then merges with a track along the western shore. Walking along the shoreline to the north, you pass a caravan site and eventually reach Belle Grange (marked by a tree with a circular seat). A signpost points out a path leading uphill to the west, with the Grange a little to the left. Climb the uphill path, which is fairly steep and rough,

The Inns

Sawrey Hotel, Far Sawrey

About the Inn: An early 18th century coaching inn a mile from the Windermere ferry, this delightful country hotel offers two oak-beamed bars and is the perfect overnight base for an extended visit. Comfortable but inexpensive accommodation (about £8 including dinner) and a friendly atmosphere created by landlord David Brayshaw make it hard to actually strap on the boots and head for the hills. A garden and bankside welcomes children. Darts; no music.

Beers and Food: Theakston's Best Bitter, 'Old Peculier' and Mild handpumped from the wood. Draught Guinness, Scotch Bitter, Tartan, Export and Stone's Bitters and a variety of lagers. Range of bar snacks, hot home-prepared lunches and table d'hôte dinners in the separate restaurant.

Tower Bank Arms, Near Sawrey

About the Inn: Nestled in a hollow beneath Hill Top, the much-visited home of Beatrix Potter, this small but cosy inn has an open-beamed, flagstoned interior. Popular with villagers, liable to get a little crowded in summer thanks to the influx of visitors to the cottage.

through a strongly-scented pine forest to a major junction. Take the left-hand fork up and over another well-used track and through Forestry Commission land. The path leads out into a clearing beside Wise Een Tarn and then descends gradually for over a mile towards Moss Eccles Tarn.

Just beyond Moss Eccles Tarn a three-way fork offers a path to the right towards Near Sawrey. The path leads right into the village and **The Tower Bank Arms,** a small, cosy inn beneath Hill Top, the one-time home of Beatrix Potter and the most visited cottage in England. Hill Top is closed to the public on Fridays.

Following the main road (B5285) leads you back to Far Sawrey and the Windermere ferry. Gluttons for further punishment can take a 4-mile detour towards the charming village of Hawkshead beside Esthwaite Water; the market village where Wordsworth went to school (the blighter even carved his name on a desk at the Grammar School which has become a museum). Take the road north-west out of Near Sawrey along Esthwaite Water.

Beers and Food: Hartleys XB and Bitter on draught. A wide range of bar snacks and simple, but wholesome home-prepared hot grub.

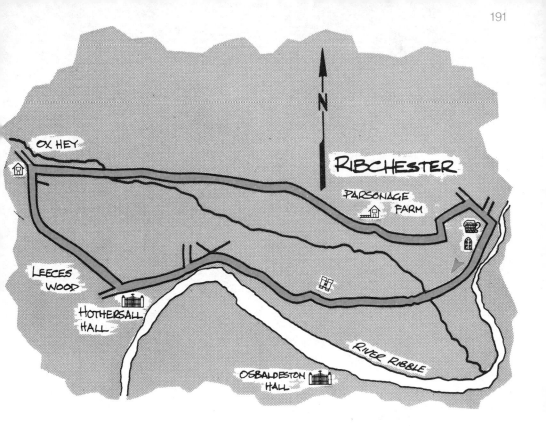

5d Ribchester

The District

Ribchester is a small, quiet Lancashire village, as yet unspoilt by tourism. It lies next to the **River Ribble**, in a circle of green hills which overlook meadows and woodland.

Listed in the Domesday Book, Ribchester's main claim to fame is that it used to be a fortified Roman encampment. The camp, known as **Bremetennacum**, was built by Agricola around 80 AD, to ward off hooligans from the neighbouring counties, as well as the odd aggressor who happened to stray over from Ireland. Nowadays there is a museum on the site which houses most of the Roman antiquities discovered throughout the years; including pottery, coins, a game of discus and the replica of a stone head thought to have been employed in some sinister form of idol worship.

A large portion of the camp lies under the **Church of St Wilfred**, dating from the thirteenth century. Indeed the two pillars which prop up the church's organ loft are believed to have been pilfered from the Roman site.

How to Get There

By car, turn off the M6 motorway at junction 31 (east of Preston). Take the A59 west towards Whalley and then turn left onto the B6245 for Ribchester. By rail to Blackburn station, and then bus to Ribchester from outside the New Hotel.

►

The Ribchester Walk

This is a relatively easy walk of about 6 miles, which includes some fine views of the River Ribble. For much of the early part of the walk you are actually walking over the site of the old Roman camp, as it used to cover an area of about six acres.

The bus from Blackburn stops right outside The Black Bull Inn. As this pub is closed at lunchtime, it seems only sensible to suggest that you make a swift left turn into Church Street and head for **The White Bull Inn**, which is on your left (past the Co-op to your right). This is an excellent pub, which has four Doric pillars on its front porch, believed to have been taken from the 'Temple of Minerva' on the Roman site. There is also the unusual sight of a large wooden carving of a white bull projecting over the porch, which serves as the inn's sign.

After visiting the pub keep walking down Church Street, passing Ribchester Museum and the church of St Wilfred to your right. A public bridlepath is indicated through a farmyard, follow this and you should see the River Ribble bending away sharply to the left. Continue along the track, passing under pylons and crossing over a stream which flows south into the Ribble. As you pass by a farmhouse (with green windows) on your right, there is a good view of the impressive-looking Osbaldeston Hall, with a driveway rising up steeply behind it.

Cross over a second stream and go through the first of a succession of three gates/stiles. The River Ribble is again clearly visible to your left. Pass through the second gate (or over the second stile, depending on how much your little tipple at lunchtime has taken out of you) and you will notice that the path now starts to climb slightly as it reaches the third gate at the edge of a small wood. After passing through the third gate, carry straight on up through the wood. The path goes off to the left and right here, so be careful to stick to the main track.

Carry on through the wood until you come to a clearing. From here, looking due south, there is a lovely view of the river as it sweeps round from left to right; with Osbaldeston Hall to the left and Hothersall Hall to the right.

Descend in the direction of Hothersall Hall, rejoining the track as it comes down from the right. Walk through the grounds of Hothersall Hall, following the driveway as it bends round to the right. At the top of this driveway turn sharp right through an iron gate and follow the well-defined track as it bends round to the left, then right. This track is used by farm vehicles, so please do not get mistaken for an errant haystack.

Eventually this track leads on to a field and here you should strike straight across the field, making for a large wooden gate with its accompanying iron kissing gate on the far side. Once through this, head for the top right-hand corner of the field, and follow the wide path, bordered on either side by tall hedgerows, which leads towards Ox Hey. At the end of this path do not turn immediately right (on account of a Barbara Woodhouse-trained farmdog — of which there are many on this walk) but take the next right across a field. Incidentally, you should see a signpost to this effect, but we would rather not guarantee it.

Follow closely a stream to your left for

about a quarter of a mile, before crossing over it, so that it is now, in fact, to your right. (Elementary dear reader!) The path now climbs slightly towards a pleasant copse with a small pond, leaving the stream to the right.

In the distance, in a south-easterly direction, you should now be able to make out the Church of St Wilfred. However, whether you can see it or not you should head off in this direction until, down to your right the buildings of Parsonage Farm hove into view. Turn down to the right towards the house on the left (otherwise you will yet again have to contend with a ferocious guard dog) and from here follow the road back into Ribchester.

The Inn

The White Bull Hotel, Ribchester

About the Inn: The evidence suggests that this inn, which was renovated in 1707, could have played host to the soldiers stationed at Bremetennacum; as there is an old mounting block out front and the remains of a Roman bath house to the rear. The pottery on display in the lounge bar was excavated from the back garden of the pub itself. The historical atmosphere is enhanced by the friendliness of landlord David Best and his wife Glynis. A large open fireplace, a beer garden with clear views over the Ribble valley and nearby Pendle Hill, and a separate restaurant dependent upon the fresh vegetables, salad stuffs and herbs grown in the garden; supplement this pub's attractions.

Beers and Food: The pub has real ale, Whitbread's Special Cask, on hand pump; plus draught Guinness, Trophy bitter and Whitbread's Best Mild. No convenience foods are ever found in The White Bull, the landlord being a firm believer in fresh home-made fare. Hot lunches are served daily, plus high teas on Sundays and a special, usually French provencale style meal is served monthly.

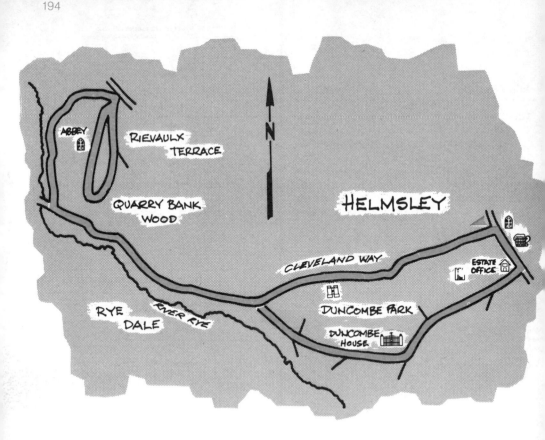

5e Helmsley

The District

Helmsley lies in a hollow of the River Rye and is a gateway to Ryedale and the North Yorkshire Moors. This part of Yorkshire was, at one time, one huge forest; which is hard to believe when you see the compact plantations of conifer and hardwood surrounding the town today.

It was a man called Helm who actually cut down many of the trees, and from 'Helm's clearing' the little market town of Helmsley sprang up. Market day, each Friday, is definitely the time to make your visit, as the pubs open early (around 10.00) and remain open throughout the day, until 11.00 at night.

Information about the historic sites in and around Helmsley will probably now slide like water off a duck's back, but neverthe-less there is much of historical and architectural interest here.

Helmsley Castle was largely dismantled after Charles I's forces were beseiged here in 1644, but it is possible to walk around the ramparts and admire the imposing keep. The castle remains are at the eastern end of the **Duncombe Park Estate;** which consists of a young plantation of beech mixed with larches, believed to be over 150 years old. The classical building itself is now a private girls' school, only the grounds of which are open to the public (during the summer months).

Rievaulx Abbey, 3 miles north-west of Helmsley, was the first large Cistercian monastery to be established in England; the isolated location being granted to a group of twelve monks in 1131. Henry VIII dissolved the monasteries in 1539 and the abbey was surrendered to the crown. There are considerable remains of both the lofty church and the monks' domestic quarters, which are best seen from **Rievaulx Terrace**, or at the top of the neighbouring hillside. This long, curving grass terrace, with its classical temples, was laid out in the 18th century and a series of vistas, cut through the trees, provide views which have entranced the visitor since Wordsworth and Turner first came here.

How to Get There
The nearest railway station is at Pickering, which is the southern terminus of the North Yorkshire Moors railway line. The northern terminus of the line is at Grosmont, where there are connections to Middlesbrough and Whitby, both served by British Rail. The 128 bus from the United Bus depot in Pickering, takes you to Helmsley, and drops you off directly outside The Feathers Hotel in the market square.

The Helmsley Walk
This walk is not for the faint-hearted, as it covers a fair amount of mileage to include the dramatic ruins of Rievaulx. However the walk is along clearly-defined paths, including the early stages of the Cleveland Way; and incorporates some fine valley and woodland scenery.

Turn left outside The Feathers Hotel, facing the market cross, and walk down the road for approximately 100 yards, to a right-hand turning. On the corner of this turning is the Duncombe Park Estate Office, where you have to obtain a visitor's permit to enter Duncombe Park.

Leave the estate office and follow the road round to the right, doubling back on your original course. This road, Castlegate, follows the course of a small stream in a deep gulley. On your left, as you follow the road, is the entrance to the castle and just beyond, on the other side of the road, is the church. Just beyond the church and next to The Feversham Arms Hotel is a footpath leading off to the left, and marked 'The Cleveland Way'.

Follow this track, noting the excellent views it gives of the castle. The track reaches the brow of a hill and the stone wall to your right disappears. Proceed along the well-defined route, across two fields to a

The Inn

The Feathers Hotel, Helmsley

About the Inn: Fronting onto Helmsley market place with the picturesque outlines of the ruined castle as a backdrop, **The Feathers Hotel** could not be more centrally or pleasantly located. The hotel has two bars, the Feversham lounge and the 15th century Pickwick bar; both have oak beamed ceilings and wooden panelling and are furnished throughout with the local Thompson wooden furniture.

Beers and Food: The bars serve a wide range of beer including Theakston's Old Peculier, Camerons, Youngers and Stones, all on pressure pumps. Sandwiches, hamburgers, soup, steak and grills are available at the bar. The restaurant is open to non-residents and offers a wide choice of traditional and Yorkshire fare, including excellent roast topside of beef with Yorkshire pudding.

▶

stile, when you turn sharp left and then right, following the edge of the field. There is a fence to your left and beyond is a steepsided valley of scrub and pine. Look out for a gate in the wall to your left and follow the path across the valley to another gate. Continue along the path, to the left of the wall until you come to a small house. Skirt the grounds to the left and continue over a stile into a field leading into Whinny Bank Wood.

There is a well-defined path through the trees, downhill leading, eventually, onto the road in Rievaulx. At the road turn left and walk along, turning sharply to the right by an old stone bridge, where the abbey ruins suddenly hove into view.

Continue along the road which follows the course of a river, to Rievaulx, and after viewing the ruins, turn right and continue up the road, your original approach route. Pass through the village and up to the main road where, at the junction with the Helmsley road, you will see a driveway off to the right, from where there are excellent views of the terraces.

However, retrace your steps to the road and walk back through the village, to the right-hand turn along Cleveland Way, through Whinny Bank Wood. Just beyond the small house, your original landmark; a beaten path leads off to the right, which, after about 100 yards, becomes a concrete road. Stay on this road through woodland until, on passing over a cattle grid, the woods open out into fields. In the distance to your left you will see Duncombe House. Continue down in direction of the house, to a T-junction and turn left along the road, passing in front of the house. The road bears right, passing through the railings and cattle grids, giving fine views of the temple on the hill above, as well as the whole length of Helmsley castle.

Continue into Helmsley, passing the Park Estate Office, and turning left for **The Feathers Hotel.**

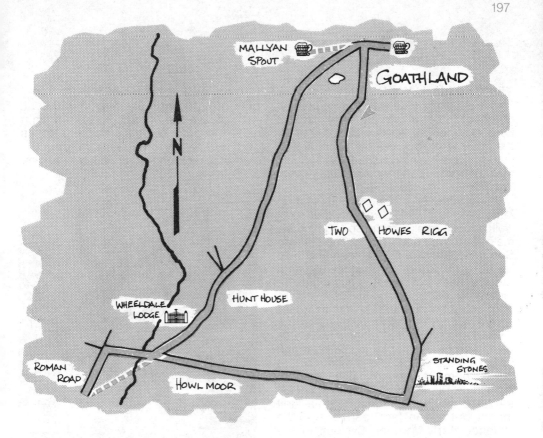

5f Goathland

The District

Goathland is a beautiful village situated high up on the North York Moors, about nine miles from Whitby, which has Viking origins, although most of the remaining buildings are comparatively modern. Unattended black face sheep graze on the village green and the Plough Stots sword dancers perform special traditional dances on certain days of the year.

Just outside the village to the south stands **Abbot House**. Here a priest established a hermitage in the 12th century to which pilgrims would often pass through the village. There are no fewer than nine waterfalls in the Goathland area, of which **Mallyan Spout** is the biggest and most well known.

George Stephenson's famous railway which passes over these moors was acquired by a preservation society in 1965. Train spotters can delight in the old steam locomotives and rolling stock that now journey regularly between Grosmont, Goathland and Pickering.

How to Get There

By car, take the A169 from Pickering and turn left just after Eller Beck bridge onto a minor road. Then turn right at the T-junction into Goathland. By train from Whitby via Grosmont on the North York Moors Historical Railway. Bus no 92 from Whitby.

The Goathland Walk

This is definitely not a walk to take granny, grandad and two-year old baby Jim on. Even experienced walkers should stay off the moor when the weather is bad for, in places, there are no landmarks and should the mist come down it would be easy to get lost. It is long — about 5-6 miles.

If you come by car or bus then start at Mallyan Spout. Those coming by train must walk about a mile up to the Spout along the main road. We commence at **The Mallyan Spout Hotel** where the Southerner should be careful ordering 'Scotch' for he'll receive beer not whisky (but might be pleasantly surprised for all that...). Turn right out of the pub and up onto the grass where a sign indicates the way to the Roman Road. Take the higher of two tracks you'll see bearing away to the right and follow it up to the brow of the hill. Over to the left there is a mound in a direct line with Fylingdale Domes. These look as though they are waiting for some celestial golf match but are in fact, part of NATO's Defence Early Warning System. In the event of a nuclear attack they will give us fifteen minutes warning so we can all rush off and build that shelter we've always been meaning to get round to, bury our heads in the sand, have a last drink, or whatever.

Follow the track round past a small lake in a dell. At the brow of the hill it disappears and from here the markers are a number of small cairns (heaps of stone). You should be able to see two mounds: the Two Howes. These are prehistoric burial mounds, of which there are thousands in the area. From the first there is a track leading up to Simon Howe which can now be discerned on the skyline. Follow it up through short heather and after a while it becomes clearer. At the cairn there is a very clear track going off to the left towards Wheeldale. Take it, with the 'golf balls' now behind you.

This stretch is part of the Lyke Wake walk, a forty mile stroll inland to the coast which is traditionally supposed to be done in its entirety, between sunset and sunrise. Press on along the track thanking your lucky stars that you're not doing all of it!

Presently we come down a steep rocky path going down to the river. If you don't wish to see the Roman Road turn right here. If you do, cross the stepping stones and up the bank opposite, taking the diagonal track on the left which takes you to the road.

The Roman Road is about 15 feet wide. The original flat surface has long since eroded away, but the rough foundation stones are still clearly visible. Turn right along it until you come to a wall, turn right again here and follow the Lyke Wake route back to the stepping stones. Cross them and turn left. There is a clear path round Wheeldale Lodge to Hunt House. Just past the house there is a tractor trail which turns off up the hillside to the right. This will take you up to a cairn and, keeping this on your left, follow the rough path below the brow into a steep-sided gulley. After the gulley, walk past a vale on your right and follow below the brow of the hill, keeping parallel with the road below to your left. After a while Goathland becomes visible once more and the path leads easily back to Mallyan Spout.

Those desperate for refreshment will stop off at **The Mallyan Spout Hotel** once more. However, should the dedicated drinker walk but half a mile down the main road, he will find a sight for sore eyes: **The Goathland Hotel**. There, in the charming Rustic Bar (also known as the 'Gun room' after its fascinating collection of firearms) he can relax with Camerons real ales and a choice of no fewer than 40 malt whiskies! Abandon hope ye who attempt to sample all these!

The Inns

Mallyan Spout Hotel, Goathland

About the Inn: This charming ivy-clad mock Tudor inn has a comfortable half-panelled bar and an open fire where darts and dominoes can be played. Bed and breakfast for around £9 a head.

Beers and Food: Dryboroughs Scottish Ales. Best Scotch, Heavy and lager plus all normal pub drinks. Bar snacks at lunchtime. Full à la carte menu at lunch and dinner for around £6 a head.

Goathland Hotel, Goathland

About the Inn: Built in the early nineteenth century, the local hunt meets outside this inn. The Rustic Bar has a fascinating collection of antique firearms as well as many early 19th century prints of local scenes. There is a small lawn with garden tables for those who can't get enough fresh air. Darts and dominoes can be played. Bed and breakfast from around £9.50 a head.

Beers and Food: Camerons Strongarm, Best Bitter, Mild and lager. Their speciality is a 'staggering' array of just about every malt whisky you can think of. Even if you are not a connoisseur, it is worth sampling a few. Wide choice of bar snacks and full à la carte luncheons and dinners.

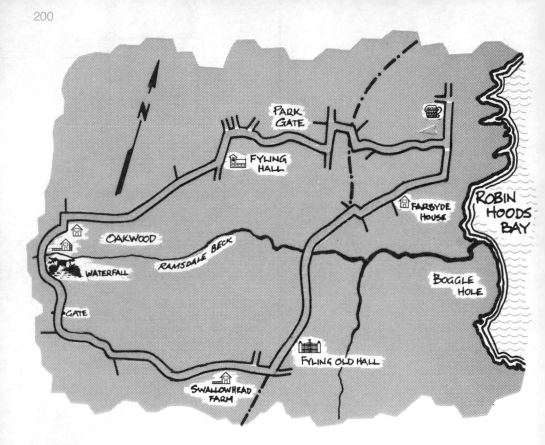

5g   Robin Hood's Bay

The District

Robin Hood's Bay — the village is perched precariously among the cliffs which sweep round from Ravenscar in the south to Ness Point in the north. It was here, you might catch a wry local telling a wide-eyed American tourist, that Robin Hood himself stood and fired an arrow the full length of the bay (some three miles, no mean feat, that...).

With its long history of smuggling and fishing, the old part of the village is a fascinating labryinth of narrow, winding alleys lined with houses of all shapes and sizes crammed into any available space. Sadly, before the sea wall was constructed in recent years, much of the village collapsed into the sea.

The bay itself is rich in fossils, and jet can be found washed up by the side (jewellery made from it can be bought locally) as well as a huge variety of seashells. Rocky ledges jut out into the sea, affording a natural habitat for all manner of seaweed and shellfish, and from where cormorants swoop and dive for fish.

How to Get There

By car, the A174 from Middlesbrough to Whitby, then A171 turning at High Hawster on to the B1447 down to the village. Train to Whitby from Middlesbrough or (for steam enthusiasts) from Pickering on the North Yorks Moors Railway, then a 93A or 93B bus (regular service) to Robin Hood's Bay.

The Robin Hood's Bay Walk

A moderately strenuous and quite long (about 6 miles) walk across moorland and along coast. The cliff tops are often muddy, so if it's been raining: be prepared.

The walk starts at **The Victoria Hotel**, where you can fortify yourself with a pint or two of Cameron's Strongarm and enjoy the excellent view from the beer garden before staggering down the steep hill into the village and on to the seafront. Ten yards before the ramp take the alley to the right marked 'To the cliffs'. Continue along it past the steps on the left to the track which runs through the wooded valley of Marna Dale Beck keeping to the right-hand side of the stream. At the top of the valley follow the path from the stile across two fields and go over the stone wall by the steps provided. The cinder-path is an old railway line converted. for walkers which we'll come across again later, but for now, turn right and go over some more steps twenty yards down on the left. (If you're sick of all these steps, don't worry. There aren't any more for a while).

Follow the path to the right past the lone oak tree and over yet more steps onto the road. Go left here and take the second turning on your right, up Middlethorpe Cresent to a rough path and then over a stile into open fields. Walk up the edge of the field with the hedge on your right, over another stile and bear away to your right. Go through the metal gate and follow the road left up the hill until you find a path on your left passing behind a row of cottages. There is a gate marked 'Public footpath'. Continue to the next gate and take a sharp right up some stone steps and then left to a gateway onto a tarmac road.

On your left there is Fyling High School, once a grand house but now overrun with screaming school children. As the road goes down past it, take the broad track to the right signposted 'Public footpath' up through the trees. Here and there you can sight Ravenscar and the Bay before the path cuts down into Oak Wood. After passing a small cottage the way winds down to the stone bridge over Ramsdale Beck, where there is an old mill and a waterfall. Follow the track over the bridge up through a gate and along the bridleway through another gate and into the woods again. The path is often muddy here and is well-used by horses. Emerging once more into open

Victoria Hotel, Robin Hood's Bay

About the Inn: Built in 1897 in Victorian Gothic style the landlord David Scrivener and his wife Wendy are both avid walkers who have drunk the length of the Pennine Way! The public bar has an open fire. Darts, dominoes and cards are played. Beer garden with a panoramic view. Accommodation for 17.

Beers and Food: Cameron's Strongarm and Best Bitter and a wide range of other drinks. The restaurant offers a four course meal for around £5 a head and there's an extensive bar menu too.

fields turn left at the cross-tracks and go through the gate into a field. Keeping the stone-wall to the right, go straight across and coming to another stone wall turn right across the next field, where the path becomes a lane. The lane turns left and opens into a field. Follow the track across this and down by the left of Swallow Head Farm picking up the farm road which runs between hedges down to an asphalt road.

Fifty yards to your right you will find Fyling Old Hall, a beautiful old 17th century house built by the Cholmleys of Whitby Abbey. Continue past the hall and then left on to the cinder track. This is the old railway-line we were on before. It used to run from Whitby to Scarborough before it disappeared along with so many of our rural railways in the fifties. Follow the track until it is eventually bridged by a tarmac road. Turn right down to a riding school. In front of the building there is a gate marked 'Public footpath' on the left which leads down to the cliff edge. Follow the cliffs back along towards the village where you will find the tops of the steps that you passed on leaving the village. Turn right at the bottom then left up the main road back to **The Victoria Hotel**.

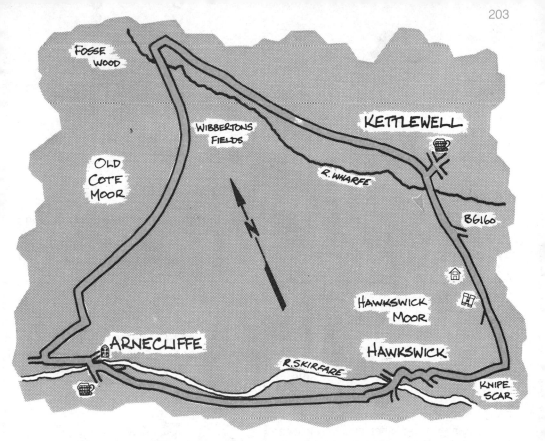

5h Kettlewell

The District

Kettlewell, one of the larger villages of Upper Wharfedale, occupies both banks of the Cam Beck. Its history dates back to Anglo-Saxon times when it was named after 'Ketel', an Irish-Norse chief. In Old Norse the name means 'bubbling spring'. By the eleventh century Kettlewell had a bubbling economy, thanks to its market and the reputation of its fairs. This prosperity came to an end with a great fire in the nearby forest during the reign of James I. Later a small textile industry flourished, but today's main source or revenue is derived from farming and the tourists who come here for the excellent fishing and the panoramic walks.

3 miles away in **Arncliffe**, just after the confluence of the River Skirfare and Cowside Beck, the river flows beneath a beautiful bow bridge and then past the churchyard. The church, though rebuilt during the sixteenth and eighteenth centuries, dates back to the eleventh century. Prior to this a wooden Saxon church occupied the site.

How to Get There

From Skipton there is a regular bus service to Kettlewell. By car, take the B6265 north from Skipton then turn left onto the B6160 for Kettlewell.

The Kettlewell Walk

With Old Cote Moor to the west and Great Whernside to the east, the walk takes you through some of the most beautiful

►

countryside in the Yorkshire Dales. But beauty does have its price and a certain amount of effort has to be put in to cope with some of the steeper ascents. Do not be deterred! If you start *inside* **The Bluebell Inn** you can fortify yourself with the appropriate beverages. From The Bluebell Hotel go over on the B6160 and cross a small humpbacked bridge, passing a car park on the right. Cross another bridge which goes over the River Wharfe, where the road bends round to the left.

After 200 yards take a right turn through a wooden gate and look for a narrower path going up through the trees. Soon you will reach a mossy stone wall, a common feature of the area. Go through the hole in the wall and leave the old stone cottage on your right as the path continues uphill. Behind you, in the distance you can see Great Whernside, an impressive peak rising to 2,310 ft. The path bends sharply to the right, then forks left across two sets of steps. Once again the path climbs steeply and at the top you will come to a wall. Follow the path across the steps and begin the descent on the other side of the scar. The path suddenly turns right and heads towards Hawkswick, a beautiful little village with traditional stone cottages. Keeping to the road, go through the village until you come to a footbridge over the River Skirfare. Once over the bridge turn sharp right and follow the footpath to Arncliffe. As you enter the village you pass the churchyard and turn left, away from the bridge, towards the village green and the beckoning portals of **The Falcon Inn.**

Head back to church and cross the bridge over the River Skirfare, following the road round to the left. After the farmhouses, take the bridleway on the right, which climbs steeply up Bradshaw scar. As you climb uphill the vegetation changes gradually from coarse pasture to heather. If you are lucky enough you may even see the residents of the numerous warrens!

At the crest you will come to a wall which you cross by some steps. The path begins to descend and you will soon see Kettlewell in the distance. The path then bends to the left and the way is clearly signposted to Starbottom. Before the footbridge, follow the footpath signposted Kettlewell.

Bluebell Hotel, Kettlewell

About the Inn: Built in 1680, this fine old inn has been transformed into a cosy, family-run hotel. With its open fire and Angus Rand paintings, the bar is tastefully and comfortably furnished.

Beers and Food: In the bar you can enjoy Younger's and Theakston's traditional ales pulled from hand-drawn pumps. The high-standard, home-cooked food is served from 7 pm and, in order to ensure a table, its a good idea to book. Alternatively, a wide selection of bar meals are available. Coffee is also served.

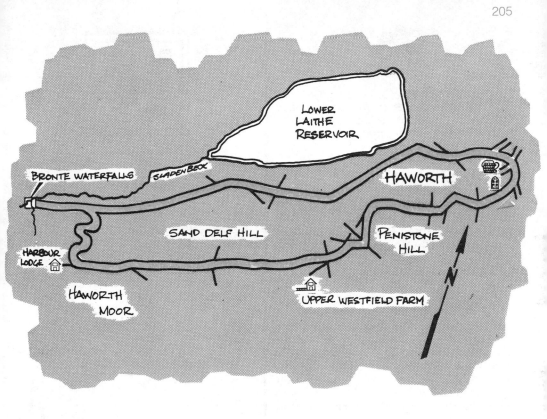

5i Haworth

The District

Haworth, 4 miles south-west of Keighley in the West Riding of Yorkshire, is best known as the home of the Brontes. With its grey-stone houses and slate roofs the town has changed little since the Brontes were in residence. The spinning and weaving industries are still carried on, but the town's main source of revenue is tourism. The steep climb up the cobblestone road of Main Street leads to the **Parsonage Museum** which houses a fine selection of 'Brontecana'. The church of St Michael and All Angels where the Reverend Patrick Bronte was incumbent has been extensively altered, but the Bronte family vault is still there, as are the Scots Pines planted by Charlotte Bronte.

The surrounding countryside is a decidedly bleak and windswept area which clearly influenced the haunting and impetuous books written by the Bronte sisters. Not surprisingly many of the areas of interest have been renamed to reflect the Bronte Association. The Waterfalls at Sladon Beck are now known as the **Bronte Falls**, while the large slab of stone where the Brontes rested during their walks on the moor is now called the 'Bronte Seal'.

For the non-literary minded the small railway museum near the station is a must for enthusiasts.

►

How to Get There

From Keighley, either by the Worth Valley Railway or by bus route 665. By road, the B6144 from Keighley then the B6142 to Haworth.

The Haworth Walk

This 6 mile walk across the hauntingly beautiful Haworth moor should not deter anyone who is aware that the Bronte girls used to walk a greater distance when they went on foot to Keighley for their shopping.

The walk begins at the Parsonage Museum and heads towards the church. A signpost to Haworth Moor takes you through the churchyard and out to Balcony Farm. At the farm turn right and follow this lane up to a minor road. Go straight across and take the path, bearing left, across the moorland. The path climbs steadily to the Penistone Hill triangulation pillar. To your left you can see a quarry from which the grey gritstone was obtained to build many of the houses in Haworth. Ahead, our route takes us to the far quarry. As you go towards the far quarry look for a path to your right which goes downhill towards Lower Laith reservoir. At the bottom of the hill bear left round the base of the hill. You will soon come to a car park on your left. Go through the car park to the Oxenhope-Stanbury road where you turn left. After 100 yards you come to some public conveniences, a welcome stop for those who have been sampling the local brews. Directly opposite is a private road which you take, to cross a cattle grid onto a stony road, which continues for about 1½ miles across Sand Delf Hill. Eventually you come to a farm house gate, turn right here and leave civilization behind as you take a narrow path which takes you towards the heart of Haworth Moor. The path crosses a small stream which is later recrossed by means of a plank. Keep on this path until you come to a track, turn left here and go up the gulley to the Bronte Waterfall. Retrace your steps after visiting the waterfalls and keep on this path all the way back to the Oxenhope-Stanbury road. Directly opposite is a metalled road which takes you straight back to Haworth's Main Street.

The Inn

The Fleece, Haworth

About the Inn: Situated at the beginning of the cobblestone section of Main Street, it is reputedly the oldest in Haworth having been built in about 1600.

The cosy front room, the old-style tap room, the oak-panelled main bar lounge and the games room provide a diverse atmosphere to satisfy most moods.

Beers and Food: A good selection of normal pub grub to be washed down by Timmy Taylor's excellent real ale.

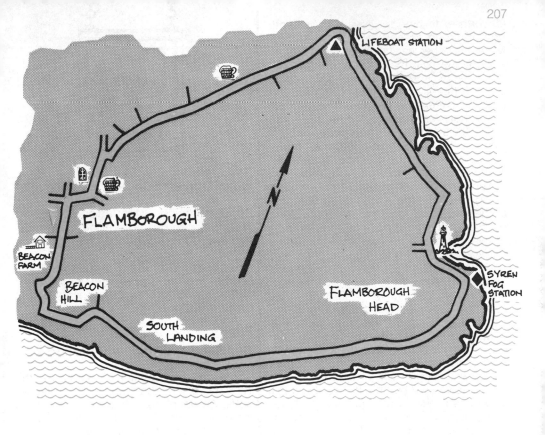

5j Flamborough

The District

Flamborough Head is an area steeped in history. It is divided from the mainland by an earthwork called **'Dane's Dyke'** which dates from the Stone Age. It was also one of the first landing-places of the Vikings who rushed ashore to sample the local brew, and because of this it is sometimes known as 'Little Denmark'.

Many sea-birds inhabit the headland: guillemots, puffins, kittiwakes and razorbills are particularly common. The cliffs in which they roost are riddled with caves, long used for smuggling.

The Head, 178 feet high, is the northernmost natural chalk formation in the British Isles.

How to Get There

By car B1255 from Bridlington (crossing over Dane's Dyke). Buses 83 and 183 go from Bridlington to Flamborough.

The Flamborough Walk

A longish walk (about 5 miles) which even a fairly mobile granny should be able to manage.

We begin at **The Royal Dog and Duck** in Flamborough High Street where the walk can get off to a fine start with a pint or two of excellent Bass or Stones real ale in this comfortable tavern. Turn left out of the pub (if you can still tell left from right), up Post Office Street and then go left along the Main Road till it joins the Bridlington Road and turn right. On the left here is the 13th century Parish Church at St Oswald which ▶

is worth examining for its superb fifteenth century rood screen. The poet Andrew Marvell's father was vicar here at one time.

Continue past the Church and turn left down West Street which will take you to Beacon Farm. Follow the Broad Way and bear right after a small copse. The footpath turns sharp left when you come to a fence and follows it to a stile. The kidney-shape of Beacon Hill stands to your left. Walk round the inside edge of the hill to a stile and then bear right to reach the cliff.

Turn left along the clearly-marked track along the cliff edge. Cross South Landing at the bridge and from here the path leads easily round the cliff edge for the next mile or two. From here until we leave the cliffs a huge variety of bird life can be observed, here and there in their hundreds, wheeling and diving below the cliffs. It is sometimes an awesome spectacle.

At the Syren fog station venture inland for a few hundred yards to skirt the lighthouse (92 feet high, it was built in 1806 without scaffolding!) If you continue up the road to the left there is a hexagonal chalk tower which was built as a lighthouse in 1673. As you will be able to see, it is a fair way off, so if you want to press on with the walk, continue round the far side of the lighthouse, and back to the cliffs on the track marked 'Public Footpath'.

From this stretch of the cliffs in 1779 the locals watched The Battle of Flamborough Head by moonlight. Paul Jones, an American pirate, recklessly attacked two warships escorting a merchant navy fleet to Hull. The story goes that at one point the English hauled down the Jolly Roger, believing Jones dead. To their embarrassment he reappeared very much alive, raised his Skull and Crossbones once more and went on to win the battle. However, shortly after the English surrendered, his boat sank! What better entertainment on a September eve in the 18th century?

Follow the cliff path to the Lifeboat Station. The road down to this continues back towards Flamborough. The left fork will bring you back to the High Street.

This time why not sample a refreshing draught of Camerons real ale in the rough and ready **Rose and Crown**. The landlord Harold Dobson is a real Yorkshire character — gruff but likeable — and his tavern is very atmospheric.

Royal Dog and Duck, Flamborough

About the Inn: A comfortable tavern about 100 years old. Beamed ceiling. Darts, pool and a yard with a sun rood.

Beers and Food: Both Stones Ales and Bass as well as a wide selection of wines and spirits. A good range of bar snacks at reasonable prices.

Rose and Crown, Flamborough

About the Inn: A genuine old ale-house, the interior is quaint and rough with half-timber walls. An open fire at the bar end forms a small snug. The landlord is a real character. Darts, dominoes and cribbage.

Beers and Food: Camerons Best Bitter, Strongarm, Mild and Lager. Many wines and spirits. Unfortunately — no food.

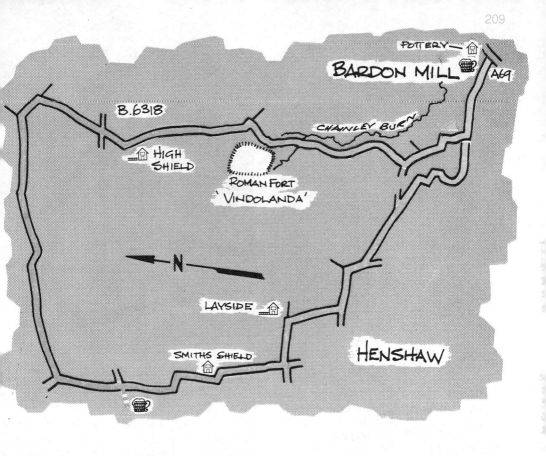

5k   Bardon Mill

The District

Bardon Mill is a small industrious village situated on the South Tyne. There is a small pottery here which sells a variety of different types of earthenware, including replicas of Roman pottery. All around this area is a profusion of Roman roads, forts, castles and supply depots, all built to service Hadrian's Wall, the impressive structure that once marked the northernmost extremity of Rome's far-reaching Empire. It was built between AD122-30 and was occupied till the end of the fourth century. It was often extensively damaged and built again after the attacks. Much of what is left was reconstructed in the 19th century, using the original stone.

To the north-east of the village on top of the wall lies **Housteads**, the most visited Roman site in Britain. It once housed a 1000 infantry, and is the most complete surviving fort in the country. It has a small museum and the latrines and granary are still surprisingly complete.

Just north of Bardon Mill is the fort of **Vindolanda** where much excavation is taking place and where the army, seemingly for want of anything better to do, have constructed a replica Roman fort.

How to Get There

By car, A69 from Newcastle. By train from Newcastle central station or bus no 685 from Marlborough Crescent bus station.

►

The Bardon Mill Walk

There are lots of ups and downs, especially along the Wall part, and less agile members of the family should perhaps be encouraged to stay at home.

The Bowes Hotel at Bardon Mill affords an appropriate starting place with its choice of five Newcastle beers and two lagers. If you can still walk after that lot, turn right out of the pub and right again up to the path just after the pottery. It veers left, and at the top of the field go over the stile. The path turns right and connects with a lane by another stile. Turn left along the lane and right along the road after the white gate. Walk down the hill and take the left fork up the other side. Where the road bears sharp left, go through the gate on the right-hand side. Turn right and walk round the hill until the path meets Chainley Burn and continue up the path as it runs parallel with the stream.

The path descends and crosses a smaller stream in a gap between the two clumps of woodland. Continue following the course of the burn and you will come to a path leading left to the Roman Fort Vindolanda where, on a clear day, you can sometimes spot Magnus Magnusson doing a TV documentary or two. Leaving Vindolanda continue up the path going north rising to High Shield. Here the footpath veers right and crosses the Military Road (so-named because it was built by General Wade during the Civil War to ferry his poor troops back and forth across the country).

Here you can see the line of a raised Roman rampart crossing the road diagonally. The footpath follows it, but continues on the same line where the rampart veers to the right. The path continues to a lane up which you should turn left until come to the eastern end of Crag Lough. At the corner of the woodland on the Lough's southern edge turn left along the footpath leading towards the woods.

The next part of the walk follows some of the best remaining parts of Hadrians's Wall. If you're wondering why so little of the wall is left, just look at any building hereabouts. They're all made of nice angular stones plundered from the wall. Turning right here would take you eastwards to Housteads. Turning left takes you over Steel Rigg with its spectacular views of the moorland to the north. Many kestrels, buzzards and hawks can be observed here hunting for prey. The rocky ridge on which the wall is built here is part of the Great Whin Sill, a volcanic outcrop which is evident right across Northumberland. Holy Island Castle is built on its northern extremity.

The path goes up through some woods, through which Crag Lough can be

The Inn

glimpsed below to your right. Steel Rigg, after the woods, has something approaching 100 different climbs in the cliffs below. In the summer scores of climbers can be seen clambering excitedly among the rocks and swinging about on ropes. At end of the cliffs, the path goes sharply down and meets a lane. Turn left down this until you are back on the Military Road. Turn right here, past the Youth Hostel on your left and go straight into **The Twice Brewed Inn,** where you can relax for a while with their wide selection of draught beers, lagers and ciders and enjoy some of their excellent bar food. This pub is the centre of walking round here, and they are genuinely welcoming to hikers.

Turn right out of The Twice Brewed and right again after the Youth Hostel. Follow the road down past the Roman Camp on the right and over an old Roman road (turning left here would take you back to Vindolanda) then turn left along a track to Layside. Follow the track to Layside Farm and there turn right onto a path that leads down to another small road. Turn left here and right at the T-junction. When the road forks, take the left one and at the next fork, go right. Follow this past houses, over the crossing, and where it ends you'll find the footpath that leads back down past the pottery to **The Bowes Hotel.**

The Twiced Brewed Inn, Bardon Mill

About the Inn: An old pub, built in 1409 with stone taken from the Roman Wall. One of the rooms has a ghost called the Grey Lady who never bothers anyone. However, she likes the door of her room left open and if it isn't, then she opens it herself! The Twice Brewed is a centre for walkers, both on the wall and on the Pennine Way which cuts across here. They are well-used to hikers but would prefer it if you left your packs outside (there's often so many walkers in here, that if they all brought their gear in, it would clog up the bar!) Darts and dominoes are played and there are 26 bedrooms.

Beers and Food: A wide selection of local beers and lagers are on offer, plus a variety of bar foods — soup, ploughman's lunches etc — their speciality is home-made pies.

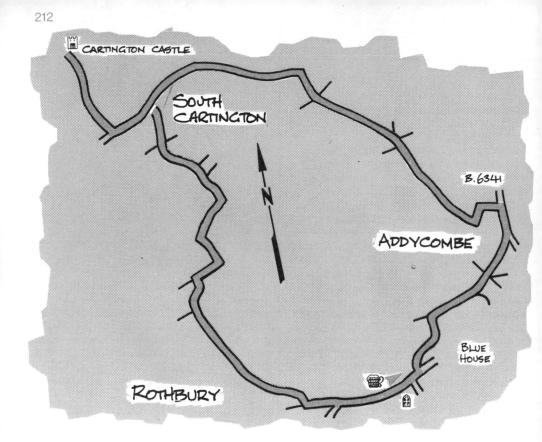

51 Rothbury

The District

Rothbury is a busy market town lying in the heart of Coquetdale where the River Coquet forces through the sandstone in a ravine called 'The Thrum'. Surrounded by heatherclad and wooded hills, it offers walking, touring, golf at nearby Whitton and game fishing (salmon and trout, licence available from Soulsby's in Rothbury High Street).

The town dates back to Saxon times of which only the famous cross in All Saints Church (about AD 800) survives. This in itself is well worth examining as a fine example of early Saxon carving. There are also the remains of some prehistoric settlements, most notably 'Old Rothbury' to the north-west of the town.

Cragside Hall to the west of the village was founded in 1870 by the first Lord Armstrong. Apart from its extensive landscaped grounds and intriguing hotchpotch of mock Tudor and Norman architecture, the house boasts some William Morris glass in the library and the first domestic lights in the world!

Cartington Castle (on the walk) to the north was built in the fifteenth century and, despite having been sacked in various battles and skirmishes, is still worth a visit.

How to Get There

By car, A1 north from Newcastle turning left on to A697 after Morpeth, then B6344 from Longshorsley. By bus, the no 416 from Newcastle's Haymarket Bus Station.

The Rothbury Walk

Although for the most part on clearly marked paths, this is a long and hilly walk. It would probably be wise to persuade young Carol to wear those ugly walking shoes after all.

We begin at **The Queens Head** on Rothbury's sycamore-lined High Street and, after sampling their excellent Vaux beers, you should feel more than ready to set out for a stroll. Turn left out of the pub and left again up Addycombe Gardens. As the road bears right take the first turning left, at the end of which is a footpath. Follow the path along the left-hand side of the hedge and over the stile that takes you into the next field, now on the right-hand side of the hedge. Cross the stile at the top of the field and turn right along the lane. Pass some houses on the left and then a copse where there are some stone steps going up left. Take them, go over the stile at the top and continue up the hill. Cross stile on to the lane, cross another stile on the other side, after which you can forget about stiles for a while. Go into the woods and down the hill, till the path brings you out on to a road. Over on the right here is a lake that is part of the Cragside Estate. Go left up the road for a few yards and then left up a track that skirts round the southern edge of Debdon Lake. The path soon leaves woodland, crosses a stream and meets another track on the right. Go past this and continue on up the hill past another track on the right. Go through more woodland and, on the other side of the trees, go over the crossing, following the track around the hillside and along the north edge of the woods.

At the point where the track has trees on both sides you have a choice. Continuing along the track takes you to Cartington Castle. Turn right to South Cartington and after the buildings onto a footpath that takes you up to the castle ruins. The castle is in an imposing position commanding the Debdon pass. A survey of 1541 describes it as a 'goode fortresse of two towers and other strong houses'. It suffered badly in the English Civil War when it was a Royalist stronghold taken by Cromwell in 1648. In 1887 Lord Armstrong strengthened and preserved the remains. There is still a 14th century tower. Retrace your steps to come back to the main route. Turn left (or right if you have just come from the castle) and follow the path as it climbs through the

The Inns

The Queens Head, Rothbury

About the Inn: About 200 years old, this is a family pub with a warm and friendly atmosphere. A figurehead (reputed to be Mary Queen of Scots) graces the grey stone wall outside, inside there's a large stone fireplace and a beamed ceiling. Darts and dominoes are played. Accommodation, two double rooms and one family room.

Beers and Food: Vaux London Draught Bitter, Lorimers, Draught Guinness and many wines and spirits. A selection of reasonably priced meals can be had at the bar: Ploughmans' lunches, steak and kidney pie, curries, sandwiches and salads.

Railway Hotel, Rothbury

About the Inn: Constructed of local stone about 100 years ago at the same time as the railway — hence its name. Bed and breakfast is available — there is one family room and two doubles. Darts and dominoes are played. So is occasional live traditional music. Stabling is available too.

Beers and Food: Scottish and Newcastle beers: Exhibition, Tartan Bitter and Eighty Shillings (recommended!). During summer there are bar meals — fish and chips etc — as well as a variety of sandwiches and salads.

woods and emerges to meet a bridleway. Turn right here and follow it round past the cairn.

Just before the triangulation point, turn right onto a path which meets a track. Here turn left and follow it round the hill where it drops to skirt some woodland.

Here the path passes through the pre-historic settlement at Old Rothbury, which occupies a strong position on the hills which encircle the town. It is now covered with bracken, but traces of a double ditch and rampart can still be seen. The track continues past the quarry back into Rothbury where a pint of McEwans excellent 'Eighty Shillings' at **The Railway Hotel** will slake that thirst.

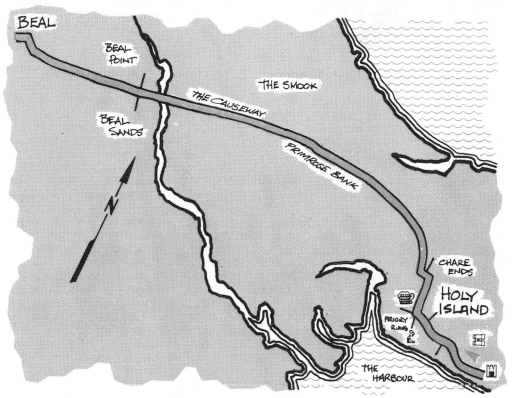

5m Holy Island

The District
Also known as **Lindisfarne**, the island lies a mile off the Northumbrian coast. It was one of the early centres of Christianity in England and boasts a 12th century priory and a 16th century castle as well as beautiful beaches and a nature reserve.

Six miles to the south lies the charming village of **Bamburgh**, where those who don't want to examine its impressive castle can laze around on the expansive white beach and rolling dunes, or visit the **Grace Darling museum** which commemorates her heroic rescue of the SS Forfarshire on September 7th 1838.

From **Seahouses**, a fishing village a little further south, regular boat trips can be had to the Farne islands, the famous Sea Bird Sanctuary which also has a huge colony of Atlantic Grey Seals.

How to Get There
By car, straight up the A1 from Newcastle through Alnwick, minor road to Beal from West Mains. Trains from Newcastle to Berwick-upon-Tweed then a bus to Beal.

The Holy Island Walk
Holy Island is a tidal island, which means at high tide there ain't no way back to the mainland. Those unwilling to check out the rumour that when cut off, the island's pubs stay open all night, should make sure the tides will be in their favour before setting off (a glance at a local paper will suffice). This aside it is a longish but very flat walk, which all the family can enjoy.

►

Begin at Beal and walk down the lane about a mile to the beach. If you've got it right the tide will be out and there's a clearly defined metalled causeway which goes over a bridge and sweeps across to the sand dunes of the island's Primrose Bank. As you follow the track around the coast and across the sands, to your left is the **Holy Island Nature Reserve** which harbours no less than 311 species of bird: elders, fulmars, kittiwakes, puffins, greylag geese and whooper swans... you name them. In fact, Lindisfarne, among British estuaries, is second in importance for its bird population. On reaching the western end of the isle, the track meets a lane at Chare Ends. Turn left up this which brings you into the north end of the village. Turn right at the end and you can enjoy that drink you've been waiting for at **The Castle Hotel**. Now, when in the village little Johnny finishes his second ice-cream and demands a third and you're about to call him 'pig', restrain yourself; this is about the worst thing you can say to annoy the locals, call him 'grunty' (the preferred term) instead. Although the inhabitants have many old superstitions (if a fisherman sees a woman on the way to the beach in the morning, he won't put out to sea) they are a friendly bunch.

Turn right out of the pub, then right again, and you'll find the Priory. Besides the more visible ruins of this beautiful Saxon building (once painted by Turner) ghosts of monks and dogs are said to stalk around, as well as the ghost of a nun who was bricked into a wall for the heinous crime of having an affair with one of the monks (of what happened to him, there is no record). The most famous of all the Lindisfarne bishops was St Cuthbert who died in 687. His coffin became a holy relic and was literally carted around by his followers for centuries! It now rests at Durham Cathedral.

From the Priory walk back to the centre of the village, turn right and follow the southern coastal path past the coastguard station towards Castle Point. There is a fine view of the castle, resting on its volcanic outcrop, all the way along this stretch. The castle was built in 1583 as a bulwark, like so many castles in Northumberland, against the marauding Scots.

It was derelict for a long time until Sir Edward Lutyens converted it into a private house in 1903, and it now contains some fine seventeenth century English and Flemish oak furniture, as well as some contemporary pieces designed by Lutyens.

The coastal path back into the village leads one directly to **The Northumberland Arms** where you can fortify yourself for the stroll back. Autograph hunters please note: famous customers here have included Lindisfarne (the group), Roman Polanski and the Nolan Sisters!

The Inns

Castle Hotel, Holy Island

About the Inn: About a 100 yards from the village green with its 1828 market cross, The Castle Hotel is frequented by many local characters. The wood for the panelled walls and ceiling came from the wreck of the ship Mauritania. Darts, pool, dominoes and cards can be played.

Beers and Food: A selection of Dryboroughs beers, wines and spirits. Tides permitting, all kinds of food are also available. Accommodation for four.

Northumberland Arms, Holy Island

About the Inn: Approximately 300 years old. The bar, with its open fire and oak beams, contains a fascinating collection of paintings and photographs of local characters and scenes. Darts and dominoes.

Beers and Food: Selection of Scottish and Newcastle beers and other drinks. Try the Special Lindisfarne Mead. Many sandwiches and bar snacks.

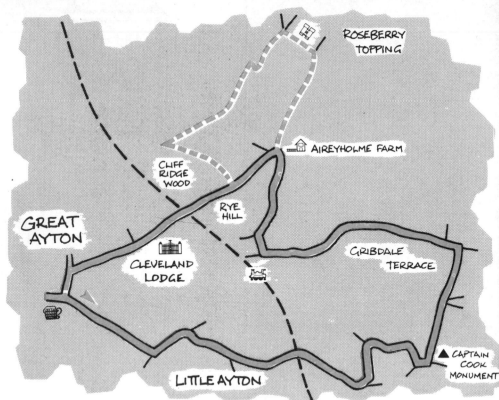

5n Great Ayton

The District

Great Ayton is one of a series of market towns at the foot of the Cleveland hills. Its main claim to fame is that Captain Cook, erstwhile discoverer of Australia and all-round seafaring chap, spent his childhood here. At the age of 13 he moved to Whitby to begin his life on the ocean wave. Cook's family tomb can be found at All Saints Church and there is a small museum dedicated to him at the old School House. The village is cut through by the River Leven and narrow streets with stone houses run into the spacious village green.

To the north-east is **Guisborough**, a slightly larger market-town with a broad main street, along which there are often stalls selling a wide variety of curios. It also boasts a ruined 12th century Abbey.

How to Get There

By car, take the A172 from Middlesbrough and turn down the B1292 into Great Ayton. By bus (avoids an initial long walk from the station) no 290 from Middlesbrough (good service) stops right outside The Royal Oak.

The Great Ayton Walk

Quite a long (about 6 miles) but rewarding walk along clearly defined though sometimes muddy paths. If the more infirm members of the family are accompanying you, then the most strenuous part of the walk — the climb up Roseberry Topping — can be avoided.

We begin with the serious stuff at **The Royal Oak Hotel**. After partaking of sufficient liquid refreshment turn right out of the pub and right again by Cleveland Lodge and follow the road to Little Ayton. Turn left before the bridge and the path will lead you into open fields. When the track forks, take the right-hand path and, after crossing three fields, turn left to the railway-line. Cross the line and follow the path up by the copse and go right where it forks up the hillside. It soon joins a broad path which continues upwards and when it reaches a wide gate, go through and follow the track up and around the hill. Where the track begins its descent, go off right along a path through the pines. Emerging at the top of the hill the Captain Cook monument can be seen and a well-marked track leads to it off to the right.

The monument was built in 1827 by Robert Campion of Whitby 'In memory of the celebrated circumnavigator Captain James Cook FRS, a man in nautical knowledge inferior to none...' From here, turn left and follow the broad sand-finished road downwards. At the ending of the wall on the left, turn left and follow the field to the brow of the hill, where you can look down on to Gribdale Gate.

Go down to the Park fence and, turning left, follow it to a row of terraced cottages crossing the fence into Gribdale Terrace. At the end, where the road bends to the right keep straight on to White House Farm. Turn right after the farmhouse and follow the road past Aireyholme Farm, where Captain Cook's father was once foreman labourer. Those who wish to avoid Roseberry Topping can turn left here and walk down to the wood where we will meet

The Inn

The Royal Oak Hotel, Great Ayton

About the Inn: This white-painted stone building beside the village green was built in 1771, the date which is on the old sundial outside. The interior is beamed and contains a lot of attractive brass-work. Darts and dominoes are played, and there is overnight accommodation.

Beers and Food: Scottish and Newcastle Ales: Exhibition, Tartan, Bitter, McEwan's Lager and the famous local 'Brown Ale'. Lunchtime bar meals are extensive, usually 3 hot dishes (quiches, curries etc) for about £1.30, (on Sunday there are only sandwiches). The restaurant which is in the same building offers a full à la carte meal for around £5 a head.

them later. Follow the road past the farm to its end, going through a series of gates. Venture off the path here at your peril — your intrepid author once did and was chased by a bull for his pains! Turn left up the path that leads past a small stone pillar directly to the top of Roseberry Topping.

From here there's a commanding view of the surrounding countryside, not to mention the industrial panorama of Teesside. Thornaby chemical works are particularly prominent. Turning your back on the urban vista, you can see the moors beyond Eskdale and the tops which the Lyke Wake Walk follows.

Take the path which goes down towards Ayton at right-angles to the one you came up by, running parallel to the road you took from Aireyholme Farm. At the last gate turn right, until you arrive at an 18th century summer house. From the window opposite the entrance you can see, slightly to your left, a small gate in a fence leading to a wood. Go through it and follow the path through the wood and out into the open. Keep the fence to your left, and when the path forks move left up the hill. By a small stone ruin the path meets a broader way, and, just after the ruin, another leads up to the left. Take the latter up to the escarpment and follow the valley leftwards. As it ends, don't go round, but drop down into

the valley turning right at the bottom. You can see the opening of a pothole under the cliff.

Leave the valley going left and follow the escarpment edge on your right and the fence on your left until it reaches a stile. Don't go over it, but follow the path on your right until it joins a bridleway well down the slope. At this junction there is an iron gate opposite. (This is where you would arrive from the other direction if you had turned to avoid Roseberry Topping — aren't you glad you didn't!). Go through the gate and down through the woods to a stile into an open field. Follow the path to your right crossing a signposted private road and over the railway line into open fields, keep the hedge to your right going through the Cleveland Lodge Estate. At the last latch-gate in a small copse go straight across the road to an opening in the woods. After the wood turn left on to the main road which bends to the right, back to a welcome at **The Royal Oak.**

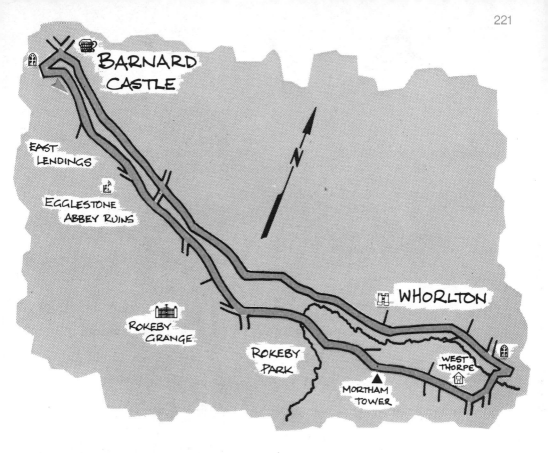

5o Barnard Castle

The District

Barnard Castle, situated by the River Tees in one of the most beautiful parts of Co Durham, is a busy market town. Almost exclusively built in local stone, the predominant style is elegant early Georgian. The town takes its name from the 12th century castle founded by Bernard, son of Guy de Baliol, a Norman knight who fought alongside William the Conqueror at the Battle of Hastings. It is on a 80ft bluff and has an imposing 14th century tower.

Blagraves House is the most famous house in the town. Standing in The Bank, it's easily recognisable by its Tudor bay windows. It has recently been renovated and the downstairs is now an excellent restaurant. Visited by Cromwell in 1648, it takes its name from the Blagrave family who lived there from 1672.

Bowes Museum a little way out of the centre along Newgate, was founded by John Bowes in the late 19th century. John apparently wanted to build it in Calais, but political unrest prevented this and Barnard Castle was his second choice. The museum houses paintings by El Greco, Goya, Sassetta, Tiepolo, Boucher, Gainsborough and others, as well as collections of porcelain, china, pottery and tapestries. There are also period rooms and parts dedicated to local history. John Bowes satisfied his Francophile ambitions somewhat by constructing the place in the style of a second empire chateau.

Egglestone Abbey along the river was founded in 1190 and sits on a hill on the south bank.

How to Get There

By car, A67 from Darlington. Buses 75, 76 and 77 from Darlington bus station.

The Barnard Castle Walk

This is a long walk (about 6 miles) but fairly flat along well-defined pathways.

The bus terminates in Galgate. Walking from here towards the chapel, down Horse Market (which becomes Market Place) to the 1747 Market Cross, will eventually bring you to **The Ruby Hotel** on the left. And what better place to begin than here, with a choice of Camerons and Newcastle Ales?

When you've had enough of that (if ever ...) or once it is drinking-up time, continue on down the street which keeps on changing names to try and confuse the hapless visitor, past Blagraves House on the left. Presently you come to a metal bridge over the Tees. Cross it, turn left, and follow the footpath along the river.

After some houses and a caravan park, turn right and follow the path up the hill. At the top, turn left in a field just before the trees on the left. The path is well-defined for a mile or so, running through fields connected by stiles. When the path meets a road, turn left along it. It soon passes **Egglestone Abbey**, romantic ruins which were painted by Turner and provide the setting for the final scene of Sir Walter Scott's *Rokeby*. Just after a packhorse bridge over the river the road veers to the right, but the path continues along the same bank, going off to the left. Continue along this path until it comes out at a road junction. Turn left along the smaller road which runs past Rokeby Park and 'The Waters Meet' where the Rivers Tees and Greta come together. This is the setting for the rest of Scott's poem, a similarly romantic location.

The path turns left and follows the bank of the Greta for about 50 yards to where a small bridge crosses the river. Go across the cattle grid on the far side (I hope granny didn't bring those *naughty* stilettoes with her) and **Mortham Tower** (as featured in... you've guessed it: Scott's *Rokeby* again) becomes visible. Take the road which

describes an arc towards the tower, and at the entrance to the grounds follow the wall up and then left and across more fields connected by stiles. You can see the river here, about half a mile away, and the path stays parallel to it.

Soon the Whorlton suspension bridge comes into view. Turn left along the road which the path runs into and over the bridge. On the other bank the road turns right. Climb the steps opposite and you'll meet it at the top of the hill on the outskirts of Whorlton. To the left is a stile which puts you on a pathway over more stile-connected fields. At first the path is on high ground with an excellent view of the river. Stay on high ground and soon the path comes down to the Tees again. From here back to the town the path stays beside the river bank opposite the one you walked out on. At Barnard Castle the path becomes a lane which brings the intrepid traveller out on to Grey Lane. Go straight over Thorngate, down Bridegate opposite and turn left at the bottom over County Bridge below the castle on your right. This will bring you to **The White Swan Inn** where a choice of four hand-drawn real ales in this historic tavern will help you forget those blisters on your feet. Keep an eye out for the ghost of a young lady who stalks the bridge; she was pushed from here to her doom by her lover.

The Inns

Ruby Hotel, Barnard Castle

About the Inn: Reputedly haunted by a previous landlord who hung himself in the bottle store. The current landlord — James Gardiner — has no such morbid ambition and offers a warm welcome in this friendly tavern. There's accommodation for four people at the moment (for 12 when alterations currently under way are completed). Dominoes, pool and skittles can be played.

Beers and Food: Cameron's Strongarm and Best Bitter, two lagers and many wines and spirits. A variety of toasted sandwiches and snacks are available at the bar.

White Swan Inn, Barnard Castle

About the Inn: A 16th century tavern built into a bridge over the River Tees in Elizabethan style. Heavy beamed interior with an open fire and oak panelling. There is a beer garden on the river bank which overlooks the 12th century castle. Darts and dominoes are played. A historic pub in a beautiful setting. Full of character.

Beers and Food: Theakston's and Cameron's Best Bitter, Castle Eden Bitter and Kelly's Golden Bitter all hand drawn. Also keg Newcastle Exhibition, Younger's Tartan and Carlsberg and Carling lagers on keg. Bottled beers include Theakston's Old Peculiar and Worthington White Shield. There is a full restaurant; also many sandwiches and bar snacks.

Wales

As moody and romantic as Ireland, as awe-inspiring as Scotland and with coastal scenery equalling that of Cornwall, Wales is probably the most underrated part of the Celtic fringe. Yet its accessibility does not deny its essential separateness; the tongue-twisting place names, the musical lilt of its language and the strong Druidic roots.

But Wales is not just one region. The border counties; still guarded by the imposing Norman castles, built to control the fiercely nationalistic princes, but now only presiding over lush farmland and wealthy market towns. South Wales; deeply scarred by past generations pillaging the gentle green slopes for black gold, leaving only disused mines and row upon row of small houses. North Wales; dotted with charming old-fashioned seaside resorts and offset by ancient rugged hills. And finally Mid Wales, alive with lakes, waterfalls, streams and birdsong.

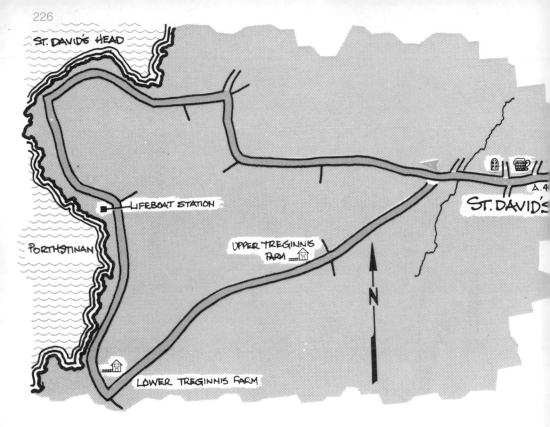

6a   St David's

The District

Guaranteed to make your nose run in any but the kindest weather, this walk begins in the smallest city in Britain, **St David's**, and takes you round a small section of the windswept Pembrokeshire coastline. A pleasure ground for botanists, the landscape is dominated by yellow gorse flowers which respond to the traditional saying that 'when the gorse is out of bloom, kissing's out of fashion' (a daft traditional saying, if ever one was coined).

The city's imposing cathedral was begun in about 1182 by the Norman bishop, Peter de Leia, and features artifacts from all periods: a stone choir screen from the 14th century, misereres in the choir stalls from the 15th, the beautifully carved oak of the nave roof and the fan-vaulted ceiling of the

Holy Trinity Chapel from the 16th. There are even some early Christian monuments dating from the 5th century, and St David's relics are kept in a moveable shrine behind the High Altar.

In the summer boat trips are run, on an informal basis, around **Ramsey Island**, starting at **St Justinian**, the halfway point of the walk. If you are interested in taking the trip, find out the times from the newsagent in the square. Allow an hour and half to walk to St Justinian, excluding any time spent in the cathedral.

How to Get There

By car, the A478 down the coast from Cardigan or west from Haverfordwest. The car park costs 20p and is down Quickwell Hill. Walk back to the road and turn right for the city's main square. By train to Haverfordwest station; buses leave from the station and take almost an hour to St David's Square.

The St David's Walk

A 6 mile walk from the tiny city of St David's out onto the desolate Pembrokeshire coast. The walk begins in the city square. Walk down, with craft shops on your left, through an archway to the cathedral and Bishop's Palace.

On leaving the Palace, go right along the tarmac path to join the road. Turn right and follow the road alongside the cathedral's boundary wall. Cross a stream and pass another car park on your left.

This part of the walk, and the closing section, take you along typical Pembrokeshire lanes, the hedgerows of which are renowned for the proliferation of wild flowers along them. Many of the species are quite rare and localised, and visitors are expected to refrain from picking any flowers unless they grow in great abundance.

Pass a turning signposted for Traeth-Mawr, or Whitesand, and a little further take a right fork in the road, signposted for St Justianian. Pass a turning left and at a fork go right to Treleddyn. Walk straight through the farmyard and through a gate marked 'Caerheydyn'. Keep along the right edge of this field. Pass a gate to a field containing a standing stone, but cross through the next gate, and skirt this field to the gate in the opposite corner. Taking this gate, keep to the track on your left and after another gate turn sharp right towards the sea. Follow the stream down to the beach. Just before a life-buoy in front of you turn left, crossing the stream. You are now on the Pembrokeshire coastal path.

Treat this route with respect; the erosion

➤

The Inn

Farmer's Arms, St David's

About the Inn: A fine, though simple century-old inn on Goat Street, with pebble-dash exterior and seating in good weather on the pavement outside. A small car park at rear with a perfect view of the cathedral. Darts, pool and chasing women are listed as the pub games on offer! Background music, children welcomed.

Beers and Food: Double Dragon, Worthington Best Bitter from Llanelli hand pumped. Very fresh, basic pub grub all home-made: sarnies, salads, Ploughman's lunch.

of the coastline provides you with views of magnificent rock formations and strata all along this stretch, but be aware that the process of erosion continues and **stick to the path**. Stiles are provided to take the path away from the edge where necessary. As long as you follow these, and take the left path whenever it forks, you will enjoy the walk in complete safety. The rocks which line the coast, a little way out to sea, are known as the 'Bishops and Deacons', as each clump consists of a large 'Bishop' surrounded by several smaller 'deacons'. As you round the headland, Point St John, the hills which you have been able to see to the west for some time are revealed as the contours of Ramsey Island, not part of the mainland at all.

Follow the path until you come into sight of the lifeboat station at St Justinian. This bay, called Porthstinian, is where the boat trips are made from. Legend states that 20,000 saints are buried on Ramsey Island. St Justinian was reputedly a friend of St David, a hermit born in Brittany, and murdered on the island. The story goes that he walked back across the sound, carrying his head under his arm, to be buried at the site of the now-ruined chapel, which can be seen above the lifeboat station. His remains were later removed to the cathedal. The bells of the chapel were stolen by Puritans, and subsequently lost when their ship was wrecked in the sound, giving rise to the legend that the bells can be heard chiming under the sea during strong gales.

Ramsey Island is now owned by the Royal Society for the Protection of Birds, the Pembrokeshire coast being richer in sea-bird life than any other part of mainland Britain. Seals also breed on the island under protection.

Continue along the coastal path until you reach stile 269. This is a kissing-gate. Cross it; on your left is a metal gate. Cross the kissing gate beside this metal gate and follow the track to Lower Treginnis Farm. Bear left through the farmyard, ignoring the track which forks right, and follow the path which passes a building on the right. You are now on a direct course for St David's.

Walk through Upper Treginnis Farm and follow the road on which the walk began. Pass the road to Whitesand on your left, and on reaching the entrance to the Bishop's Palace, continue on the road, bearing left up a steep hill and keeping left again when it joins the main road. On the left, about 200 yards further up the road, is **The Farmer's Arms**. A simple Welsh inn, with pebble-dash front and slate roof, and an excellent view of the cathedral from the small car park at its rear, the Farmer's is managed with pride by David Owen-Richards. It offers good beer, solid pub food and a friendly atmosphere that completes an adventurous day's excursion.

Continue up Goat Street back to the city square.

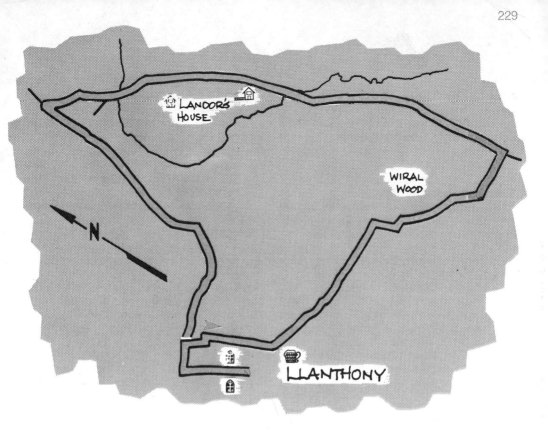

6b   Llanthony

The District

Nestling deep in the Vale of Ewyas in the heart of the Black Mountains in Gwent, **Llanthony** takes its name from the Welsh **Llandewi Nant Honddu** — 'St David's church by the Honddu stream'. St David, the patron saint of Wales, is thought to have spent much of his life here in the 6th century. The Church of St David dates from the second half of the 12th century and is probably built on the site of the saint's monastic cell. The church was so aligned that the altar could face directly towards the rising sun on March 1, St David's Day. During the Middle Ages the building served as a hospital for the Priory and the surrounding district. Today it is the parish church and holds regular Sunday services.

Most of what remains of the Priory dates back to the mid-12th century. Founded by the Earl of Hereford in 1108 after, it is said, a kinsman of his had been so moved by the grandeur of the valley that he abandoned his worldly possessions to become a hermit there. **Wiral Wood**, through which our walk route takes you, is small but sufficiently secluded to attract a number of birds, including the wood warbler, a rare inhabitant of the British isles distinguished by his yellow breast and white belly. Another inhabitant of the wood, the nuthatch, clambers down trees head first — the only British bird crazy enough to do so! Green and greater spotted woodpeckers, redstarts, pied flycatchers and goldcrests are easier to spot than the well-camouflaged treecreeper. Red grouse breed on the moorland above the valley.

►

How to Get There

By road, from Abergavenny, go north along the B4423 to Llanthony. By rail from London (Euston) to Newport and change for Abergavenny Station. Then bus to Llanthony.

The Llanthony Walk

This is a shortish (about 2½ miles) walk, not very strenuous but liable to be very muddy in parts, crossing several streams that flow down from the Black Mountains and that pass over the path as often as they pass under it. Please keep dogs on a lead.

Starting at the free car park walk between the Abbey and St David's Church to a gate. Cross the stile and turn right along the Drystone Wall. Cross a second stile, by a sign for Longtown, and follow the arrow marked 'Way to Hill'. Across a second stile follow the footpath sign up through a field. Continue uphill through Wiral Wood.

At the top of the wood cross the stile on your left and keep climbing along the edge of the field. Away down the valley to your right you can see the characteristic shape of Sugar Loaf Mountain. Cross a stile at the top and follow the path left (we wouldn't be so cruel as to send you trekking up the mountain!). This is where the stream you have been following emerges from underneath the mountain. Follow the path to a stile and pass through the enclosure of a stone farmhouse, over another stile and onto a track. Cross another stile and follow the track down to Landor's House.

Walter Savage Landor was a wild gentleman whose antics came close to justifying his middle name. Best known for his book of *Imaginary Conversations* between anachronistic historical figures, he fought for the Spanish against Napoleon and bought Llanthony Estate in 1802. He did much to shape the district in the early 19th century, importing merino sheep from Spain, improving roads, bridges and communications and planting much of the woodland in the area. But his fiery temper put him out of favour with the locals, and he left the area in 1814 having been thrown from a first-floor window of his house by an incensed neighbour.

The Inn

Past the house cross the bridge, a stile and then turn right, skirting the field to a gate. Go through the gate and follow the track a few yards to a marking post. Turn left, on to a footpath which takes you down to a stile at the bottom of the field. Walk through the copse to a second stile. Climb the stile and simply follow your eyes back to the Abbey, crossing one more stile at the end of the field.

By the end of the walk, adjournment to **The Abbey Hotel**, a charming hostelry actually built into a wing of the Abbey, is almost mandatory. It boasts a bar in one of the Abbey's original cellars, and accommodation in the tower part of the West Front. The top room is reached by 62 spiral steps (not for visitors with too much luggage) and boasts a four-poster bed, a Victorian toilet seat and some 19th century graffiti. The landlord, Lawrence Fancourt, has written an interesting pamphlet on the history of the Priory, the first Augustinian Priory in Wales; copies of which are available at the bar.

Abbey Hotel, Llanthony

About the Inn: Built into part of the west range of the 12th century Augustinian Priory, this small hostelry, set amid the Black Mountains, is an ideal base for pony trekking and walking in the region. Frequented by the composer Vaughn Williams, the playwright George Bernard Shaw, numerous politicians, actors, journalists and a few relatively normal people, its accommodation is sited in the Priory's tower. No ordinary garden is good enough for this romantic establishment: in summer drinks are taken in the cloisters and on the green lawns amid the Priory ruins. The kitchen boasts a 19th century range, with a spit of similar vintage in the dining room. Children are welcomed. No games, music (often live in summer).

Beers and Food: Ruddles County, Samuel Smith's Old Brewery by hand-pumps, Hancock's Pale, Whitbread's Best Bitter, Brain's Bitter by gravity. Stella Artois on draught in the summer. Symonds Cider and Bulmer's West Country Cider by gravity — enough choice for anyone. A wide range of food, from simple snacks to restaurant menu, large selection of liqueurs. The restaurant is closed November to March.

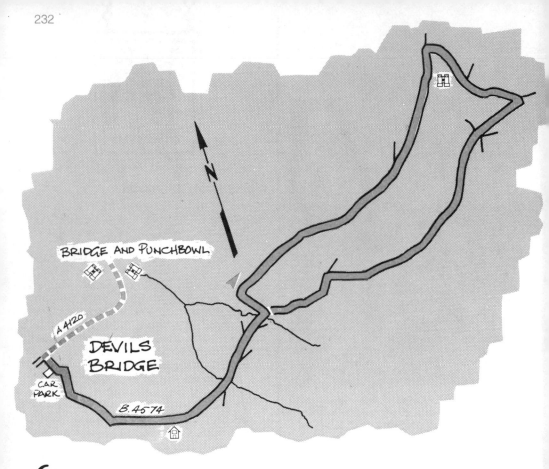

6c   Devil's Bridge

The District

This walk, set in the picturesque **Rheidol Valley** near **Aberystwyth** and **Aberdovey** is a must for enthusiasts of the 'black arts' and devil-worship! For the aptly-named **Devil's Bridge** is, according to legend, the work of Satan himself.

In the early Middle Ages there was no bridge across the Mynach river at all. An old widow named Marged lived in a cottage on the bank of the stream, with a dog and a cow as her only company. She relied on the cow to supply her with the dairy products from which to eek a modest living. The cow usually grazed in a pasture close to the cottage but one day, after ceaseless and heavy rainfall, the cow strayed upstream and across the gorge. Recognizing her plight, Marged cried (as widows do all the

time): 'I'd give anything for a bridge!'

'I'll build you a bridge,' responded the deep voice of a monk from the nearby abbey, 'within the hour. It will cost you nothing. As for recompense, I ask only to be given the first living thing that crosses it'.

Enthused at the prospect of rescuing her cow, the widow took little notice of this last sentence. The miracle was completed on schedule, a fine stone bridge now crossed the gorge. But the monk (you don't really believe it was a monk, surely?) announced to Marged that her cow would not cross. 'You will have to come over and fetch her'.

The widow was about to trip gaily over the bridge when a gust of wind blew the cowl from the monk's head, to reveal horns on either side of his face. Realizing just in time that she had almost fallen victim to the

Devil the widow threw a crust of bread across the bridge, which enticed her little dog to scamper over in pursuit. The Devil gave a tremendous howl of rage: 'What use is a *!+*/! dog to me!' he shrieked and disappeared in a cloud of smoke and flame.

This is also a walk for railway enthusiasts, and we recommend taking the narrow gauge railway up the Vale of Rheidol from Aberystwyth to Devil's Bridge.

How to Get There

By car, from Aberystwyth to the village of Devil's Bridge on A44(T) turning right at Pont Erwyd. From Aberdovey drive on A493 to Machynlleth, then onto A487(T) to Bow Street, where you bear left to join A44(T) for Pont Erwyd and the right turn to Devil's Bridge. In the quiet season you can park on the Pont Erwyd side of the Bridge; otherwise, cross the bridge and turn left to the car park on B4574. By rail, we recommend taking the Rheidol Valley narow gauge run from Aberystwyth.

The Vale of Rheidol Railway was built in 1902 and runs from April to October. It is now the only surviving steam railway operated by British Rail. Twelve miles long, it climbs 650 feet, and was originally used for carrying zinc ore and lead from the Rheidol Valley Mines to Aberystwyth. The last four miles of track are seated on a ledge carved out from the rock face.

The Inns

Devil's Bridge Hotel

About the Inn: Site of the Mynach Falls, this hostelry is a sprawling building with the look of a swiss chalet outside and the atmosphere of a Welsh manor within. Built in 1787, it offers a lazy female ghost (who has not been sighted this century) and an additional dose of ghoulage for those who cross the Devil's Bridge at night without a crucifix and bible. The inn offers three bars (including a cocktail bar) and restaurant, accommodation for 35, darts, pool and a welcome for children (but not dogs). Kites, buzzards and sparrowhawks can be seen in the surrounding countryside.

Beers and Food: Whitbread Flowers on handpump. Welsh Bitter and Heineken lager on draught. Bar snacks, tea room (soon to be open in the evenings for children) and full restaurant (lunch about £ 4, four-course dinner about £ 6).

Angel Inn, Aberystwyth

About the Inn: For those based in Aberystwyth, this inn in Great Darkside Street is full of character, interesting ales and fresh, inexpensive pub grub. Darts, fruit machines and TV are a boon to some, an intrusion to others, but varied live music adds to the Angel's friendly atmosphere.

Beers and Food: Bass, Mitchells & Butlers, Allbright, Worthington E on draught, draught cider and Guinness. Good simple pub grub, hot and cold. Pies and pasties, sarnies and salads, Ploughman's; all very good value.

The Devil's Bridge Walk

A fairly light (about 4½ miles) walk, following the valley of the River Mynach through some countryside unique in the British Isles. Shaded forestry land gives way at the end of the walk to staggering views of the beautiful Mynach Falls below the three spans of the Devil's Bridge itself. Occasional steep climbs.

Those arriving by rail have the choice of completing the full walk, or leaving out the first section. Turn left out of the station and at the fork turn right for the complete walk (which begins at the car park) or left for the shorter walk (beginning at the bridge).

Starting at the car park, turn right onto the B4574, pass through the second metal gate on the left opposite the beginning of the forest. Follow the clearly marked track, through a gate marked 'Aberbodcoll'. Pass some stone buildings on the left, then a stone cottage on the right, and cross a footbridge. Cross a wooden gate, then bear left onto a farm track at the junction. Turn right at the fork, through two gates and into the forest. On joining another track continue left. Bear left across a concrete bridge then turn left, taking the lower track. Follow this back along the other side of the gorge, passing through a wooden gate and some farm buildings on your left. Cross the bridge marked 'Unsafe' (applies to vehicles and elephants only). Pass through another gate and follow the track, bearing right onto the main path. From here, retrace your steps back towards the beginning of the walk, keeping right at the fork and turning left onto the main road. Walk past the car park and the T-junction, turn right for the bridge.

At the bridge, take the right-hand turnstile (20p) to the Devil's Punchbowl and follow the descent down a steep flight of steps — called Jacob's Ladder — to the floor of the bowl. Small children and the elderly may find these steps difficult. From here you will enjoy a good view of the three bridges that now straddle the gorge; the iron bridge at the top, which carries the main road and was built in 1901; the stone bridge below it, of 18th century vintage; and the Devil's Bridge itself, a 12th century job.

Return to the road and cross to the other turnstile, for the Mynach Falls. These are probably the highspot of the visit. A clearly marked footpath takes you all the way round the falls and back to the main road. The falls are on grounds belonging to **The Devil's Bridge Hotel**, an ideal inn in which to savour some Welsh bitter in a Welsh manorial setting. The hotel is haunted by a female ghost, who appears to have been on strike for the last century or so — who knows, you may be the first person in living memory to meet her over a pint!

Motorists then turn left and return to the car park; train passengers turn right for the station and the train back to Aberystwyth. **The Angel Inn** will be waiting to receive you there.

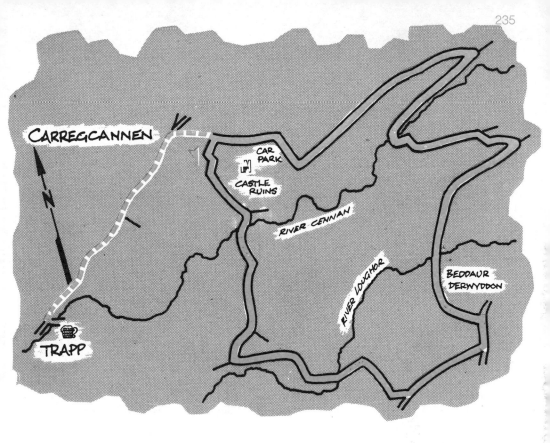

6d Carreg Cennen

The District

Set under the Black Mountain against the River Cennen valley in Dyfed, **Carreg Cennen** — which means simply 'Cennen Rock' — is a limestone crag towering 300 feet above the valley. There is hardly a point on the circular walk we have chosen when this great landmark does not dominate the skyline. It is the site of the ruins of a majestic castle which dates from the 13th and 14th centuries. Built against the almost sheer wall of the cliff, the castle is an example of a sophisticated fortification, with the side of its easiest approach protected by a system of double walls which trapped would-be invaders in a strip of open ground between them.

The original castle is thought to have been built in the 12th century by the Welsh prince Rhys ap Gruffydd; it changed hands several times in the next century, passing to John of Gaunt and his heir, the exiled Henry of Bolingbroke. When Henry acceded to the throne, the castle became Crown property as part of the Duchy of Lancaster. In 1403 the castle fell, after a long siege, to the Welsh army of Owen Glendower, and was eventually demolished by Yorkists during the Wars of the Roses, in 1462.

➤

How to Get There

By car, for Aberystwyth A487 south to Aberaeron, then A482 south-east to Llanwrda and A40 to Llandeilo. From London, A40 to Llandeilo, the drive to the car park on the lane leading from Trapp to the castle. Carreg Cennen is not easily accessible by public transport: nearest station, Llandeilo, about 4 miles away.

The Carreg Cennen Walk

A fairly strenuous 5 mile walk, compensated by sensational views of and from the crag, a visit to the castle and impressive countryside. Strong shoes (boots in wet weather) are recommended.

The castle can be seen from the front of **The Cennen Arms** in Trapp. This charming inn serves a range of Welsh bitters and an excellent, fortifying pub menu essential for anyone tackling this walk on a fresh, winter's day. The castle dominates the landscape. Walk (or drive) across the bridge beside the inn bearing right towards the car park below the castle.

Turn left back down the lane, taking a sharp turn left onto a track below the castle. Just before a cottage turn right over a stile and walk straight to a second stile. Cross it and bear left down a very steep hill. Crossing a third stile, head for the wooden footbridge which takes you across the River Cennen. Bear left, climbing steeply to a metal stile in a hedge. Climb the hill and turn right, along the track to the right of the farm. Follow this track for almost a mile as it crosses a ford and bears right then left. Then turn left through a gate. After crossing a stile, you will see a stream trickling alongside the path ahead of you.

Follow the stream, which becomes the River Loughor, over a stile until you can see below you the source of the river flowing out from deep beneath the rock. This is a limestone cave, known as Llygad Llwchwr — the Eye of the Loughor. The ruined kiln on your left was built for the manufacture of quicklime, an alkaline used to neutralise the

acidity of the local peat soil.

Follow the track to the right of this kiln. After serpentining the track opens into a grassy pathway. Pass through a gate and bear right between two wooded hollows. Then bear to the left, following a dry stone wall. When it becomes a fence, keep following towards a stile beyond which you take the tarmac road to the left. Where this road bears right, keep to the left, following a track hugging the wall. On your right is a cluster of man-made rabbit warrens, called Beddau'r Derwyddon. Rabbits are unable to dig their own homes in this thin soil.

Cross a stile and head towards a lone bush in the middle of the field. Past the bush, the path leads over a stream to a fence. Don't take the gap through the fence, but follow it to the corner of the field and the path downhill. At a fork bear left, keeping to the path as it hairpins left down to a farmyard. Cross the farmyard, down over a bridge to the bottom of the hill. Turn right past a ruin on the left, and follow the river through a field, across a stile, through another field and up some steps to another stile. Continue along this track until you reach a fence; turn sharp left and, keeping to the left of an outcrop at the top of the crag, begin the long haul up to the castle.

Return through Castel Farm — at which Bernard Llewellyn serves tea and the most incredible fresh milkshakes in summer — to the car park. An alternative to milkshakes is offered at **The Three Tuns** in Market Street, Llandeilo, at a fine bar fashioned from old church pews.

The Inns

Three Tuns, Llandeilo

About the Inn: Tucked away in Market Street, this fine old inn is a thriving centre for refreshment and conversation, popular with locals. Indeed, it boasts 'conversation' as its specialist pub game! Two bars, both with open fires; the lounge bar is made from church pews and features a collection of beer bottles (full) from all over England — they certainly taste better than stamps! Background music.

Beers and Food: Felinfoel and Marstone handpumped real ales; several lagers and Guinness on draught. Wide selection of bottled beers. Home-made hot lunches, as well as a variety of sandwiches and other cold snacks.

Cennen Arms, Trapp

About the Inn: A charming, farmhouse-style two-storey inn, featuring a snug main bar and a music room 'with occasional singing' — by whom, is not quite clear. Good views from foot of the Black Mountain. Occasional live music, darts and dominoes. Children welcomed (they have a special playground within the rear garden).

Beers and Food: Buckley's Best, Whitbread Welsh Bitter and Tankard pumped electrically. Heineken and Kronenberg lagers on draught. Draught Strongbow, Guinness and Buckley's Mild. Usual pub snacks and hot lunches (gammon, scampi, chicken, plaice etc.).

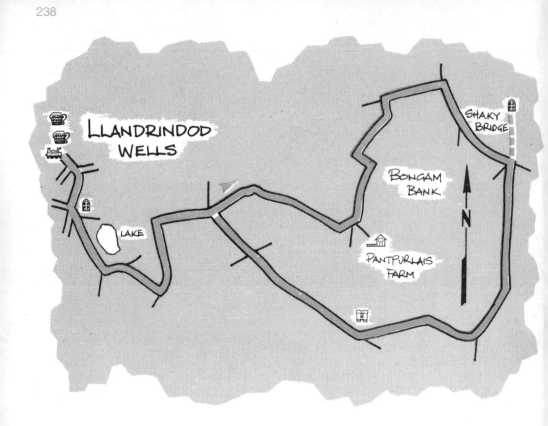

6e Llandrindod Wells

The District

Llandrindod Wells was built on a green hill far away in the Middle Ages. Originally known as 'The Church of Trinity' (referring to the old parish church near the lake) it overlooks the confluence of the River Ithon and the River Avon.

By the 17th century the town was well known for the virtue of its springs and before long a pump-house was erected, with ballrooms and gaming rooms, in the grandiose fashion of Bath. The pump-house, pavillion, springs and bowling greens are all within Rock Park, which is situated in a picturesque part of this now fading spa. A path from the pump-house leads to a spot known as Lover's Leap, a projecting rock of about 30 feet.

Two miles to the east is the site of Cefnl-lys Castle, which was built around 1242. Nowadays there is just the earthwork on top of a grassy hill, offering impressive views.

How to Get There

Llandrindod Wells is easily accessible by road; from the north on the A483, the east and west off the A44 and from the south via the A470. It is a Golden Rail Resort served by the Mid Wales line which runs through the heart of the Welsh countryside. National Coach services run from London and Aberystwyth daily.

The Llandrindod Wells Walk

This is an easy walk across unspoilt contryside, incorporating some magnificent views of the Welsh Hills.

Starting at the railway station, walk up the station crescent into the centre of town. Turn right down Temple Street and continue to **The Metropole Hotel**. Take the first left after the hotel and then after about 20 yards, turn right into Princes Avenue. This leads up and around the side of the lake passing an unusual sign announcing 'Toads — slow migratory crossing'. You'd be forgiven for thinking this was a joke, but it was actually erected after local naturalists complained about the number of toads squashed by road traffic.

Follow the road as it veers to the left and right and, when it veers right, turn left through a kissing gate, follow the path for about 100 yards, where you should fork right through a wood. When the path emerges from the wood keep on the right-hand side of the fence and continue over a stile into a small meadow. Pick up the track on the far side and turn left and walk towards a house. However, you should turn off to the right before reaching the house, passing through 2 kissing gates.

Follow the path into oak woodland, along a ravine. It climbs uphill and out of the wood into a field. Take a diagonal left course across the field to an iron stile, and proceed straight ahead to another stile.

The Inns

The Hotel Metropole, Llandrindod Wells

About the Inn: This spacious hotel was built by the Great Grandmother of the present owners, in the Edwardian heydey of 'Taking the Waters' at Llandrindod Wells. The imposing facade, with its white-painted wrought ironwork, overlooks the lawns of Temple gardens and has an air of tranquillity integral to this Spa. The Lantern Bar, with its oak-panelled finish and large open fireplace, is popular with locals and visitors alike.

Beers and Food: Wide range of beers, plus a comprehensive bar menu, with separate restaurant facilities readily available.

The Llanerch Hotel, Llandrindod Wells

About the Inn: Originally a staging post, dating back to the 16th century, the Llanerch is by far the oldest tavern in the area. It occupies a comparatively isolated position in the High Street and overlooks some fine scenery. Built of local stone, the

Turn left onto the track (almost opposite the entrance to Pantpurlais Farm) and follow this for about quarter of a mile to a T-junction. Turn right here and walk down the lane for 200 yards, before turning left over a stile, just after a small clump of trees. The path continues across a field to a stile, where you emerge onto a lane, by Shaky Bridge and Cefynllys Church. Cefynllys Castle is to your right, uphill.

Return across the Shaky Bridge and immediately turn left along the metalled lane to a picnic area. After 20 yards a sign indicates the 'Forest Walk' to your right. Follow the path through the trees and, after the second gate, turn right onto a track, which forges uphill, past a bungalow and a stile on the right. After about 200 yards, cross the stile on your right and walk towards a triangulation post for a beautiful view.

Behind you, in the distance is Radnor Forest, with the craggy outline of Llandegly Rocks in the foreground. In front of you lie the hills, which comprise the so-called 'wilderness' of mid Wales; and to your left can be seen the ridges of the Black Mountains.

However, even awe-struck walkers have to get home, so continue in the same direction to a fence and by keeping to the left of it, drop downhill over a stile. Keep heading in the same direction downhill, over two more stiles, to the woods below. Follow the path for about 200 yards and you will find yourself in a field which should look familiar. You can return to Llandrindod Wells as you like now; either by returning the way you came (by turning left across the meadow and then downhill) or by walking across the meadow towards a house, where you can make a short-cut through woods.

interior has a warm and friendly atmosphere and some interesting old features, including a Jacobean staircase and Georgian partitions and glasswork. The pub is reputedly haunted by a bishop, although the Landlord declares not to know him intimately.

Beers and Food: The cellar has spring water running through, which is ideal for the conditioning of real ale. A Whitbread house, with draught Bass and Whitbread Flowers Bitter on hand pump. The Landlord, Ken Leach, also serves a select range of 'modern' cocktails. A wide range of food is available, from sandwiches to grills, with the occasional seasonal speciality dish.

The Drinkers' Guide to Walking

Readers' Comments and Suggestions

As it says on the side of the packet, this book left the typewriter in a state of perfect freshness, and we want you to enjoy it in that condition. But Nature and Man can change the face of the countryside quite rapidly, and in keeping THE DRINKERS' GUIDE TO WALKING as reliable and up-to-date as possible we would welcome readers' comments on any aspects of the featured walks and inns that might need amending in future editions. Any help will be gratefully acknowledged in the next edition of the guide.

We are also most receptive to readers' suggestions for new walks. If you should be wily enough to come up with a walk that we would like to publish, you will be the lucky recipient of £10, a free copy of the next edition of THE DRINKERS' GUIDE consigned at no little risk to the Royal Mail, a generous acknowledgement in the book and... overnight fame!

Walks should be within reach of a major town or city, preferably accessible by public transport. They must offer local places of interest for all the family and, of course, interesting watering-holes at the base or en route. We require:

1) Brief details of the geography, places of interest, flora and fauna of the district (about 300 words).

2) Information on how to get to the starting point by road and public transport from major towns and cities in the area.

3) A detailed talk-round, including a note of the approximate distance and the kind of terrain, explaining whether the route is easy or for Chris Bonington only, prone to muddiness, etc. (about 800 words).

4) An outline sketch of the route (preferably based on an Ordnance Survey map) from which an artist can develop a map.

We also require details on the pubs selected: address and a description of the precise location, name of the landlord, history, architecture, atmosphere and facilities, as well as the beers and food on offer. Photographs and copies of any literature prepared by the pubs would be appreciated. Copies of a standard questionnaire are available from the publishers if required.

Please send any correspondence to the editor; Nicola Hodge, care of the publishers:

Proteus (Publishing) Limited,
Bremar House,
Sale Place,
London, W2 1PT.